Development and Public Banks

Development financing institutions (DFIs), are public financial institutions initiated and steered by governments with explicit official missions to promote public policy objectives, and public development banks (PDBs) are the main category. DFIs are experiencing a renaissance worldwide, but there is limited academic research examining their roles, operations, and effectiveness.

This book attempts to fill this gap by bringing together world-renowned scholars who discuss in detail the economics and the social consequences of both development banks and public banks. Combining together, the chapters in this volume discuss topics from sustainability, development impact of financial instruments, a new development financial architecture, and the interaction with existing international rules like the Basel Accord. This book will be of particular interest to students, scholars, and researchers of development finance, global governance, and international political economy.

The chapters in this book were originally published in the *Review of Political Economy.*

Stephany Griffith-Jones is the Financial Markets Program Director at the Initiative for Policy Dialogue at Columbia University, USA. She is also a Board Member of the Central Bank of Chile. Her research interests include global capital flows, with special reference to flows to emerging markets; macro-economic management of capital flows in Latin America, Eastern Europe, and sub-Saharan Africa; proposals for international measures to diminish volatility of capital flows and reduce likelihood of currency crises; analysis of national and international capital markets; and proposals for international financial reform.

Régis Marodon is Senior Advisor on Sustainable Finance at the Agence Française de Développement (AFD), France. With a Ph.D in Development Economics, he previously performed research assignments for the World Bank. At the AFD, he contributed extensively to development financing in many African, Mediterranean, and Latin American countries, and was consecutively the Director for Turkey, Mexico, and Latin America. He joined the CEO Advisory Staff of the AFD in 2016 on sustainable finance matters and is an active Member of many international networks on that issue.

Louis-Philippe Rochon is Full Professor of Economics at Laurentian University, Canada, where he has been teaching since 2004. He is the Editor-in-Chief of the *Review of Political Economy.* He is the Founding Editor (now Emeritus) of the *Review of Keynesian Economics.* He has widely published in post-Keynesian economics, and monetary theory and policy. He has been a visiting professor in over a dozen universities around the world.

Jiajun Xu is Assistant Professor and the Executive Deputy Dean of the Institute of New Structural Economics at Peking University, China. Xu initiates the International Research Initiative of Development Financing Institutions Working Groups, and currently acts as the General Secretary of the Global Research Consortium on Economic Structural Transformation (GReCEST) and the Invited Researcher at the Public Policy Research Center of the Counsellors' Office of the State Council of the People's Republic of China. Her research focuses on development financing and global economic governance.

Development and Public Banks

Edited by
Stephany Griffith-Jones, Régis Marodon,
Louis-Philippe Rochon and Jiajun Xu

Routledge
Taylor & Francis Group
LONDON AND NEW YORK

First published 2023
by Routledge
4 Park Square, Milton Park, Abingdon, Oxon, OX14 4RN

and by Routledge
605 Third Avenue, New York, NY 10158

Routledge is an imprint of the Taylor & Francis Group, an informa business

British Library Cataloguing-in-Publication Data
A catalogue record for this book is available from the British Library

ISBN13: 978-1-032-35970-0 (hbk)
ISBN13: 978-1-032-35971-7 (pbk)
ISBN13: 978-1-003-32960-2 (ebk)

DOI: 10.4324/9781003329602

Typeset in Minion Pro
by codeMantra

Publisher's Note
The publisher accepts responsibility for any inconsistencies that may have arisen during the conversion of this book from journal articles to book chapters, namely the inclusion of journal terminology.

Contents

Citation Information vii
Notes on Contributors ix

Introduction: Unleashing the Potential of Public Development Banks for Achieving Sustainable Development Goals 1
Stephany Griffith-Jones, Régis Marodon, Louis-Philippe Rochon and Jiajun Xu

PART I
Development Banks

1 Matching Risks with Instruments in Development Banks 7
Stephany Griffith-Jones, Shari Spiegel, Jiajun Xu, Marco Carreras and Natalya Naqvi

2 The Global Development Banks' Architecture 34
José Antonio Ocampo and Victor Ortega

3 Should National Development Banks be Subject to Basel III? 59
Ricardo Gottschalk, Lavinia B. Castro and Jiajun Xu

4 Can Development Banks Step Up to the Challenge of Sustainable Development? 78
Régis Marodon

5 Scaling Up Public Development Banks' Transformative Alignment with the 2030 Agenda for Sustainable Development 96
Maria Alejandra Riaño, Jihane Boutaybi, Damien Barchiche and Sébastien Treyer

6 From Global to Local: Subnational Development Banks in the Era of Sustainable Development Goals 128
Sergio Gusmão Suchodolski, Adauto Modesto Junior, Cinthia Helena de Oliveira Bechelaine and Leila Maria Bedeschi Costa

PART II
Public Banks

7 Understanding Full Investment and the Potential Role of Public Banks 153
Wesley C. Marshall and Louis-Philippe Rochon

8 A Dynamic Theory of Public Banks (and Why it Matters) 169
Thomas Marois

9 Public Banks, Public Purpose, and Early Actions in the Face of Covid-19 185
Diana V. Barrowclough and Thomas Marois

Index 205

Citation Information

The following chapters were originally published in the journal *Review of Political Economy*, volume 34, issue 2 (2022). When citing this material, please use the original page numbering for each article, as follows:

Chapter 1
Matching Risks with Instruments in Development Banks
Stephany Griffith-Jones, Shari Spiegel, Jiajun Xu, Marco Carreras and Natalya Naqvi
Review of Political Economy, volume 34, issue 2 (2022) pp. 197–223

Chapter 2
The Global Development Banks' Architecture
José Antonio Ocampo and Victor Ortega
Review of Political Economy, volume 34, issue 2 (2022) pp. 224–248

Chapter 3
Should National Development Banks be Subject to Basel III?
Ricardo Gottschalk, Lavinia B. Castro and Jiajun Xu
Review of Political Economy, volume 34, issue 2 (2022) pp. 249–267

Chapter 4
Can Development Banks Step Up to the Challenge of Sustainable Development?
Régis Marodon
Review of Political Economy, volume 34, issue 2 (2022) pp. 268–285

Chapter 5
Scaling Up Public Development Banks' Transformative Alignment with the 2030 Agenda for Sustainable Development
Maria Alejandra Riaño, Jihane Boutaybi, Damien Barchiche and Sébastien Treyer
Review of Political Economy, volume 34, issue 2 (2022) pp. 286–317

Chapter 6
From Global to Local: Subnational Development Banks in the Era of Sustainable Development Goals
Sergio Gusmão Suchodolski, Adauto Modesto Junior, Cinthia Helena de Oliveira Bechelaine and Leila Maria Bedeschi Costa
Review of Political Economy, volume 34, issue 2 (2022) pp. 318–339

Chapter 7
Understanding Full Investment and the Potential Role of Public Banks
Wesley C. Marshall and Louis-Philippe Rochon
Review of Political Economy, volume 34, issue 2 (2022) pp. 340–355

Chapter 8
A Dynamic Theory of Public Banks (and Why it Matters)
Thomas Marois
Review of Political Economy, volume 34, issue 2 (2022) pp. 356–371

Chapter 9
Public Banks, Public Purpose, and Early Actions in the Face of Covid-19
Diana V. Barrowclough and Thomas Marois
Review of Political Economy, volume 34, issue 2 (2022) pp. 372–390

Notes on Contributors

Damien Barchiche, Institute for Sustainable Development and International Relations (IDDRI), Paris, France.

Diana V. Barrowclough, United Nations Conference on Trade and Development, Geneva, Switzerland.

Cinthia Helena de Oliveira Bechelaine, Development Bank of Minas Gerais, Belo Horizonte, Brazil.

Jihane Boutaybi, Institute for Sustainable Development and International Relations (IDDRI), Paris, France.

Marco Carreras, Institute of Development Studies, Brighton, UK.

Lavinia B. Castro, The Brazilian Development Bank, Rio de Janeiro, Brazil.

Leila Maria Bedeschi Costa, Development Bank of Minas Gerais, Belo Horizonte, Brazil.

Ricardo Gottschalk, United Nations, Office of the Resident Coordinator, Pretoria, South Africa.

Stephany Griffith-Jones, Financial Markets Program, Initiative for Policy Dialogue, Columbia University, USA.

Régis Marodon, Sustainable Finance, Agence Française de Développement (AFD), Paris, France.

Thomas Marois, Department of Development Studies, SOAS University of London, UK.

Wesley C. Marshall, Universidad Autónoma Metropolitana – Iztapalapa, Mexico.

Adauto Modesto Junior, Development Bank of Minas Gerais, Belo Horizonte, Brazil.

Natalya Naqvi, LSE – London School of Economics, UK.

José Antonio Ocampo, School of International and Public Affairs, Columbia University, USA.

Victor Ortega, Inter-American Development Bank, Washington, DC, USA.

Maria Alejandra Riaño, Institute for Sustainable Development and International Relations (IDDRI), Paris, France.

Louis-Philippe Rochon, Economics, Laurentian University, Canada.

Shari Spiegel, UN Department of Economic and Social Affairs at the United Nations (UN-DESA), USA.

Sergio Gusmão Suchodolski, Development Bank of Minas Gerais, Belo Horizonte, Brazil.

Sébastien Treyer, Institute for Sustainable Development and International Relations (IDDRI), Paris, France.

Jiajun Xu, Institute of New Structural Economics, Peking University, Beijing, China.

Introduction: Unleashing the Potential of Public Development Banks for Achieving Sustainable Development Goals

Stephany Griffith-Jones, Régis Marodon, Louis-Philippe Rochon and Jiajun Xu

Introduction

The collection of chapters in this book first appeared in the *Review of Political Economy* in April 2022 (34; 2). It contained two separate but related sections: the first on development banks (six articles) and the second on public banks (three articles).

Financing Development

Development financing institutions (DFIs) are public financial institutions initiated, owned, and steered by governments with explicit official missions to promote public policy objectives, and public development banks (PDBs) are the main category (Xu et al., 2021).

Major planetary concerns, including climate, loss of nature, and inequalities among human beings, call for very large-scale concerted action at all levels. The challenge is to favor major structural transformation of all economies to achieving higher productivity, while becoming low carbon and more inclusive. PDBs and DFIs, whether at a local, national, continental, or international scale, are key instruments to help governments finance the rapid recovery from the COVID-19 crisis and achieve long-run transformation of existing economic models to ones that serve people and planet far better. By providing direct public financing and mobilizing private finance, PDBs and DFIs should transform themselves with tools and indicators that allow them to proactively select and support long-term productive investments and low-carbon operations, as well as those that support poorer regions and people. They should set up a "sustainable development analysis grid" to select operations, based on criteria that help maximize development impact of all their transactions; financial returns are also important but secondary to maximizing development impact for PDBs and DFIs.

DFIs are experiencing a renaissance worldwide, but there is limited academic research examining their roles, operations, and effectiveness. To fill the gap, the Institute of New Structural Economics at Peking University (INSE) in collaboration with key stakeholders set up the International Research Initiative on PDBs and DFIs in 2019, sponsored by the Agence Française de Développement (AFD), the Ford Foundation, and the International Development Finance Club (IDFC). This Initiative has been coordinated by Stephany Griffith-Jones, Financial Markets Director of Initiative for Policy Dialogue at Columbia University; Régis Marodon, Special Adviser on Sustainable Finance of AFD; and Jiajun Xu, Executive Deputy Dean of INSE. It aims to create a global community of academics and practitioners in the field of PDBs and DFIs and to foster rigorous academic research and propose concrete policy recommendations for unleashing the full potential of PDBs and DFIs to the SDGs. To lay the foundation for the original research, INSE started to build the world's first development financing institution database and then collaborated with AFD to strengthen first ever comprehensive database on PDBs and DFIs worldwide. Based on the first-hand data collection, the pilot database has identified over 550 PDBs and DFIs from more than 160 countries, with aggregate total assets of about 22 trillion USD.[1]

The International Research Initiative has set up five working groups, namely, SDG-compatible investments, global development finance architecture, business model, financial regulation, and governance of DFIs. The effort in the pilot years has culminated in the production of 14 working papers after going through two rounds of rigorous external peer reviews and disseminated in the inaugural Finance in Common Summit.

The pilot effort is truly a global endeavor with the wide-ranging participation of researchers, experts, and practitioners from (but not limited to) 10 universities (Peking University, Boston University, Columbia University, University of Melbourne, Toulouse School of Economics, The London School of Economics and Political Science, George Washington University, Cass Business School, SOAS University of London, and The Graduate Institute of International and Development Studies), 2 international organizations (United Nations-Department of Economic and Social Affairs and International Monetary Fund), 7 DFIs (Asian Infrastructure Development Bank, The Brazilian Development Bank, Inter-American Development Bank, Development Bank of Minas Gerais, Asian Infrastructure Development Bank, Banque de France, and French Development Agency), and 8 Think tanks and research institutions (Foundation for Studies and Research on International Development, Overseas Development Institute, African Center for Economic Transformation, Institute of Research for Development, Institute for Sustainable Development and International Relations, Institute of Development Studies, ETH Zurich Center for Development and Cooperation, and World Resources Institute). Six papers were selected and published as a special issue of the renowned peer-reviewed journal, *Review of Political Economy*. These six papers lay the foundation for this book volume.

The key message from this book volume is that PDBs and DFIs, under certain conditions such as being sufficiently capitalized and having good governance, are crucial to play a leading role in helping fund investment, essential for a just transition to sustainable development. Based on the academic research, we synthesize the following 10 policy recommendations:

1. Make National Development Banks (NDBs) the forefront for transitions: Multilateral development banks, donors, and climate funds should use national development banks, especially small ones in low-income countries, to channel funds. The report of the G20 Eminent Person Group on Global Finance Governance calls for nothing different from the setting of "country platforms". Both non-concessional and concessional funds are relevant, provided that they are dedicated to transitional projects and programs, part of national trajectories to low-carbon economies. While on-lending helps credit-constrained NDBs to gain access to international resources, international lenders should foster export-enhancing investment projects in line with latent comparative advantages of host countries to mitigate the risk of potential balance of payment crises; alternatively, it would be crucial to develop financial instruments denominated in local currency.
2. Make sure capital is at scale: existing PDBs and DFIs should have sufficient scale to perform their functions. In particular, all regional and subregional multilateral development banks (MDBs), which had their capital significantly increased in the wake of the

[1] INSE and AFD, Public Development Banks and Development Financing Institutions Database, http://www.dfi-database.pku.edu.cn/index.htm.

2008 financial crisis, need urgent and significant capitalization following the far worse COVID-19 crisis and the negative effects of the Russian invasion of Ukraine. National development banks also need further capitalization. Some of the funds mobilized as to alleviate the COVID-19 crisis could be devoted to that end. The three Chinese policy banks' total assets account for 26% of China's GDP, while in Africa, assets of development banks range from 2 to 4% of GDP. PDBs and DFIs need to be provided with sufficient capital, as well as other financial support to make them able to provide crucial counter-cyclical finance in difficult times, like COVID-19, and to support the structural transformation to low-carbon and inclusive development. In countries that do not have PDBs, it would seem key to create one.

3. Measure to manage: PDBs and DFIs should incorporate the imperative of transitions towards low-carbon, resilient, and equitable socio-economic models in all their financing decisions and project cycles. It implies that each development bank should equip itself with the necessary analytical tools to allow monitoring and accountability for the impacts of its financing.
4. Shape the future: PDBs and DFIs need to move from being just "project-takers" to "project makers". Once goals are defined, e.g. for climate and SDG action, it is essential for them to take a proactive role in acting as the first-mover to overcome uncertainties and risks and define programs and projects, including creating special funds for project preparation. Development banks could even become "development hubs" to originate and develop more sustainable projects, which they could turn to private sector investment once matured.
5. Blend with private sector: PDBs and DFIs should help mobilize private sector finance, helping fund what private sectors alone would otherwise not fund, so as to bring together all actors towards sustainable development objectives. This should be done in ways that maximize the sustainable development impact of these flows, which is the main goal of PDBs and DFIs.
6. Apply regulations appropriate to DBs: The existing framework of financial regulation does not consider PDBs' role in providing long-term and high-risk capital for achieving development goals and mitigating financial stability concerns. Regulators should consider differentiating prudential rules to account for PDBs' contributions to future financial stability and economic structural transformation in an equitable and sustainable manner. It is in the long-term interest of financial regulators to encourage investments that enhance climate change resilience and sustainable development. PDBs often cannot use market-based responses to tighter regulation by issuing common equity. Alternatives should be promoted that, based on transparent governance and international cooperation, widen PDBs access to capital markets without creating systemic stability hazards.
7. Enforce an independent and strong governance: Good governance matters for NDBs to fulfill their mission to promote development and achieve development impact. But it is not destiny that NDBs are afflicted with poor governance in poorly governed countries. With the support of farsighted leadership even poorly governed countries can have well-governed NDBs. Furthermore, some NDBs evolved and undertook reforms to restructure their internal organization and significantly improved their governance despite relatively constant low institutional indices at a country level.
8. Do not stay isolated, integrate the community: PDBs and DFIs should be encouraged to build a global and united coalition committed to the transition for sustainable development and the operationalization of the Paris agreement on climate change. Going beyond isolated initiatives is essential to tackle problems at a global scale. Cooperation between multilateral, regional, and national banks is crucial, and networking better

within themselves will secure a better access to the international system of grants and global funds, especially the green climate fund. This will help in financing more projects with positive environmental externalities. The world needs a horizon of solutions and of actors capable of embodying new forms of collective action, in support of multilateralism, to instill optimism and positive dynamics around sustainability.

9. Give preference to instruments that maximize development impact: it is important that risks taken are focused on the real economy, such as investing in impactful innovative projects, rather than financial engineering risks, derived from instruments themselves. While loans are the main and simplest instrument used by PDBs in case of market failures, guarantees may however perform a useful role when there is a high uncertainty, like in COVID times. For innovative technology and high risk projects with potentially high development and profit potential, it seems desirable to use more intensively equity investments, so PDBs can capture the upside.
10. Call on development banks to design and finance SDGs' policy objectives: Projects matter, but they are not all. The setting of proper multi-sectoral policies is key, given the inter-connections existing between all SDGs. A water project is never simply producing water, as its impacts affect directly nature, rivers, gender equality, poverty, job creation, energy, cities, and almost all SDGs. National development trajectories should be aligned with international agreements. PDBs should actively support governments, including policy loans instruments not assigned to particular projects.

As a general standpoint, PDBs should align their mandates with SDGs. Policies and counter-cyclical financing to support recovery should be explicitly aligned with SDGs, with a particular priority in supporting the mitigation and adaptation to climate change. The role of PDBs should be enhanced in (i) supporting countries and regions that lag behind; (ii) promoting innovation and structural transformation; (iii) enhancing social development; (iv) increasing financial inclusion; (v) financing infrastructure investment; and (vi) supporting the provision of global public goods.

Reference

Xu, Jiajun, Régis Marodon, Xinshun Ru, Xiaomeng Ren, and Xinyue Wu. 2021. "What are Public Development Banks and Development Financing Institutions?——Qualification Criteria, Stylized Facts and Development Trends." *China Economic Quarterly International*, volume 1, issue 4: 271–294.

Part I

Development Banks

Matching Risks with Instruments in Development Banks

Stephany Griffith-Jones, Shari Spiegel, Jiajun Xu, Marco Carreras and Natalya Naqvi

ABSTRACT
This paper explores how development banks should deploy appropriate financial instruments to encourage real economic risk-taking while minimizing financial engineering risks. We distinguish real economic risks from financial engineering or intermediary risks and argue that using complex financial instruments to leverage additional private financing may undermine policy steer and lead to too much risk being taken by development banks. We then explore comparative advantages of different financial instruments such as loans, guarantees, equity, and insurance in tackling risks in normal times. Then we synthesize common features of development banks' responses to the COVID-19 crisis. Finally, we propose future research directions.

1. Introduction

This paper explores appropriate financial instruments for mitigating different types of risks to maximize development impacts. It first provides an analytical framework for studying development banks' (DBs) risks and development impact, including theoretical considerations, for evaluating appropriate instruments that development banks do and should use, to maximize development impact. The second part builds on this framework to examine analytically the instruments DBs use in normal times, looking at their advantages and challenges; it draws on extensive data collection, which INSE at Beijing University is carrying out. The third part details the response of DBs to the COVID-19 crisis; especially this section, but also the previous one, draws on extended interviews carried out with senior officials of sub-national, national, regional and bilateral DBs, which provided very valuable insights and information.

2. Analytical Framework for Studying Development Banks' Risks and Development Impact

A key difference between development banks (DBs) and purely commercial banks is that the main (and usually only) aim of commercial banks and other private investors is to maximize risk-adjusted expected returns, often short-term ones. Thus, they generally do not aim to pursue development goals. Their focus is on minimizing risks that may lead to financial losses or reduce profits. While commercial banks need to manage the full range of economic, environmental, and social risks, they generally only do so to the extent that these risks impact financial returns.

In contrast, DBs have a double mandate. They mainly aim to maximize sustainable and inclusive development impact (including economic, environmental and social impacts), while maintaining some financial profits or avoiding financial losses.

In simple terms, the development bank aims to maximize a:

$$\text{Dual Ratio} = \frac{\text{(sustainable developmental impact)}}{\text{(risks to that impact or developmental risks)}},$$

evaluated subject to a minimum or positive risk adjusted financial return (RAFR)

A key point is that for DBs the main goal is to achieve a high level of development impact — making a major contribution to meeting the SDGs. Though important, achieving a good financial return is somewhat secondary to the dominant aim of development impact. In addition, DBs should evaluate investments over a longer period as their liability structure and projects are long-term, and because sustainable development results need to be evaluated over a longer time horizon to be sustained.

Measuring this dual ratio can be difficult. There is literature and experience on how to evaluate financial returns — though financial crises and other shocks show this literature and experience do not at all guarantee precision or even approximation to future evolution. Though there is a lot of valuable research being done in this area, consensus on measurements of sustainable development impact is still being developed.

While some risks can be managed through financial instruments and/or through strengthened public policies, others are unavoidable. In addition, some risks (especially those linked to financial engineering, or insufficient development impact) are strongly influenced by the financial instruments that development banks may use. Identifying and categorizing different types of risks can thus help DBs determine the when and how best to use different financial instruments.

2.1. Identify Risks

2.1.1. Uncertainty vs. Risk

Before studying different categories of risk, we first make a fundamental distinction between uncertainty and risk.

Uncertainty cannot be valued, as Knight (1921) argued, as it is not susceptible to measurement. More uncertainty makes it harder to measure and manage risks. Events that are difficult to predict are characterized by uncertainty, such as questions surrounding the impact of digitalization on employment, unpredictable exogenous shocks, or difficult to predict political risks. COVID-19 can be seen as an example of extreme uncertainty, both with regards to it happening in the first case, as well as its evolution in different countries and its resulting overall negative economic effects.

The more uncertain the risk, the more difficult it is to raise private financing, and the more finely it needs to be distributed. In principle, this is one reason for public action (Arrow and Lind 1970).

Risk can be valued, based on the probability of an event and the potential losses/gains (or their expected values). However, as the financial crisis of 2008/2009 reminded us, and COVID-19 is reminding us again, it is difficult to measure risk precisely, even using complex modeling techniques. In particular, markets tend to underestimate or neglect to incorporate 'tail risk' — the risk of low probability events with severe outcomes — in part due to short-term investment horizons, uncertainty and relative difficulty of predicting such events.

Certain types of risk are positive; indeed, such risks may stimulate innovation and are at the core of investment decision-making, as investors seek return for taking risks. There are clear development impacts/benefits of taking certain types of investment risks, such as lending/investing in projects that spur technological and other innovations, often with important positive externalities, which are beneficial for development. We call risk that generates investment, which creates value and development impact 'real economy' risk.

These real economy risks, as we discuss below, need to be clearly distinguished from other risks, such as financial engineering risks, originating mainly from the type of financial instruments used. Financial engineering aims to attract and leverage additional private financial flows. In theory, financial engineering should help distribute risks to those best able to manage them. For example, financial engineering can create tranches that meet different investors' risk appetites. A positive example is attracting institutional investors to invest in projects with long-term maturities, which match their long-term liabilities. However, the use of such instruments risk extracting value, by for example redistributing such value from development banks (and ultimately governments and taxpayers) to private financial institutions (Mazzucato 2018).

A key question is how development banks should deploy appropriate financial instruments to encourage real economic risk-taking, while minimizing financial engineering risks, as illustrated in Figure 1. Quadrant 4 (bottom right) shows the ideal outcome that DBs pursue (in general and in individual transactions) — i.e., to maximize development impact, whilst at the same time minimizing financial engineering risk.

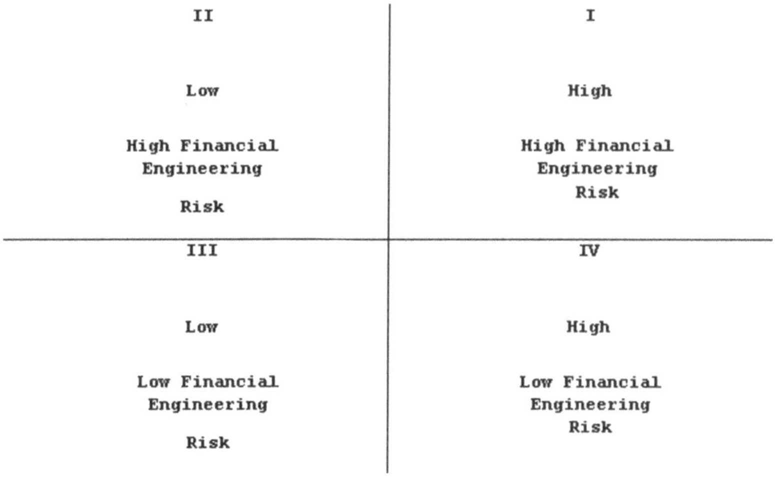

Figure 1. Achieving high development impact (see horizontal axis) with low financial engineering risk (see vertical axis). Source: Authors' elaboration.

For instance, with $1 million of capital a DB has the option of using a simple instrument, such as a direct loan or direct equity vs. a more complex option-based financial instrument, such as a guarantee or first loss tranche of an SPV. A direct loan or direct equity would maximize the development bank's policy steer to try to ensure maximum development impact of the transaction, though it would use more of a bank's capital. Equity could be particularly well suited for ambitious projects, e.g., development of a new technology, which may have difficulty attracting private finance due to high levels of risk and uncertainty; here an equity instrument could be particularly valuable, as it would allow the DB to capture the upside if the project is very successful.

The DB can, alternatively, use a financial instrument or derivative product that is engineered or created to attract additional financing and add leverage. The aim, from the DB angle, is often to maximize development impact by increasing volume and value of activity. The use of such instruments, however, poses several challenges. First, it may lead to too much risk being taken by the DB, including through contingent liabilities. Indeed, there may be too much risk transfer from the private financial intermediary to the DB, and therefore potential losses to the DB and ultimately taxpayers. Second, there may be a reduction of policy steer aimed at maximizing development impact, particularly when contracts are opaque.

The potential of long-term losses to DBs and governments is particularly high when the additional risk to the DB is not accurately compensated (e.g., through sharing in potential upside in a project) or priced (e.g., due to uncertainty, tail risk, and/or complexity of structured products which can obscure risks). When the risk is not provisioned against there is a likely trade-off between needing less fiscal resources in the short term, and potentially more in the long term (Griffith-Jones and Naqvi 2020).

It is important to stress that DBs can involve private finance in different ways, some of which will be more desirable in terms of maximizing development impact, and minimizing future contingency risk (see Figure 1). For example, when DBs borrow on private capital markets and give direct loans or grants, or co-finance with commercial banks or private investors, DBs can keep their policy steer, and thus aim to maximize development impact, whilst increasing leverage of scarce public resources. Another useful mechanism of DB/private financial sector collaboration can be DBs on-lending via commercial banks, if the programs have clear aims (e.g., loans for green transformation), and effective monitoring to ensure such development targets are met.

These mechanisms potentially give DBs greater policy steer than complex instruments, especially when such instruments are opaque. It could thus be argued that there is a loose hierarchy of involving private finance in development funding in terms of impact, with most impactful mechanisms being DBs borrowing on private capital markets to offer direct loans; private lenders and investors co-lending or co-investing with DBs; on-lending to commercial institutions; and complex opaque financial engineering products least attractive in terms of development impact, while also creating contingent liabilities. However, the precise impact will depend on the specifics of the projects, risks and instruments.

One of the aims of using financial engineering is 'doing more with less (fiscal resources)', which is attractive to governments that are (or see themselves as) fiscally constrained, especially during and after crises. As discussed below, one of the perceived advantages of guarantees, securitization and other more complex instruments is that they can achieve more leverage, given a certain amount of capital.

Instead of using guarantees, or other instruments, to achieve more leverage, and thus greater level of activity, there is the option of increasing the capital of DBs, as was done for many DBs in the wake of the 2007/2009 financial crisis. An increase of capital allows a DB to increase activity without risking increased contingent liabilities and deterioration of its credit rating. This is especially needed when DBs take on more economic risks, for example to encourage more innovation and/or to go into new sectors; or in circumstances, like COVID-19, where general uncertainty and different risks are perceived as increasing. An increase in capital will allow greater level of transactions, and/or assuming more risks by the DB, without leading to lowering of credit ratings or increasing contingent liabilities. We think increasing the capital of DBs is an important avenue worth pursuing, both at the national and multilateral level, especially in times of crisis, such as the COVID-19 related one, and given major challenges for structural transformation to a low carbon and more equitable economy.

As pointed out, increasing the paid-in capital of DBs, for a given level of transactions, at a particular level of risk, will reduce the possibility that rating agencies will downgrade DBs, thus reducing the cost of borrowing on capital markets. An important issue for further research is whether the methodologies that rating agencies use are appropriate for DBs. For example, if a DB introduces a debt standstill policy, due to unexpected shocks like COVID, rating agencies may wish to downgrade the DB; in fact, a standstill may increase the chances of the debtors paying back in the medium term, as will have more breathing space to recover during a major shock, and therefore increase capacity to service debt in future. This is one of many examples why rating agencies, and their methodologies may need to be regulated, in general and especially for their rating of DBs.

2.2. Risk Categorization

We now focus on different categories of risk that DBs face, with the aim of better understanding the most appropriate instruments for managing different investment risks (as well as mitigating new risks that some instruments might create).

In analyzing these different risk categories, we draw on some of the theoretical and policy literature, which gives valuable insights into this discussion. Below we distinguish between: exogenous shocks and endogenous risks (or policy risks); risks that are diversifiable (e.g., idiosyncratic risks) and risks that are not diversifiable (e.g., systemic or systematic risks); and project level 'real economy' risks and financial engineering risks.

In Section Four, we examine more specific criteria for how DBs can help reduce, manage, and share risks for projects/companies that have high economic risks and a large development impact potential, and how this could be reflected in the type of instruments that DBs should deploy.

2.2.1. Global/National; Exogenous/Endogenous (or Policy); and Systematic/ Idiosyncratic (or Diversifiable Risks)

Global systemic risks include the risk of shocks or volatility that impact countries around the world at the same time. These include macroeconomic shocks, such as commodity price shocks, global interest rate volatility, etc. that are determined by the evolution of the international economy and external events, such as policy decisions in major developed economies. They also include non-economic risks, such as disasters and pandemics that defy and cross national borders.

NDBs tend to have concentrated exposures to systematic risks, whether on the global or national level, making it difficult for them to manage these risks or offer hedging to private investors, especially when markets are incomplete, as is the case in many developing countries.

When markets (e.g., insurance and capital markets) to hedge some of these risks exist, private entities could be best placed to take the risk, but this may be expensive, especially in developing countries where markets may be thinner. In some countries, such markets do not exist at all. In addition, hedging instruments tend to have short tenors, especially in some developing and emerging economies, making it difficult to hedge a project over its lifetime, and costly to roll over hedges during crises (e.g., the cost, and even availability of hedging is pro-cyclical). Many developing countries will need international support, especially during systemic shocks as liquidity dries up. This underscores the need for strengthening the *system* of development banks, for example with MDBs broadening their support of NDBs in this aspect.

National risks include domestic endogenous or policy-related risks, such as macroeconomic policy and political risk, as well as exogenous shocks that do not cross borders (e.g., forest fires that impact individual countries). Such national risks raise risk premiums and deter investment in a country.

A feature of endogenous risks is that policy-making impacts these risks (e.g., governments can reduce risks by pursuing good macroeconomic policies, strengthening enabling environments etc.). While financial instruments NDBs use cannot reduce these risks per se, they can play a role in encouraging improved policy-making aimed at risk reduction. For example, if the government lends to or guarantees the payment by the public utility to an independent power producer (IPP), it has an interest in this public utility remaining financially sustainable, for instance by addressing inefficiencies in the utility.

Even though these national risks are systemic to the domestic economy, they can be idiosyncratic from a global perspective. This means that external actors (MDBs or international private actors) can manage some of these risks through diversification. For example, political risk is often uncorrelated across countries, making political risk insurance diversifiable. Similarly, when currency volatility is linked to national policies and events, it is uncorrelated with other currencies (i.e., the portion of the correlation that is less than one indicates some level of idiosyncratic risk) and thus diversifiable. Indeed, historically, a diversified portfolio of 20 or more currencies tends to have significantly lower volatility than individual currencies, and outperforms other asset classes. National disaster risks that are not globally systemic, e.g., hurricanes that impact countries independently and randomly, can also be managed through diversification — which is the basis of insurance.

A strengthened system of development banks, along with improved global insurance markets, could thus help NDBs better manage these risks. For example, MDBs could create portfolios of projects with relatively short maturities from a range of countries, which they could securitize and sell to international investors to diversify risk internationally (see Ketterer and Powell 2018).

2.2.2. Real Economy Risks vs. Financial Market Risks

There are a wide range of investment-specific real economy risks, depending on the project and the timing in the investment cycle. For example, different stages of infrastructure projects, including preparation, construction and operation generate different types of cost overruns and are exposed to other important commercial risks. There are also technology and geological risks, particularly in the construction phase (see Griffith-Jones 1993; Ketterer and Powell 2018).

Financial engineering or intermediary risks refers to those risks that are related to counterparties and financial intermediaries, or are generated through investment structures. Financial market risk management implies matching risks with those best able or willing to take them. As discussed above, financial products (e.g., tranching in structured products etc.) can themselves create new risks for the guarantor (in this case the DB, thus implying potential costs to taxpayers). As noted, this can be because the use of instruments increases leverage and/or transfers risks from private entities to DBs.

Financial engineering products may also have less sustainable development impact, as policy steer is often very indirect, and may become diffused or inexistent, especially when instruments are opaque. (See Griffith-Jones and Naqvi 2020) In addition, public subsidies can also engage the private sector in the investment process when it is not the most cost-efficient solution, and can create perverse incentives, such as excessive risk-taking by financial institutions (i.e., increasing the debt leverage of a company to a point where it jeopardizes its long-term viability).

This does not mean that financial products do not have some possible role to play. But that the choice of instruments needs to take into account the full range of risks, both financial and developmental.

3. Financial Instruments Deployed by NDBs in Normal Times

As noted in the previous section, where risk is well compensated (high return to risk ratio), risks should be taken by private investors without need for public support or finance. But if investment returns are not competitive with other opportunities on a risk-adjusted basis, and there are clear positive externalities/developmental impacts, government/NDB interventions and support is warranted.

NDBs use 5 main instruments to support investment: (i) loans (concessional and ordinary); (ii) guarantees; (iii) grants; (iv) equity investments (including venture capital and private equity); and (v) insurance type products, securitization and other diversified products. Most of these are reflected in Table 1.

3.1. Loans (Including Concessional Ones) and Grant Financing

Loans are the primary financial instrument of all NDBs. Practically all NDBs in the INSE survey discussed below, and most NDBs worldwide, provide loans (see Table 1). An

Table 1. Types of Financial Instruments of Selected NDBs.

No.	Name	Original Name	Income Level	Loan (Yes/no)	Concessional loans (Yes/no)	Guarantee (Yes/no)	Grants (Yes/no)	Equity Investment (Yes/no)	Venture capital or Private equity (Yes/no)	Insurance assets (Yes/no)
1	British Business Bank	British Business Bank	HIC	Yes	NI	Yes	NI	NI	Yes	NI
2	Business Development Bank of Canada	Business Development Bank of Canada	HIC	Yes	NI	Yes	NI	Yes	Yes	NI
3	Croatian Bank for Reconstruction and Development	Hrvatska banka za obnovu i razvitakt	HIC	Yes	NI	Yes	Yes	Yes	NI	Yes
4	Production Development Corporation	Corporación de Fomento de la Producción	HIC	NI	NI	NI	NI	NI	NI	NI
5	Development Bank of Japan, Inc.	日本政策投資銀行	HIC	Yes	NI	Yes	NI	NI	NI	NI
6	FINNISH FUND FOR INDUSTRIAL COOPERATION LTD	Teollisen yhteistyön rahasto Oy	HIC	Yes	NI	Yes	Yes	Yes	NI	NI
7	KfW Banking Group	KfW Bankengruppe	HIC	Yes	Yes	Yes	Yes	Yes	Yes	NI
8	KOMMUNALBANKEN AS - NORWAY	KOMMUNALBANKEN AS - NORWAY	HIC	Yes	NI	Yes	NI	NI	NI	NI
9	KOREA DEVELOPMENT BANK	산업은행	HIC	Yes	NI	Yes	NI	Yes	Yes	Yes
10	National Development Bank of Palau	National Development Bank of Palau	HIC	Yes	NI	NI	NI	NI	NI	NI
11	Public Investment Bank	Banque publique d'investissement	HIC	Yes	Yes	Yes	Yes	Yes	Yes	Yes
12	Slovak Guarantee and Development Bank	Slovenská záručná a rozvojová banka	HIC	Yes	NI	Yes	NI	NI	NI	NI
13	Turkish Republic of Northern Cyprus Development Bank	Turkish Republic of Northern Cyprus Development Bank	HIC	Yes	NI	Yes	NI	NI	NI	NI
14	Oman Development Bank	بنك التنمية العماني	HIC	Yes	Yes	Yes	NI	NI	NI	NI
15	Agricultural Bank of Namibia	Agricultural Bank of Namibia	UMIC	Yes	NI	Yes	NI	Yes	NI	NI
16	Bulgarian Development Bank	Българската банка за развитие	UMIC	Yes	NI	Yes	NI	Yes	Yes	NI
17	China Development Bank	国家开发银行	UMIC	Yes	NI	Yes	NI	Yes	NI	NI

(Continued)

Table 1. Continued.

No.	Name	Original Name	Income Level	Loan (Yes/no)	Concessional loans (Yes/no)	Guarantee (Yes/no)	Grants (Yes/no)	Equity Investment (Yes/no)	Venture capital or Private equity (Yes/no)	Insurance assets (Yes/no)
18	DEVELOPMENT BANK OF SOUTHERN AFRICA	DEVELOPMENT BANK OF SOUTHERN AFRICA	UMIC	Yes	NI	Yes	Yes	Yes	NI	NI
19	Fiji Development Bank	Fiji Development Bank	UMIC	Yes	NI	Yes	NI	NI	NI	NI
20	Fund for the Financing of the Agricultural Sector	Fondo para el Financiamiento del Sector Agropecuario	UMIC	Yes	NI	NI	NI	NI	Yes	NI
21	Funding Authority for Development	Financiera del Desarrollo Nacional	UMIC	Yes	Yes	NI	NI	Yes	NI	NI
22	Industrial Development Bank of Turkey	Industrial Development Bank of Turkey	UMIC	Yes	NI	Yes	Yes	Yes	Yes	NI
23	MY HOUSING Fund	Fondo MIVIVIENDA S.A.	UMIC	Yes	Yes	NI	NI	NI	NI	NI
24	NATIONAL DEVELOPMENT BANK	Nacional Financiera S.N.C.	UMIC	Yes	NI	Yes	NI	Yes	NI	NI
25	Rural and Urban Production Development Bank	BanEcuador B.P.	UMIC	Yes	Yes	NI	NI	NI	NI	NI
26	The Brazilian Development Bank	Banco Nacional de Desenvolvimento Econômico e Social	UMIC	Yes	NI	Yes	NI	Yes	Yes	NI
27	The Development Bank of Minas Gerais S.A.	Banco de Desenvolvimento de Minas Gerais S.A.	UMIC	Yes	NI	Yes	NI	Yes	NI	NI
28	Bangladesh Development Bank Ltd.	Bangladesh Development Bank Ltd.	LMIC	Yes	NI	NI	NI	NI	NI	NI
29	Bhutan Development Bank Ltd.	Bhutan Development Bank Ltd.	LMIC	Yes	NI	Yes	NI	Yes	NI	NI
30	Development Bank of the Philippines	Development Bank of the Philippines	LMIC	Yes	NI	Yes	NI	Yes	NI	Yes
31	Federated States of Micronesia Development Bank	Federated States of Micronesia Development Bank	LMIC	Yes	NI	NI	NI	Yes	NI	NI
32	National Agricultural Credit Fund of Senegal	Caisse Nationale de Crédit Agricole du Sénégal	LMIC	Yes	NI	Yes	NI	NI	NI	NI
33			LMIC	Yes	NI	Yes	NI	NI	NI	NI

(Continued)

Table 1. Continued.

No.	Name	Original Name	Income Level	Loan (Yes/no)	Concessional loans (Yes/no)	Guarantee (Yes/no)	Grants (Yes/no)	Equity Investment (Yes/no)	Venture capital or Private equity (Yes/no)	Insurance assets (Yes/no)
	National Bank of Economic Development	Banque Nationale pour le Développement Economique								
34	National Development Bank of Papua New Guinea	National Development Bank	LMIC	Yes	Yes	NI	NI	NI	NI	NI
35	PT. Multi-Infrastructure Facility	PT. Sarana Multi Infrastruktur	LMIC	Yes	Yes	Yes	Yes	Yes	NI	NI
36	Rural Development Bank	ធនាគារ អភិវឌ្ឍន៍ជនបទ	LMIC	Yes	NI	Yes	NI	NI	Yes	Yes
37	Small Industries Development Bank of India	Small Industries Development Bank of India	LMIC	Yes	NI	Yes	NI	Yes	Yes	NI
38	The Development Bank for Production	Banco de Fomento a la Producción	LMIC	Yes	Yes	Yes	NI	Yes	NI	NI
39	Vietnam Development Bank	Vietnam Development Bank	LMIC	Yes	NI	Yes	NI	NI	NI	NI
40	Vanuatu Agricultural Development Bank	Vanuatu Agricultural Development Bank	LMIC	Yes	NI	NI	NI	NI	NI	NI
41	Cooperative & Agricultural Credit Bank	بنك التسليف التعاوني والزراعي	LIC	Yes	Yes	Yes	Yes	NI	NI	NI
42	Development Bank of Ethiopia	የኢትዮጵያ ልማት ባንክ በሊዝ	LIC	Yes	NI	Yes	NI	NI	NI	NI
43	Development Bank of Rwanda	Development Bank of Rwanda	LIC	Yes	NI	NI	Yes	Yes	NI	NI
44	Liberian Bank for Development and Investment	Liberian Bank for Development and Investment	LIC	Yes	NI	Yes	NI	Yes	NI	NI
45	National Bank of Agricultural Development	Banque Nationale De Developpement Agricole (Bnda)	LIC	Yes	NI	Yes	NI	NI	NI	NI
46	National Investment Bank	Banco Nacional de Investimento	LIC	Yes	NI	Yes	NI	Yes	NI	NI

(Continued)

Table 1. Continued.

No.	Name	Original Name	Income Level	Loan (Yes/no)	Concessional loans (Yes/no)	Guarantee (Yes/no)	Grants (Yes/no)	Equity Investment (Yes/no)	Venture capital or Private equity (Yes/no)	Insurance assets (Yes/no)
47	Tanzania Agricultural Development Bank	Tanzania Agricultural Development Bank	LIC	Yes	NI	NI	NI	Yes	NI	NI
48	TIB Development Bank Limited	TIB Development Bank Limited	LIC	Yes	NI	NI	NI	Yes	NI	NI
49	Uganda Development Bank	Uganda Development Bank	LIC	Yes	NI	NI	NI	Yes	NI	NI
50	Financial Development Company	Société Financière de Développement	LIC	NI	NI	NI	NI	NI	NI	NI

Note: NI Refers To 'No Information' After the Thorough Search Of Official Websites Or Annual Reports.
Source: Authors.

important distinction is that loans can be first tier (i.e., directly granted by the DB) or second tier (i.e., channeled through on-lending by other financial institutions, usually commercial banks, but also cooperative banks, sub-national development banks and others). First tier loans may have important advantages, particularly for larger and more strategic projects, by granting higher policy steer to the DB. Second tier loans are valuable for smaller loans, and where local knowledge may be important, due to asymmetries of information.

Most NDB loans are provided on a non-concessional basis, though NDB loans are generally cheaper than those provided by commercial banks, because the funding costs for DBs tend to be cheaper than those obtained by commercial banks due to the guarantee of the publicly owned capital.

Concessional loans are a relatively low proportion of total loans. Among 50 selected NDBs, only 10 reported that they provide concessional loans (including 21 per cent of HICs, 23 per cent of MICs and 19 per cent of LICs). However, the low numbers could reflect inconsistent definitions of concessionality. In addition, 9 NDBs report using grants (including 29 per cent in HICs, 15 per cent in UMICs, 8 per cent in LMICs, and 20 per cent in LICs). Concessionality of loans may be carried out by either subsidizing the principal or the interest payments, with the former being better in many cases, as it implies lower transaction costs.

Subsidized credit is a particularly useful mechanism *when there is insufficient return on an investment to attract private investors, but positive social or environmental externalities*. For example, in case of important development impact externalities, (e.g., positive effects on reducing carbon emissions) subsidized credit or partial grants, for example in the project design stage, seem to be most appropriate. Given its direct nature, subsidized loans and grants can have strong policy steer, and can be used to direct lending toward sustainable development impacts, with appropriate reporting and monitoring. Subsidies can be used to stimulate investment in new markets or to encourage higher financial inclusion. In new markets or sectors, such subsidies are meant to be temporary and can be withdrawn when new activities become competitive, with solar and wind energy providing a good example.

Subsidized lending is also often used to reach underserved market segments, such as MSMEs (UN 2020). These subsidies, which target areas of high risk or low return due to structural issues (such as poverty), might be kept in place for extended periods. For example, microfinance firms generally depend on subsidies to cover the difference between revenues and the cost of providing services and revenues obtained.

When subsidies are used, they should be just sufficient to induce private actors to invest, without over-compensating the private investor. One way to address this is through an auction, where the NDB might set a quantity and give the project to the lowest bidder. For example, viability gap funding mechanism have been created in infrastructure sectors to make projects financially attractive without raising user fees. In these mechanisms, the eligible private sector bidder requiring the lowest subsidy is selected. Another mechanism to help strengthen subsidy allocation is strong governance structures, which benchmark concessionality to projects in similar industries and countries (UN 2020).

3.2. Guarantees

Guarantees are another primary financial instrument of NDBs. Of the 50 NDBs studied in the INSE Survey, 35 use guarantees, including 86 per cent of HICs, 69 per cent of MICs, and 50 per cent of LICs. This indicates that NDBs are more likely to use guarantees as countries move to more advanced stages of development.

Arrow and Lind (1970) show that, when risk is spread in small amounts over large numbers of investors, capital can be priced at risk-neutral prices. This implies that the state's inter-temporal tax and borrowing capacity gives it a unique ability to spread risk across large populations. Therefore, development bank guarantees can help manage idiosyncratic risk by encouraging private investment or lending in the face of high risk or high-risk aversion by private investors or lenders. Excessive risk aversion may arise in reaction to risks, real or perceived of specific new projects/sectors, or in situations of high overall uncertainty, national or international, such as the 2008/2009 financial crises and the current COVID crisis. In more mature markets, they can be effective in addressing fat tails in idiosyncratic risks, which markets do not tend to price on their own (Anginer, de la Torre, and Ize 2011). Guarantees can also potentially be used to crowd in private investment on a temporary basis when financial systems are underdeveloped, though the lower use in lower income countries suggests that they are not being used as much in this manner.

However, the case for using guarantees to help overcome credit rationing is not clear once the potential cost to the taxpayers of such guarantees is taken into account, and if credit rationing is caused by adverse selection linked to asymmetric information (Stiglitz and Weiss 1981). Thus, Greenwald and Stiglitz (1989), as well as Lacker (1994) and Anginer, de la Torre, and Ize (2011), conclude that, without an informational advantage and the ability to cross-subsidize, it is not possible for public guarantees to help produce socially better outcomes.

Furthermore, when there is extreme uncertainty, guarantees may not be sufficient to overcome investors' heightened risk aversion, unless governments/development banks are willing to assume most of the risk, which could subject them to unacceptably high losses. Indeed, the level of guarantee needed to catalyze private lending in conditions of high uncertainty may be close to 100 per cent (Interview material, see list of interviewees, in Appendix). Therefore guarantee programs may fail to provide an effective countercyclical tool. In those cases, first-tier development loans may provide the only reliable channel to increase lending.

It is also often harder for the government to assess the development impact of on-lending or guarantees. This underscores the importance of sufficient information on the final beneficiaries (for instance by requiring appropriate reporting from these banks). A reward system could help address risks of lending to projects with low development impact. For example, the AFAWA initiative from the African Development Bank offers preferential terms to institutions performing well on pre-defined objectives regarding women's access to financing (UN 2020).

Box 1
INSE NDB Study
In order to map financial instruments deployed by NDBs, INSE selected 50 NDBs out of the full population of 220 NDBs worldwide[1] based on three main criteria, income levels, size and mandate, to ensure that the selected cases are as representative as possible.

All NDBs were divided into four income levels, high income countries (HICs), upper middle income countries (UMICs), lower middle income countries (LMICs) and low income countries (LICs), in line with the World Bank's country classification. Development stages matter, as countries at different stages of developments have different industrial structures and financing needs (Lin, Xifang, and Ye 2013; Allen et al. 2018). Hence, NDBs from different income levels should have distinct missions and instruments.

Second, NDBs at each income level were ranked by total assets, then divided NDBs into quintile, and select about two NDBs from each quintile to ensure that both big and small NDBs are represented. Size matters, as banks of different sizes may face divergent challenges and opportunities. For instance, small banks may be undercapitalized and resource constrained.

When selecting NDBs from each quintile, different mandates to ensure representativeness were considered. Mandates of NDBs have two categories: one is general purpose and the other is single purpose including agriculture, infrastructure, housing, SMEs and entrepreneurship, trade, etc.

In total, 50 NDBs were selected to ensure their representativeness as far as the income level, size, and mandate are concerned. In addition, the selected NDBs come from different regions being also representative in terms of geographical scope. The results for type of financial instruments of these 50 banks selected are presented in Table 1.

3.3. Equity Investment

Unlike grants or loans, equity financing allows the NDB to capture upside potential. Assuming more risks may require higher provisioning against DB capital, but has the advantage that if the company/project becomes very profitable, the DB will obtain part of the profits, which it can use to cross-subsidize socially or environmentally desirable operations and/or increase the DB's own capital, leading to the future increased ability to carry out larger or more transactions. It also allows significant policy steer.

If the objective is to support innovation and innovative business models, the right instrument seems to be equity financing, either directly in individual companies, or through a diversified portfolio — or a Venture Capital model. While some of the businesses seeking investment may ultimately fail, the gains from a few winners should compensate the failures of the losers, and may generate significant net profits.

Equity investment is the third NDB financial instrument in terms of the importance of use by DBs. Out of the 50 selected NDBs in the INSE Survey, 27 deploy equity investments. These NDBs seem to be evenly distributed across income levels (42 per cent of HICs, 69 per cent of UMICs, 46 per cent of LMICs and 60 per cent of LICs).

In the INSE Survey, 11 NDBs provide Venture Capital or Private Equity investment to high-risk firms. These 11 NDBs include 35 per cent of HICs, 30 per cent of UMICs, 15 per cent of LMICs, and 0 per cent of LICs. This implies that there may be more demand for VC or PE for countries at the technological frontier.

There are other mechanisms through which DBs can 'capture the upside', such as debt instruments with equity kickers. One such instrument, currently used by the European

[1]The Institute of New Structural Economics at Peking University (INSE) has built a comprehensive database on development finance institutions worldwide (Xu, Ren, and Wu 2019). In total, 378 NDBs have been identified worldwide. In order to use the basic financial indicators, we have rigorously matched these NDBs from the INSE list with banks from Bank focus — a very comprehensive bank-level database based on publicly available annual reports and financial statements. Out of 263 matched NDBs, 220 have information on total assets as we need to use total assets as a proxy of bank size to select representative NDBs.

Investment Bank (EIB), is venture debt to support 'innovative enterprises'. If a business does well, the EIB gets part of that higher profit as compensation for taking a higher risk. This is usually done by a loan that is converted into an equity-linked instrument (warrants) or profit participation. Venture debt also has the virtue of financing the growth stages of companies, for example for scaling up from pilot to mass manufacturing, further development of R&D, and international expansion.

When capital markets do not develop on their own, DBs can support investments in sustainable development via equity, and catalyze market creation. Injections of equity via DBs can lower debt leverage for companies, especially valuable in COVID times, when companies have borrowed so much. Such investment could also be structured to cap the entrepreneur's upside, so that entrepreneurs will not use public money, especially if some degree of concessionality is involved, unless they really need it (Carter and Plant 2020). Nonetheless, finding the appropriate risk-reward sharing mechanism can be difficult. This requires transparency and monitoring systems in place to assess the results of public support mechanisms.

3.4. Resource Financed Infrastructure Instrument

One interesting infrastructure loan instrument deployed by CDB and China Exim Bank is known as resource-financed infrastructure (RFI). RFI is an instrument whereby a government pledges future revenues from a resource project to repay an existing construction loan, linking two separate activities, infrastructure building and resource extraction. The size of China's overseas RFI is significant. Over half of CDB and China Eximbank very large infrastructure lending was in the form of RFI.

RFI helps fill the infrastructure-financing gap, including in low-income countries. Traditionally, developing country governments often borrowed from foreign creditors to build public infrastructure and used tax revenues to repay their loans. However, debtor governments often cannot make credible commitments to repay their loans.

RFI loans are much larger than conventional sovereign loans. Second, countries with RFI loans are seen to be more poorly governed than those without. Though poor country-level governance often exacerbates credit rationing, RFI helps alleviate this (Xu, Ru, and Song forthcoming).

There are two channels through which RFI protects itself against limited commitment while mitigating credit rationing in poorly governed, resource-rich developing countries. First, Chinese development banks allocate funding directly to construction companies rather than borrowing governments. Second, the resource revenue goes directly to an independent escrow account established to service the debt of infrastructure loans. These two mechanisms reassure creditors that loans will finance infrastructure and that sufficient revenues from separate resource-extraction projects will be secured to repay infrastructure loans (Xu, Ru, and Song forthcoming).

Whilst this instrument has the advantage of reducing credit rationing for funding infrastructure projects important for development, it reduces flexibility for debtor governments. Many countries/companies may have debt servicing difficulties for reasons other than poor governance, for example, these may be due to commodity price shocks, international financial crisis and most recently COVID. These shocks are not the fault of the government, because they are external. Therefore, the RFI mechanism is clearly good for creditors as it ensures repayment to them; it is partially good for borrowers, as it may enable/facilitate more lending to them. However, borrowers may lose flexibility in managing their foreign exchange resources, as part of their export revenue goes automatically into an escrow account, for repaying their infrastructure loans. If the country experiences an external shock, and may need to defer or reduce payments to creditors so as to use scarce foreign exchange for essential spending, it would be unable to do so. Debt restructuring/debt relief may also become more difficult.

3.5. Insurance Type Products, Securitization and Other Diversified Products

Insurance, which is based on diversifying risks, is the least used financial instrument. Amongst the 50 NDBs studied, only 5 NDBs report the usage of insurance including 3 from HICs and 2 from LIMCs.

Investors might be reluctant to invest if certain risks are deemed too high and cannot be properly managed. Insurance can enable the transfer of risk to entities better equipped to hold that risk. Certain risks are, however, difficult to manage nationally. For example, NDBs do not have the tools to insure clients against *global systemic risks and global shocks*. In these cases, international markets may provide some hedging instruments, though these might be expensive, and also may become illiquid during global shocks. MDBs may be well placed to provide insurance, eg on currency risk, which they can diversify.

Securitization: Securitization is another way of sharing risks with investors by bundling deals and taking advantage of diversification. In these structures, a DB could sell a portfolio of loans to investors by issuing a security. This allows the issuing banks to free up space on its balance sheet, increasing their lending capacity. Such bundling makes use of diversification by combining different assets with idiosyncratic risks.

Nonetheless, securitization is not without risk as demonstrated by the 2008 financial crisis. In the lead up to the global financial crisis, many sub-prime mortgage-backed securities were issued with highly correlated loans, so that in an event of a downturn, that is an increase of systemic risk, it was likely that most homeowners would default at the same time (which is what happened).

Securitizations can be structured to try to overcome some of these risks, but countries need regulatory and supervisory capacity to issue such instruments effectively. A wider application of such financial engineering by DBs in developing countries, therefore, warrants more research.

3.6. Additional Factors that Impact Instrument Choice

The type of instruments chosen is often linked to the funding, which DBs get (Interview material). For example, one DB, which works under the principle of capital preservation, cannot undertake operations, which could break capital preservation, such as first loss guarantees. In this case, the only source of the DB's funding is government grants (coming from the aid budget, which are not recorded as fiscal expenditure), and the type of instruments that can be used requires a counterpart of assets. NDBs that rely heavily on capital markets also reported linking instrument choice (and the level or risk taken) to funding choices, especially when ratings may be threatened in situations like COVID-19. Unless these DB's capital is increased, or other funds provided, e.g., from MDBs, the DB's ability to use instruments and lend to sectors that imply greater risks will be limited.

As the economy develops, the appropriate financial structure for the economy evolves correspondingly (Lin, Xifang, and Ye 2013). Applied to DBs, this means that their business models, and specifically, the instruments used, need to reflect the level of development as well as the overall characteristics of their economy. As noted above, different missions, e.g., innovation, may require different instruments. Similarly, funding different sectors, e.g., agriculture vs. infrastructure, may require different instruments. Further research is required here.

4. Development Banks' Response to COVID-19: Instruments for the Short and Long Term[2]

The COVID-19 pandemic presents a systemic crisis worldwide that will have deeper economic and social impacts compared to the 2008 economic downturn — '15 years of progress destroyed in less than a year' (IADB interview referring to Latin American economies). The economic policy focus in the short-term is on: saving companies and jobs; economic recovery; and medium to long-term structural transformation of the economy, with sustainable and inclusive development as key targets — 'build back better' as the motto for many DBs. At the same time, countries face risk of international capital flight due to risk aversion, especially in poorer regions like Sub-Saharan Africa, causing stock market downturns, weakening of exchange rates, making international finance more expensive or unavailable, and forcing governments to rely mainly on domestic borrowing.

Common factors across countries that impact DB activity include: the need of companies for liquidity (working capital) to pay workers and suppliers; the need for specific financial instruments, including those with sectorial priorities (e.g., health); and a focus on avoiding disruption to value chains.

In this context, DBs are facing a greater complexity in risk management, with increasing needs and uncertainty, and in the identification of their role and targets as financial institutions for development. The current dilemma is between a possible deterioration of the credit loan portfolio, as companies' financial situations compromise their ability to repay, vs. the imperative of granting credit for companies' survival and maintenance of jobs.

A positive aspect of the COVID response is that DBs can — and have been — using the instruments they developed in the 2007/2009 crisis. In our interviews, DBs also stressed that it is easier to lend directly and quickly to companies with whom they already have a relationship, hence deeper knowledge. Several international DBs use national DBs as intermediaries for this reason.

DBs noted that equity instruments compared to loans are harder to roll out: their due diligence takes longer; tend to have higher transaction costs and are harder to price in today's context of uncertainty. Therefore, most DBs are concentrating more on lending

[2]The content of this chapter is the result of semi-structured interviews with the top-level management of Appendix mentioned Development Banks.

than equity, even though lending increases company leverage and may lead to excessive debt. A major problem, especially for poorer developing economies is the scale of the informal sector, which is only partially included in national emergency programs.

Meanwhile, commercial banks, especially in developed economies, but also in developing ones, are reportedly facing problems of capital more than of liquidity, hence more related to their insufficient capacity to absorb risk in a context of growing risk aversion than due to a lack of liquid financial resources. Therefore, guarantees covering credit risk seem especially valuable in current circumstances. A problem is that commercial banks' alleged risk aversion (and fear of uncertainty) is so great in COVID times, that they will often lend only with 100 per cent of public guarantees, when in normal times they may do the same transaction with 80 per cent guarantee or less (as indicated, for example by EAPB).

In this context, DBs have the capacity to intervene and absorb the effects of the socio-economic downturn caused by the COVID- 19 pandemic because, compared to commercial banks, they have:

- More efficient risk bearing activity due to their shareholder structure;
- Higher degree of repayment from investments with the same credit risk due, as debtors often have a greater willingness to repay to them, due in part to their preferred creditor status;
- More efficient structure in taking risk because DBs are not listed on equity markets and thus not subject to short term volatility of stock prices, and because DBs are long term lending institutions that can hold an equity portfolio for the long term (when the volatility is lower) without liquidating it.

Given the peculiarity of the situation, the reaction of DBs to the COVID-19 pandemic does not follow a linear or pre-defined strategy but is more like a *learning-by-doing* process in which the financial institutions are constantly evaluating whether the tools need to be adapted. Nonetheless, during the first phase of the COVID-19 pandemic, there have been some common measures adopted by National and Multilateral DBs, as shown in Figure 2.

4.1. Fast-Track Procedures

To speed-up the process and allow for a quicker distribution of resources, various DBs have put in place *fast-track procedures*, shortening the time between the request and the disbursement. The extent of time reduction differs across institutions, but among the most notable measures, we identified:

- **IDB** reduced the time of the process by 2/3 on average, by developing prototypes to pre-approve the economic analysis and the monitoring and evaluation, 'so to have the back work already done' and approve/disburse within one month and a half, maximum two months.
- **CDB** set a fast-response rule — within 24 hours for central and local leadership groups or command offices for epidemic prevention and control, including their various divisions; and within 48 hours to those of enterprises participating in epidemic prevention and control.

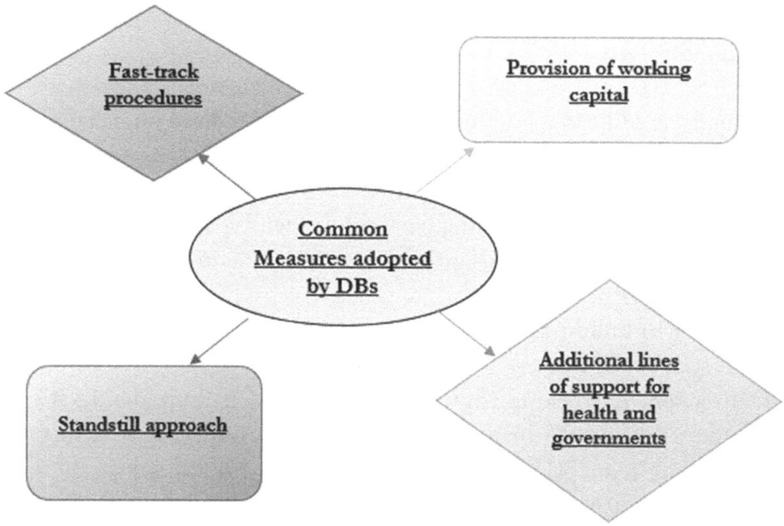

Figure 2. Common measures adopted by DBs. Source: Authors' elaboration.

- **KfW** launched a new program targeted at SMEs, the 'KfW Instant Loan 2020', to provide liquidity through an 'easy-to-apply immediate loan'[3] with no further risk assessment by KfW.
- **Caisse des dépôts** is promoting the use of digital services to make loan applications, disbursements and signatures more fluid.
- **BDMG** launched a digital platform for SMEs, to accelerate all background work and to facilitate access for companies; loans for SMEs can be disbursed in around 1 hour.
- **AFD** launched a fast-track procedure, allowing the banks to halve the time of disbursement compared to the pre-COVID-19 situation.

4.2. Provision of Working Capital with Loans, Grants and Guarantees

The COVID-19 pandemic has increased companies' demand for short-term loans, mainly working capital. In this light, and opposite to what is usually done in normal times, DBs have drastically increased this type of disbursement, to help enterprises pay workers and suppliers. The instruments to disburse working capital and general liquidity include loans, grants and guarantees, similar to instruments used in normal times. In terms of provision of working capital, loans and grants are currently usually accompanied by conditions, such as maintaining stable levels of employment and salaries.

4.3. Loans and Grants

Loans are the preferred mechanism in the short-term due to the nature of the instrument, which is easier to roll out. At the same time, as pointed out above, high usage of debt instruments implies high leverage for debtor companies.

[3]In this context, DBs are increasingly worried that regulators and rating agencies are not making any discount for long-term holding in the requirements for equity of DBs. The horizon at which DBs mark to market is usually longer, and in the long term DBs are better at bearing this type of risk.

Among the most noteworthy measures put in place by DBs during the first COVID-19 phase, we highlight:

- **BNDES** issued a credit extension for SMEs through accredited financial institutions in loans and grants with 2-months no firing and no cutting salary conditions by the companies, for an overall cost of R$ 5 billion (U$ 1 billion).
- **IDB** increased liquidity and working capital lines with a specific focus on SMEs and specific sectors such as tourism, agribusiness, manufacturing, the financial sector, trade and supply chain.
- **EIB** mobilized €40 billion as first immediate response to the COVID-19 pandemic, primarily to support SMEs.
- **CDB** set up a special working capital loan facility to help epidemic-affected enterprises resume work and to bring stability to the economy. The facility consists of RMB 130 billion loans (U$ 18 billion) and U$5 billion loans, to be adjusted based on planning, progress and needs for work and production resumption. By the end of February 2020, CDB had issued RMB 10.8 billion (U$ 1.4 billion) of special loans from the people's Bank of China, and RMB 144.1 billion (U$ 20.3 billion) of special loans for epidemic prevention and socioeconomic development of all regions.
- **KfW** will disburse up to €100 billion, through the European Recovery Fund, for refinancing of special guarantees programs. In addition, KfW also launched a program of syndicated loans for SMEs, the 'KfW Special Program for Syndicate Financing', for projects of minimum € 25 million.[4]
- **CDP** made up to € 3 billion available to Italian banks for granting new loans to SMEs together with a new 18-months liquidity line of up to 2 €/bn directly provided to medium and large companies.
- **Caisse des dépôts** focused its attention primarily on SMEs and specific sectors, mainly legal professions and social housing with an exceptional cash envelope of €500 million for the former and €2 billion for the latter.
- **CDC** launched the 'COVID-19 Business Response Facility' and the 'COVID-19 Emergency Technical Assistance Facility', to distribute grants and technical/advisory assistance to businesses. Healthcare businesses will be prioritized in the first round of funding, followed by businesses adapting to address the basic needs of underserved groups, up to £160,000 per company.

4.4. Guarantees

Guarantees are becoming more important in the COVID-19 phase, with an increasing emphasis on portfolio guarantees. As noted above, guarantees have the same credit risk/risk of default as loans, but can offer higher leverage at lower liquidity risk, which however comes at the price of a higher risk of contingent liabilities for National DBs. As the lender of last resort for DBs is the National Treasury or the Ministry of Finance, there is higher overall systemic risk embedded in guarantees. Further,

[4]https://www.kfw.de/inlandsfoerderung/Companies/KfW-Corona-Hilfe/.

guarantees work in a different manner depending on when they are used (Anginer, de la Torre, and Ize 2011), providing insurance against idiosyncratic risks during normal times but, with aggregate systemic risk and strong correlation between defaults, guarantee schemes may also need subsidies or financial resources from the State.

The most important guarantee programs put in place by DBs during the COVID-19 pandemic include:

- **BNDES** launched a new program of guarantees with an overall disbursement equal to R$ 100 billion (U$ 20 billion), equal to 20 per cent of the total credit for SMEs in Brazil. BNDES also has a program to distribute resources to certain sectors (e.g., aviation) through value chains of big Brazilian enterprises.
- **EIB** delivers a portion of the budget of the European Recovery Fund (around €200bln).
- **KfW** launched the 'KfW Special Program 2020', a package of instruments with guarantees from the State including new, considerably modified, and extended financial support for German companies. The program 'started on 23 March 2020 and registered around 2,000 applications and EUR 0.5 billion in commitments in just one week'.[5]
- **CDP** issued a guarantee covering up to 80 per cent of new bank loans for Italian companies with a turnover greater than €50 million.
- **BGK** has put in place several schemes to increase the disbursement of working capital, mainly through guarantees. BGK will increase the eligibility, the amounts and coverage of 3 guarantee programs (for SMEs, other companies, and liquidity) together with a program of loans.

4.5. Standstill Approach

Another common instrument used by DBs during the COVID-19 pandemic has been a standstill approach on existing loans, with extended grace periods. The reasons behind the choice of this (passive) instrument have to do with the current difficulty of renegotiating the terms of contract, which would increase the costs for DBs. However, this passive instrument is often seen as a negative signal by rating agencies, that tend to lower the rating of the credit institutions implementing it. At the same time, different scholars and senior officials have argued that such instrument, as for GDP linked bonds (for a detailed overview, please refer to Benford, Ostry, and Shiller (2018)), is usually aimed at increasing the quality of the credit that, consequently, will be more likely to be repaid. Therefore, it would be desirable for rating agencies to adapt their methodologies to take account of these insights by academics and policymakers.

Generally, almost all DBs have offered a standstill approach, including an introduction of grace periods. Among the most important examples, we report:

- **BNDES** offered an extended grace periods of 6 months.
- **BGK** applied a reduction in interest rates on existing loans.

[5]https://www.kfw.de/KfW-Group/Newsroom/Latest-News/Pressemitteilungen-Details_583809.html (accessed on 8 June 2020).

- **CDP** allowed for a greater flexibility of payment on installments of mortgages by local authorities and regions.
- **Caisse des dépôts** introduced an automatic deferral of six months' maturities for interest-free loans and a deferral, on request, of the repayment deadlines on loans of specific programs.
- **AFD** adopted a flexible policy on the terms of contracts for existing guarantees.

4.6. Additional Lines of Support for Health Sector and Governments

During the COVID-19 pandemic, DBs have also played a crucial role in providing liquidity to central governments and supporting the health sector with injections of liquidity. A list of the most important measures put in place by DBs over the first months of 2020, includes:

- **IADB** issued country-specific credit lines for health systems, for example, in Uruguay (U$ 1.7 billion)[6] and Belize (U$ 6.2 million).[7]
- **BNDES** announced a new special credit line of R$ 2 billion (U$ 0.4 billion) to support healthcare and life science manufacturers of medical equipment; it is also currently providing liquidity to the central government.
- **CAF** issued a contingent credit line of up to US$ 50 million per country for public health systems.
- **CDB** issued a loan of RMB 2 billion (US$ 0.3 billion) for healthcare assistance, purchases of emergency equipment, and funding for work; by the end of February, CDB had also issued RMB 27.2 billion (U$ 3.8 billion) of emergency loans for epidemic prevention and control.
- **AfDB** launched country-specific lines of credit, disbursing an overall amount of U $1.35 billion for private sector operations; U$5.5 billion for sovereign operations; and an additional U$3.1 billion for sovereign and regional operations as part of the African Development Fund.[8]
- **CDC** launched the 'COVID-19 Business Response Facility' that will prioritize healthcare businesses in the first round of funding.

4.7. Other Regional DBs and Municipal Funding Banks and Agencies

Local public financial institutions are also playing an important role during the COVID-19 pandemic. Compared to national and multinational DBs, sub-national regional DBs and municipal funding banks have a different nature, size and way of raising funding. Differences are also notable within local financial institutions, due to their different scopes, countries' credit worthiness and company statutes.

[6]https://en.mercopress.com/2020/05/28/idb-us-1-7bn-loan-for-uruguay-to-address-the-covid-19-pandemic (accessed on 7 June 2020).
[7]https://www.iadb.org/en/news/idb-approves-loan-support-belizes-covid-19-immediate-health-response (accessed on 20 May 2020).
[8]https://www.afdb.org/en/news-and-events/press-releases/african-development-bank-group-unveils-10-billion-response-facility-curb-covid-19-35174 (accessed on 3 June 2020).

The group of German regional DBs (Nordrhein-Westfalen- NRW, WIBank, Investitionsbank Berlin, Thüringer Aufbaubank, L-Bank, Förderbank-SAB, Rentenbank) has been particularly active during the first phase of the pandemic. The common instruments used in the short term are a combination of: (a) guarantee schemes, generally for specific companies in terms of size or sector; (b) working capital programs to increase the liquidity through loans, grants and bridging loans; (c) standstill approach on existing loans and an extension of the investing periods.

Outside the European continent, the regional Brazilian DB, **BDMG,** has provided strong financial support to local companies. With a combination of guarantees, loans, grants, fast-track procedures and standstill approaches, BDMG has expanded its counter-cyclical program for the health sector, and issued an emergency program for tourism and a multi-sectorial emergency line for SMEs. Further, by, inserting the 'COVID-19 impact on the sector' as an additional variable, BDMG has also adjusted its risk appetite to balance collateral with other attributes of the credit operations (rating, term, size and purpose) and provide guidelines for decision-making process. Finally, the Brazilian DB has been also working on new guarantee funds, one in partnership with the State of Minas Gerais — the Minas Investe Garantidor[9] to support operations for MSMEs, but eventually may be applicable in credit operations with large companies for strategic projects.

4.8. Recovery Phase and Instruments for the Medium-Long Term

One of the main challenges faced by DBs is meeting climate targets during the crisis response. In particular, the current debate is on whether there is a need to soften these targets, avoiding additional costs for companies during the crisis, or whether keeping these targets might represent the right push towards a greener economy 'to rebuild better'. The overall perception is that DBs will attempt the latter approach. Ongoing discussions are also about the possibility for DBs of using different reporting with regard to climate, pre and post COVID-19, keeping climate targets in the existing portfolio of instruments and relaxing targets in new emergency instruments during the pandemic.

In this context and looking towards the recovery phase, DBs agree that the medium to long-term approach must be focused on rebuilding the private sector, while moving back to an environmentally sustainable path. This can be achieved by large long-term investments, supported by appropriate instruments to provide adequate liquidity and absorb the risk in a long-term time frame. Infrastructure represents one of the main areas of interest for these types of investments and there is a wide agreement among DBs that syndicated loans can be a useful funding tool for these projects, especially in the construction phase. There are multiple advantages of using syndicated loans, usually partnered with international banks and the National Treasury, as they help DBs leverage capital and allow better risk absorption in the long term.

[9]https://www.almg.gov.br/consulte/legislacao/completa/completa.html?tipo=DEC&num=47939&comp=&ano=2020 (accessed on 10 June 2020).

5. Conclusion and Further Research Suggestions

A key question is how development banks should deploy appropriate financial instruments to encourage real economic risk-taking while minimizing financial engineering risks. The outcome that DBs need to pursue is to maximize development impact.

A DB has the option of using simple instruments, such as a direct loans or direct equity vs. more complex financial instruments, such as a guarantees or securitization. A direct loan or equity would likely maximize the development bank's policy steer to try to ensure maximum development impact of the transaction, though the latter would use more of a bank's capital. Equity could be particularly well suited for ambitious projects, e.g., development of a new technology, which may have difficulty attracting private finance, due to high levels of risk and uncertainty; an equity instrument would allow the DB to capture the upside if project very successful. Guarantees have a useful role to play in times of high uncertainty, such as COVID times or after financial crises.

The DB can, alternatively, use more complex financial instrument engineered or created to attract additional financing and add leverage. The aim, from the DB angle, is to maximize development impact by increasing volume of activity. The use of such instruments, however, poses several challenges. First, it may lead to too much risk transfer from the private financial intermediary to the DB, and therefore potential losses to the DB. Second, there may be a reduction of policy steer aimed at maximizing sustainable development impact. The potential of long-term losses to DBs and governments is particularly problematic if the additional risk to the DB is not accurately compensated (e.g., through sharing in potential upside in a project) or priced. There may be a likely trade-off between needing less fiscal resources in the short term, and potentially more in the long term.

DBs can involve private finance in different ways, some more desirable in terms of maximizing development impact, and minimizing future contingency losses. When DBs borrow on private capital markets and give direct loans or grants, or co-finance with commercial banks or private investors, DBs can keep their policy steer, and thus aim to maximize development impact, whilst increasing leverage. Another useful mechanism of DB/private financial sector collaboration is DBs on-lending via commercial banks, if the programs have clear aims (e.g., loans for green transformation), and effective monitoring so such development targets are met.

These mechanisms potentially give DBs greater policy steer than complex instruments, especially when such instruments are opaque, and for which the developmental impact may be more difficult to ascertain. It could thus be argued that there is a loose hierarchy of involving private finance in development funding in terms of impact, with most impactful mechanisms being DBs borrowing on private capital markets to offer direct loans and equity; private lenders and investors co-lending or co-investing with DBs; on-lending to commercial institutions.

More leverage and higher levels of financing of investment by DBs can also be achieved via increasing the paid-in capital of DBs. An increase of capital allows increases of DB activity, without risking increased contingent liabilities and deterioration of its' credit rating. This is the case also when the DB takes on more economic risks, for example to encourage innovation and/or investment in new sectors for a green and just transformation, and is appropriate in circumstances, like COVID, where general uncertainty and different risks are perceived as increasing. Increasing the capital of DBs is worth pursuing, both at the national and multilateral level, especially in COVID times, and given major challenges for structural transformation to a low carbon and more equitable economy.

5.1. Further Research Questions

This paper was conceived as an umbrella paper, partly with the aim of defining key topics for a future research program. These include:

(1) The role of different equity instruments for DBs as mechanisms to encourage innovative activities, better share risks and returns between DBs and private investors, and help reduce leverage for companies.
(2) How can the analytical framework developed in this paper for defining appropriate instruments be applied to different sectors, e.g., green infrastructure, agriculture, innovation, and industry? How should it be applied to DBs in countries with different levels of income?
(3) Rating agencies, and their methodologies impact the cost of funds for DBs. Are rating agencies using appropriate methodologies for evaluating risk of DBs? One example is if a DB applies a standstill on some of its debts, rating agencies may downgrade it. Is this appropriate, as this may actually increase the debtor's future ability to pay? Should rating agencies be regulated?
(4) How can grants/concessional resources channeled to DBs be used most effectively? To what extent should they subsidize new activities with potential major sustainable development impact? To what extent should they support poorer regions and smaller companies? Should they be given upfront or reduce the cost of credit? To what extent should they directly subsidize activities, and to what extent should they provide guarantees against specific risks to encourage private investors and lenders to increase their activity? Are there cases where longer-term subsidies are warranted?
(5) What are advantages and disadvantages of using direct (retail) and indirect (wholesale) instruments? In what type of scale and sector are either of these instruments more appropriate? How does this balance change, when there is a greater emphasis on speedily disbursing funds (counter-cyclical role), like in COVID times? Or if the balance shifts to supporting a major structural transformation to a low carbon and inclusive economy, requiring greater policy steer?
(6) There is a need for greater understanding of DBs in specific country and regional contexts. A study on DBs in Sub-Saharan Africa seems essential. Research on the European Investment Bank, its valuable experience, and how it can be best transformed into further supporting the European Green Deal, as well as green transformation internationally, is also important to study. The Chinese Development Bank, as the largest DB and one which has made important contributions in China and internationally seems important to study in depth.

Acknowledgements

We greatly thank all the senior officials of development banks we interviewed for valuable insights and information provided, as well as our commentators, on a previous draft, Jose Antonio Ocampo and Daniel Titelman.

Disclosure Statement

No potential conflict of interest was reported by the author(s).

Funding

We are deeply grateful for the financial and intellectual support provided by AFD, and in particular by Regis Marodon for the writing of this paper.

References

Allen, F., L. Bartiloro, X. Gu, and O. Kowalewski. 2018. 'Does Economic Structure Determine Financial Structure?' *Journal of International Economics* 114: 389–409.

Anginer, D., A. de la Torre, and A. Ize. 2011. 'Risk Absorption by the State: When Is It Good Public Policy?' World Bank Policy Research Working Paper No. 5893. http://documents.worldbank.org/curated/en/231941468134726378/pdf/WPS5893.pdf.

Arrow, K. J., and R. C. Lind. 1970. 'Uncertainty and the Evaluation of Public Investment Decisions.' *American Economic Review* 60: 364–378.

Benford, J., J. D. Ostry, and R. Shiller. 2018. *Sovereign GDP-Linked Bonds: Rationale and Design, a VoxEU.org EBook*. London: CEPR Press.

Carter, P., and M. Plant. 2020. 'The Subsidy Sorting Hat.' Center for Global Development Note.

Greenwald, B. C., and J. E. Stiglitz. 1989. 'Toward a Theory of Rigidities.' National Bureau of Economic Research, No. w2938.

Griffith-Jones, S. 1993. *Loan Guarantees for Large Infrastructure Projects: The Issues and Possible Lessons for a European Facility*. Luxembourg: Office for Official Publications of the European Communities.

Griffith-Jones, S., and N. Naqvi. 2020. 'Leveraging Policy Steer? Industrial Policy, Risk-Sharing and the European Investment Bank.' Working Paper 43 GEG Oxford. https://www.geg.ox.ac.uk/sites/geg.bsg.ox.ac.uk/files/2020-07/GEG%20WP%20143%20July%202020%20Industrial%20policy%20and%20risk%20sharing%20in%20public%20development%20banks.pdf and in M. Thiemann, D. Martens and P. Volberding, eds. 2021. *The Reinvention of Development Banking in the European Union*. OUP.

Ketterer, J., and A. Powell. 2018. 'Financing Infrastructure.' IADB.

Knight, F. H. 1921. 'Cost of Production and Price Over Long and Short Periods.' *Journal of Political Economy* 29 (4): 304–335.

Lacker, J. M. 1994. 'Does Adverse Selection Justify Government Intervention in Loan Markets?' *FRB Richmond Economic Quarterly* 80 (1): 61–95.

Lin, J. Y., S. Xifang, and J. Ye. 2013. 'Endowment, Industrial Structure, and Appropriate Financial Structure: A New Structural Economics Perspective.' *Journal of Economic Policy Reform* 16 (2): 109–122.

Mazzucato, M. 2018. *The Value of Everything: Making and Taking in the Global Economy*. Hachette: ABC Books.

Stiglitz, J. E., and A. Weiss. 1981. 'Credit Rationing in Markets with Imperfect Information.' *The American Economic Review* 71 (3): 393–410.

United Nations. 2020. 'The Inter-Agency Task Force on Financing for Development.' Financing for Sustainable Development Report.

Xu, J., X. Ren, and X. Wu. 2019. 'Mapping Development Finance Institutions Worldwide: Definitions, Rationale and Varieties.' New Structural Development Financing Report No. 1. https://www.nse.pku.edu.cn/docs/20190529100907766148.pdf.

Xu, J., X. Ru, and P. Song. Forthcoming. 'Resource Financed Infrastructure: Mitigating Credit Rationing in Poorly Governed Countries.' Working Paper.

Appendix

List of colleagues with whom in-depth interviews carried out

African Development Bank — AFDB

Ambert, Cecile — Chief Administrator — Private Sector Credit Enhancement Facility

Commonwealth Development Corporation — CDC

Carter, Paddy — Head of Research

Plant, Mark — Head of Center of Global Development, Europe

European Association of Public Banks — EAPB

Roy, Marcel — Secretary general

Ernoult, Julien — Adviser to the Secretary-General — Department Director Public Financing Policies and Compliance

Inter-American Development Bank — IADB

Bonilla, Juan Pablo — Manager of the IDB's Climate Change and Sustainable Development Sector (CSD).

Prada, Alejandro — Principal Advisor for Strategy and Corporate Affairs — IDB Invest

Galizia, Federico — Chief Risk Officer

Astesiano, Gaston — PPP Team Leader

Ketterer, Juan Antonio — Division Chief, Connectivity, Markets and Finance

Powell, Andrew Philip — Principal Advisor, Research Dept.

Yanez-Pagans, Patricia (on behalf of Alejandro Matioli) — Lead Economist, Development Effectiveness Division — IDB Invest

Fonseca Daniel — Financial Institutions Officer

Ramos Murillo, Erick — Consultant with the Competitive Cities team of the World Bank Group

Maria Fernanda (Marife) Merino — Operations Lead Specialist at the Office of Strategic Planning and Development Effectiveness

Sacristan Postigo, Gema — Chief Investment Officer, IDB Invest

Banco de Desenvolvimento de Minas Gerais — BDMG

Suchodolski, Sergio Gusmao — CEO

Modesto, Adauto — Chief Economist

Banco Nacional de Desenvolvimento Econômico e Social — BNDES

Machado, Vivian — Manager for international organizations — raising funds from other multilateral DBs

Machado, Luciene — Manager for institutional relationships

Barros de Castro, Lavinia — Planning and Research Area

Agence Française de Développement — AFD

Poisson, Julien — Project Manager

Drouin, Emmanuelle Riedel — Head of the Economic and Financial Transition Department

Marodon, Regis — Special Adviser on Sustainable Finance at the French Development Agency

Winckler, Cosimo — Investment Officer

Sauvageot, Tomas — Project Manager

Oliveira, Barbara — Development Finance research officer

European Investment Bank — EIB

Gereben, Aron — Senior Economist in the Policy and Strategy team of the Economics Department

Chevaillier, Julie — Advisor to Vice-President Ambroise Fayolle

Dustdar, Shiva — Head of the Innovation Finance Advisory division

The Global Development Banks' Architecture

José Antonio Ocampo and Victor Ortega

ABSTRACT
This paper looks at the role, evolution, and regional coverage of the system of multilateral and national development banks (MDBs and NDBs). It analyzes the roles that development banks should play to correct the market failures that characterize financial systems, particularly in emerging and developing countries. It concludes that MDBs should be capitalized to better support emerging and developing countries' recovery after the COVID-19 crisis. They should also be aligned with the Sustainable Development Goals, and enhance their role in promoting innovation and structural transformation, and supporting climate change mitigation and adaptation. It underscores that the development banks should work as a system and that better networking between MDBs and NDBs is essential and should be systematically monitored. Finally, it points out that MDBs should support the development of strong NDBs in the regions where these institutions are underrepresented.

1. Introduction

The system of development banks has a history that goes back to the Great Depression of the 1930s, when the collapse of global financial markets and their effects on domestic finance led governments to create public sector financial institutions to support economic activity. Their precedent in the 19th centery were the public sector banks created by some countries in Europe and Latin America.

The US Export-Import (Exim) Bank was created in 1934. The Latin American countries pushed the US to create an Inter-American institution in the late 1930s, an initiative that the US government finally accepted but was rejected by Congress. That project, which had been developed under the leadership of Harry Dexter White, served as the basis for the US proposal to create the World Bank at the Bretton Woods Conference, the first Multinational Development Bank (MDB) (Helleiner 2014). The name of the new institution, the International Bank for Reconstruction and Development (IBRD), made clear that one of its fundamental objectives was to support European reconstruction after the War. However, this task was replaced by the Marshall Plan, and the IBRD took at its main responsibility supporting developing countries.

The post-war European reconstruction also gave birth to several institutions to support their economies, the most remarkable being KfW (*Kreditanstalt für*

Wiederaufbau), created in 1948 with Marshall Plan support. There were many other National Development Banks (NDBs) created throughout the world in the early post-war period, some of which have been success stories, but others have a mixed history. The list includes the Industrial Finance Corporation of India, created in 1948, the Brazilian BNDES (*Banco Nacional de Desenvolvimento Econômico e Social*) in 1952; and the Korea Development Bank and the Industrial Development Bank of India, both in 1964. There were also several banks aimed at promoting countries' foreign trade, following the US Exim bank model, as well as to support agriculture.

The system of the MDBs was reinforced with the creation of the International Finance Corporation (IFC) in 1956 and the International Development Agency (IDA) in 1959 as part of the World Bank Group (WBG), and of the first regional development banks, the European Investment Bank (EIB) and the Inter-American Development Bank (IADB), in 1958 and 1959, respectively. The system of MDBs was expanded with the creation of the African Development Bank (AfDB) in 1964 and the Asian Development Bank (ADB) in 1966, and later by many other institutions. As an inter-regional institution, the Islamic Development Bank, formed in 1973, was also an important innovation. Latin America and the Caribbean were also very good at creating sub-regional institutions: the Central American Bank for Economic Integration, in 1960; the Andean Development Corporation (CAF) in 1968, which expanded to become a truly regional development bank and thus changed its name to Development Bank of Latin America in 2010, although it kept its old acronym; and the Caribbean Development Bank in 1969.

By the early 1970s, a truly Global Development Bank architecture had been formed, including global, regional, sub-regional, national, and sub-national institutions. This network has continued to grow and is now constituted by more than 400 institutions, according to the Agence Française de Développement.

The development banks, and more generally, the role of the state in the financial sector, came under a fierce attack with the rise of the market reform agenda in the 1980s. The basic argument, formulated by McKinnon (1973) and Shaw (1973), was that state intervention generates 'financially repressed' systems that are inefficient in the provision of financial services. As a result of the new trend, the support for development banks tended to wane, and their role was reduced sharply. Interestingly, however, no MDB was liquidated, and an important new one was created in 1991 to support the former communist countries in their transition to capitalism: the European Bank for Reconstruction and Development (EBRD). A major new NDB was also created in 1994: the China Development Bank.

Since the crisis that several emerging economies faced at the turn of the century, led by the collapse of several East Asian economies in 1997 and the Russian moratorium of 1998, and particularly since the 2007–09 North Atlantic financial crisis,[1] the interest in, and support for both MDBs and NDBs came back with a strong force. The recognition of the pro-cyclical character of private finance was the major reason for the recognition that these institutions can play a useful counter-cyclical function. The role of other market failures affecting the financial sector was also acknowledged, as well as their potential support for the provision of global public goods, in particular combating climate change.

[1] We prefer this term to the more broadly used of global financial crisis because, although it had global effects, it concentrated in the United States and Western Europe.

The crucial role of development banks at all levels received strong, and in fact, increasing attention in the United Nations Financing for Development conferences, from Monterrey in 2002 to Addis Ababa in 2015 (United Nations 2002 and 2015a). As the Action Agenda of the Addis Ababa conference states: 'We note the role that well-functioning national and regional development banks can play in financing sustainable development, particularly in credit market segments in which commercial banks are not fully engaged and where large financing gaps exist (…) We acknowledge that national and regional development banks also play a valuable counter-cyclical role, especially during financial crises, when private sector entities become highly risk-averse' (United Nations 2015a, paragraph 33).

This paper will underscore the role of MDBs that support emerging and developing countries. It will also take a look at the system of NDBs and the relation of MDBs with these national institutions. It is divided into five sections: the first is this introduction. The second looks at the role of development banks. The third focuses on MDBs, and the fourth on NDBs and their relation with multinational institutions. The last presents conclusions and recommendations.

2. The Role of Development Banks

Development banks play a crucial role in counteracting market failures and supporting sustainable development in the broader United Nations concept well captured in Agenda 2030 and its Sustainable Development Goals (SDGs) (United Nations 2015b). Financial market failures imply that financial liberalization has major flaws, as it is now broadly recognized and contrasts with the market reform agenda put forwards in the 1980s.

The first imperfection of financial markets is the tendency to experience 'boom–bust' cycles (see in particular Kindleberger and Aliber 2011; and Minsky 1982). This feature, which characterizes even well-developed financial markets, is reflected in the 'sudden stops' of external financing that emerging and developing countries experience during crises (Calvo 1998). This includes the massive flight of portfolio capital from emerging economies that took place at the onset of the COVID-19 crisis (IMF 2020).

The second set of market failures is associated with the imperfect information that characterizes financial markets, which generate adverse selection, moral hazard, and credit rationing (Stiglitz and Weiss 1981; Stiglitz 1994). These problems call for strong public sector regulation and supervision of financial institutions and mechanisms that guarantee access to finance for those nations, regions, sectors, and individuals excluded because of the high risks of lending to them perceived by financial agents.

A third market failure is associated with the high uncertainty and risks faced by innovative activities (Mazzucato 2013). This is crucial, as rapid economic growth is characterized by a transformation of the economic structure and calls, therefore, for policies that guarantee the 'dynamic efficiency' of a given economic system, understood as the capacity to generate constant waves of innovation and structural change (Ocampo 2017). This is also related to the concept of 'learning society' proposed by Stiglitz and Greenwald (2014), which implies that governments have an essential role in promoting innovation.

A final set of market failures is related to financing activities with large externalities and the provision of public goods. The first is the case of infrastructure, where long-term financing is essential, both for public sector investments and for relevant private-public partnerships. The second is particularly the case of climate change, which is, as Stern (2015) has stated, is the greatest market failure the world has ever seen.

Market failures are particularly strong in emerging and developing countries, as their domestic financial markets are characterized by a strong prevalence of short-term financial assets and liabilities and limited financial inclusion. The first of these problems implies that firms with access to finance may have to rely on short-term loans to finance their investments or limit their investments to what they can fund with retained profits. New firms and micro, small, and medium-sized enterprises (MSMEs) may lack financial access altogether, limiting their investments to what they can finance with their savings. In the case of governments, insufficient access to long-term financing may also reduce the levels of investments in infrastructure and in the fight against climate change.

Access to international financing may overcome some agents' dependence on short-term credits, but this is limited to governments and large domestic and foreign firms. A major implication of this, together with the prevalence of short-term domestic financing, is that financial markets in emerging and developing economies are characterized by variable mixes of maturity and currency mismatches in portfolios. This feature has significant financial stability implications, as they reinforce the boom–bust cycles that characterized financial markets.

Given the limitations and stability issues that financial sectors face, development banks play an essential role in the structural transformation and the stability of emerging and developing economies. Based on these market failures, development banks have seven priority functions,[2] as argued in a recent project on NDBs, but the analysis can be extended to MDBs: (i) providing counter-cyclical financing; (ii) supporting countries and regions within countries that lag behind in the development process; (iii) improving social development; (iv) enhancing financial inclusion; (v) promoting innovation and structural transformation; (vi) financing infrastructure investment; and (vii) supporting the provision of public goods, particularly combatting climate change. These functions have several links, which implies that they should be seen as integral tasks of the system of development banks.

The pro-cyclical nature of private international financing implies the need for official funds during crises, not only from the IMF and regional monetary institutions but also for MDBs (function i). The counter-cyclical financing from the MDBs should include emergency programs to mitigate crises and support recovery, particularly by financing public and private sector investments, supported in the latter case by their corporate branches or facilities. NDBs must also play an active counter-cyclical role, complementing that played by fiscal, monetary, and foreign exchange policies at the national level. The counter-cyclical function has long-term implications, as it is essential to avoid an interruption of the process of structural transformation (function v).

Function (ii) generates a case for MDBs to provide resources to countries with inadequate access to private financial markets. As this problem becomes more acute and affects many more countries during crises, it interacts with the counter-cyclical function. In low-income countries, it should be reflected in the design of facilities that provide

[2]We have added the second and third functions mentioned to the original list proposed by Griffith-Jones and Ocampo (2018).

transfers and very low-cost loans to these countries, supporting the role of official development assistance — or becoming agents of such assistance.

Functions (iii) and (iv) underscore the role that MDBs and NDBs should play to enhance social development. The first is supporting education, health, and social protection policies at the national level. The second is to help expand access to credit for MSMEs and low-income households, particularly in the latter case for housing. It is frequently supported by state-owned first-tier banks, or by guarantee funds or agencies that back lending to MSMEs provided by private financial institutions. Although these functions are tasks for NDBs, MDBs can provide funding for those activities.

Function (v) is crucial to enhance the dynamic efficiency of an economy. Again, it is particularly crucial for NDBs. However, MDBs can also help fund governments' innovation, science, and technology policies and provide equity and lending to innovative private sector firms. Through their corporate branches, MDBs can also be involved in the creation of venture capital funds in association with NDBs and private agents. As Mazzucato and Penna (2018) argue, there is mounting evidence that NDBs have fostered 'patient' long-term finance for innovative activities. It is worth adding that promoting innovative MSMEs, as part of the broader objective of financial inclusion (iii), may also have positive effects on structural change.

In turn, function (vi) supports governments' investments but also that of private agents involved in public-private infrastructure partnerships. Finance in this area is crucial for economic growth, given the large gaps in this area in many emerging and developing countries (Bhattacharya, Oppenheim, and Stern 2015). Financing provided in this area can also play an essential role in environmental sustainability.

Finally, the activities under (vii) are important in contributing to sustainable development's environmental dimensions and may include innovative activities that support function (v). Climate change is a particularly long-term phenomenon and requires an adequate mix of long-term financing, subsidies to climate-friendly activities, taxes on those that generate adverse effects, and adequate regulation of the financial risks generated by financing activities with negative environmental effects (Dikau and Volz 2019; Bernal and Ocampo 2020).

It is worth mentioning that many NDBs and public-sector banks have been created in several countries to support agriculture and rural development, as well as export activities. The fact that rural areas concentrate a large proportion of the poor population in several countries, and that rural markets may present specific problems of financial exclusion, implies that supporting rural development is an important role for NDBs, following functions (ii) and (iv), as well as by other public-sector financial institutions. The problems generated by the instability of agricultural prices has also been an argument to support the sector as an element of counter-cyclical policies (function i).

In turn, export diversification may be seen as a key factor in the structural transformation, and therefore support function (v). The lack of adequate foreign trade financing during crises may be an obstacle, particularly for developing countries, and therefore trade financing by MDBs during crises contribute to function (i).

Beyond the specific functions of development banks, it should be underscored that the broader context is vital for their success. Thus, sound macroeconomic policies — including active counter-cyclical macroeconomic policies — are essential to the success of the several activities promoted by these institutions. They are also more effective if there are clear national strategies that development banks can support, ideally linked to industrial policies promoting innovative sectors. A well-functioning financial sector is another important precondition and an essential one to guarantee the multiplier effects of financing by NDBs. Furthermore, NDBs can help develop deeper and better capital markets in emerging and developing countries, again with support from MDBs. In several countries, they have been vital in developing the domestic bond market and, more recently, that for green bonds.

3. The Evolution and Structure of MDBs

The evolution of financing by major MDBs serving emerging and developing countries over the past two decades is summarized in Table 1. The WBG –and IBRD in particular — has had the strongest role in terms of counter-cyclical financing. As we will see, the institution increased its lending most markedly during the North Atlantic financial crisis, and adopted a strong program to support emerging and developing countries during the COVID-19 crisis.

The regional development banks supporting emerging and developing countries have also played a counter-cyclical role but, more importantly, have grown faster than the WBG over the past two decades. The ADB has been the most dynamic, followed by the AfDB. IADB and the EBRD were also very dynamic prior to the North Atlantic financial crisis but have grown less than their regional counterparts over the past decade. Latin America also counts with CAF, a former sub-regional institution that, as previously noted, is now effectively a regional development bank. In turn, two new institutions have been added in recent years: the New Development Bank (NewDB) of the BRICS countries and the Asian Infrastructure Investment Bank (AIIB).

It is also worth underscoring the role of EIB, which has continued to be the largest MDB, essentially serving the European countries. It also played an essential role during the North Atlantic financial crisis and the succeeding euro crisis with significant counter-cyclical support.

These patterns reflect the relevance of the backing of the major developed countries for the WBG to guarantee the capacity to finance its lending program during crises, but also the growing support for the regional development banks by emerging and developing countries. The latter reflects the greater sense of ownership of the regional banks by these countries, which is associated with a sense that they respond more strongly to their demands.

In the area of concessional finance, the WBG, through IDA, plays the leading role, followed by the ADB and the AfDB. In contrast, the IADB and CAF provide very limited concessional financing, and neither the EBRD nor the AIIB offer this type of resources.

The broader system of MDBs (Table 2) includes, first of all, three institutions of the WBG (IBRD, IDA, and IFC), and four interregional organizations: the Islamic Development Bank, the UN International Fund for Agricultural Development, the NewDB, and the International Investment Bank.[3]

Among the regional organizations, Europe's dominance is remarkable, largely because of the EIB, complemented by the Council of Europe Development Bank, EBRD, and the

[3]This institution was created during the communist era. After a prolonged crisis, it has been restructured

Table 1. Loan Commitments of Multilateral Development Banks (Million US dollars).

	2000	2001	2002	2003	2004	2005	2006	2007	2008	2009
International Bank for Reconstruction and Development (IBRD)	10,919	10,487	11,452	11,231	11,045	13,611	14,135	12,829	13,468	32,911
International Development Association (IDA)	13,332	6,764	8,068	7,282	9,035	8,696	9,506	11,867	11,235	13,995
International Finance Corporation (IFC)	2,379	2,732	2,957	3,856	4,753	5,373	6,703	8,220	11,399	10,547
Subtotal World Bank Group	26,630	19,983	22,477	22,369	24,833	27,680	30,344	32,915	36,101	57,453
Inter-American Development Bank (IADB)	4,969	7,411	4,143	6,232	5,468	6,738	5,774	8,812	11,085	15,278
African Development Bank (AfDB)	1,984	2,372	2,039	1,766	2,787	2,294	2,597	3,098	3,529	8,064
Asian Development Bank (AsDB)	5,583	5,339	5,658	6,085	5,039	5,761	7,264	9,516	10,124	13,230
European Bank for Reconstruction and Development (EBRD)	2,465	3,312	3,676	4,180	5,093	5,346	6,149	7,664	7,464	10,987
Subtotal Regional Banks	15,001	18,434	15,516	18,263	18,387	20,139	21,784	29,090	32,202	47,559
Development Bank of Latin America (CAF)	2,323	3,196	3,291	3,304	3,504	4,746	5,521	6,607	7,947	9,170
Asian Infraestucture Investment Bank (AIIB)	-	-	-	-	-	-	-	-	-	-
New Development Bank (NewDB)	-	-	-	-	-	-	-	-	-	-
European Investment Bank (EIB)	44,500	46,027	55,604	41,251	36,919	41,094	42,358	41,208	40,335	74,747
TOTAL	**88,454**	**87,640**	**96,889**	**85,187**	**83,644**	**93,659**	**1,00,007**	**1,09,820**	**1,16,584**	**1,88,928**

	2010	**2011**	**2012**	**2013**	**2014**	**2015**	**2016**	**2017**	**2018**	**2019**	**2020**
International Bank for Reconstruction and Development (IBRD)	44,197	26,737	20,582	15,249	18,604	23,528	29,729	22,611	23,002	23,191	27,976
International Development Association (IDA)	14,550	16,269	14,753	16,298	22,239	18,966	16,171	19,513	24,010	21,932	30,365
International Finance Corporation (IFC)	12,664	12,186	15,462	18,349	17,261	10,539	11,117	11,854	11,629	8,920	11,135
Subtotal World Bank Group	71,411	55,192	50,797	49,896	58,104	53,033	57,017	53,978	58,641	54,043	69,476
Inter-American Development Bank (IADB)	12,464	10,671	11,179	13,811	13,629	11,074	11,325	13,350	14,756	13,268	14,511
African Development Bank (AfDB)	4,100	5,720	4,254	4,386	5,050	6,335	8,035	6,196	7,279	7,300	4,171
Asian Development Bank (ADB)	17,936	20,374	20,925	20,357	22,841	26,540	25,466	31,813	35,464	33,743	48,002
European Bank for Reconstruction and Development (EBRD)	11,830	10,681	11,214	11,836	12,273	11,794	11,104	12,083	12,763	13,172	13,844
Subtotal Regional Banks	46,330	47,446	47,572	50,390	53,793	55,743	55,930	63,442	70,262	67,483	80,529
Development Bank of Latin America (CAF)	10,533	10,066	9,275	11,876	11,622	11,537	12,412	12,259	13,663	13,010	14,147
Asian Infraestucture Investment Bank (AIIB)	-	-	-	-	-	-	1,694	2,502	3,304	4,576	8,006
New Development Bank (NewDB)	-	-	-	-	-	-	1,544	1,851	4,697	7,192	10,277
European Investment Bank (EIB)	62,614	38,410	48,318	1,06,098	1,19,180	1,04,259	83,420	94,612	74,076	65,746	1,08,972
TOTAL	**1,90,889**	**1,51,114**	**1,55,962**	**2,18,261**	**2,42,699**	**2,24,572**	**2,12,018**	**2,28,644**	**2,24,643**	**2,12,051**	**2,91,406**

Source: Information from each development bank.

Notes: For the WBG, the data refer to the fiscal year that ended in June. The EBRD and EIB data were originally in euros; the exchange rate used to convert to US dollars was the end-of-period rate.

Source: Annual reports of each institution

Table 2. The System of Multilateral Development Banks.

Area	Bank	Acronym	Established	Assets (Billion US$)
World	The World Bank	WB	1944	263.8
World	International Finance Corporation	IFC	1956	94.3
World	International Development Agency - WB group	IDA	1960	184.6
Inter-regional	International Investment Bank	IIB	1970	1.3
Inter-regional	Islamic Development Bank	IsDB	1974	37.6
Inter-regional	International Fund for Agricultural Development	IFAD	1977	9.0
Inter-regional	New Development Bank	NDB BRICS	2014	10.4
Africa	African Development Bank	AfDB	1964	13.1
Africa	Fonds Africain de Garantie et de Coopération Economique	FAGACE	1977	0.1
Africa	East African Development Bank	EADB	1967	0.4
Africa	Banque de Développement des Etats de l'Afrique de l'Ouest	BOAD	1973	4.6
Africa	Banque de Développement des Etats d'Afrique Centrale	BDEAC	1975	0.7
Africa	Ecowas Bank for Investment and Development	EBID	1975	0.9
Africa	Banque de Développement des Etats des Grands Lacs	BDEGL	1977	0.1
Africa	Shelter Afrique	ShelterA	1985	0.2
Africa	Trade and Development Bank	TDB	1985	5.5
Africa	African Export and Import Bank	Afreximbank	1993	13.4
Middle East and North Africa	Arab Bank for the Economic Development of Africa	BADEA	1973	4.9
Middle East and North Africa	Arab Fund for Social and Economic Development	AFESD	1974	12.2
Middle East and North Africa	OPEC Fund for International Development	OFID	1976	7.4
Middle East and North Africa	Arab Trade Financing Program	ATFP	1989	1.2
Middle East and North Africa	Islamic Corporation for the Development of Private Sector	ICD	1999	3.1
Middle East and North Africa	Banque Maghrébine d'Investissement et de Commerce Extérieur	BMICE	2015	0.3
Asia and Pacific	International Bank for Economic Cooperation	IBEC	1963	0.4
Asia and Pacific	Asian Development Bank	AsDB	1966	191.9
Asia and Pacific	Pacific Island Development Bank	PIDB	1989	0.3
Asia and Pacific	Interstate Bank	Interstate	1993	0.2
Asia and Pacific	Economic Cooperation Organization Trade and Development Bank	ECO	2005	0.7
Asia and Pacific	Eurasian Development Bank	EDB	2006	3.7
Asia and Pacific	Asian Infrastructure Investment Bank	AIIB	2016	19.6
Latin America and the Caribbean	Inter American Development Bank	IADB	1959	129.5
Latin America and the Caribbean	Banco Centroamericano de Integración Económica	CABEI	1960	10.9
Latin America and the Caribbean	Banco de Desarrollo de América Latina	CAF	1970	40.5
Latin America and the Caribbean	Caribbean Development Bank	Caribank	1970	1.7
Latin America and the Caribbean	Fondo Financiero para el Desarrollo de la Cuenca del Plata	FONPLATA	1974	0.3
Latin America and the Caribbean	Banco Latinoamericano de Comercio Exterior	BLADEX	1979	7.6
Latin America and the Caribbean	North American Development Bank	NADB	1993	2.0
Europe	Council of Europe Development Bank	CEB	1956	25.7
Europe	European Investment Bank	EIB	1958	555.8
Europe	Nordik Investment Bank	NDB	1975	34.9
Europe	Nordic Development Fund	NIB	1989	0.9
Europe	European Bank for Reconstruction and Development	EBRD	1991	68.0
Europe	Black Sea Trade and Development Bank	BSTDB	1999	2.0

Source: Database of the Agence Française de Développement.

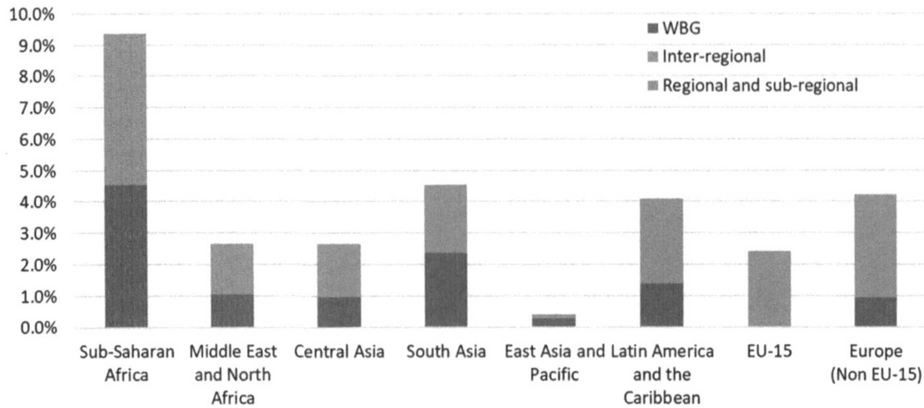

Figure 1. MDB's: outstanding loans by region, 2018–2019 (Share of regional GDPs). Source: Annual reports and financial statements of the WBG and the other MDBs.

Nordic institutions. It is followed by Asia, which includes the Arab and Islamic institutions, which are very important in regional terms, and the other Asian institutions, including some serving Central Asia. Some of the Islamic institutions can be considered interregional, as they also serve North Africa, and some of the Asian ones serve Central Asia rather than the whole continent. The Americas follow, mainly Latin America and the Caribbean — IADB, CAF and sub-regional institutions — as there is only one small North-American institution — the North-American Development Bank. Africa has a myriad of institutions, but most of them are small ones. The two most important for this continent are the AfDB and the African Export-Import Bank, created under the former's auspices. Table 2 also makes clear that most MDBs were created from the mid-1950s until the 1970s.

Most of the MDBs are wholly owned by central governments of member countries. However, some foreign trade banks have partial private ownership: the Latin American one has 84% private ownership, and the African one 22%. The only large MDB with some private sector participation is CAF, with 10%.

The relative importance of MDBs in different regions is quite heterogenous, as reflected in their size compared to the regions' GDPs shown in Figure 1. What is remarkable is the very uneven coverage of MDBs in the developing world. They are particularly important in Sub-Saharan Africa, where the outstanding loans of MDBs represent more than 9% of the region's GDP. South Asia and Latin America and the Caribbean follow, with more than 4%, and the Middle East and North Africa, and Central Asia with close to 3%. European countries also belong to this intermediate level, with shares of somewhat above 2% for the core European Union members (EU-15)[4] and around 4% for the non-core countries. The region with the least important of MDBs is East Asia and the Pacific. Hence the importance of the growth of the ADB and the new AIIB.

[4]This group includes the UK, which is now in the process of withdrawing from the EU, but we would keep it as part of the EU-15.

Regarding the weight of different types of institutions, the WBG dominates in the world's poorest regions (Sub-Saharan Africa and South Asia). The regional and sub-regional banks play an essential role in all regions. Interregional banks have an important presence in Sub-Saharan Africa and the Middle East and North Africa, reflecting the importance of the Islamic Development Bank. They are also relevant for in the non-EU-15 European countries, reflecting the EBRD's relevance in that region.

The MDBs follow two basic models. The first is the traditional division of shareholders between borrowers and non-borrowers that the IBRD established, and which a large number of institutions have followed. In this model, the non-borrowers provide not only paid-in capital but also callable capital, which effectively operates as a kind of insurance provided to the institutions' portfolios. The second can be called the 'cooperative' model. In this case, all countries contribute to the capital and can also borrow from the institution. This is the model of the EIB and CAF. It should be added that all MDBs enjoy a privileged credit status, which supports their credit ratings.

In terms of MDBs' role during crises, there is a remarkable difference between the North Atlantic financial crisis and the current COVID-19 turbulence, reflecting a broader issue about the extent of multilateral cooperation (Ocampo 2020b). The actions launched by the 'Global Plan for Recovery and Reform' adopted by the G20 Heads of State in London on April 2 2009, to address the North Atlantic financial crisis were very ambitious. The MDBs were central to the agenda, as the G20 endorsed the capitalization and massive increase in the lending of these institutions and their role in supporting trade finance and a green recovery (G20 2009, paragraphs 5, 7, 22 and 27).

In contrast, the agenda adopted by the G20 Heads of State at the end of March 2020 only included a general reference to the need for development banks to deploy robust and coordinated financial packages (G20 2020a). The Ministers of Finance and Central Bank Directors of the G20 said something similar during the 2020 Spring Meetings of the Bretton Woods institutions, essentially supporting the programs that the MDBs had already announced (G20 2020b). There was no reference to these institutions' capitalization or their role in supporting green projects in either this or the Annual Meetings' declaration (G20 2020c).

MDBs indeed played a vital counter-cyclical role during the North Atlantic crisis, partially offsetting the contraction of private international financing to emerging and developing countries (Ocampo et al. 2012). Furthermore, the counter-cyclical role that these institutions should play was explicitly recognized for the first time by the MDBs and economic authorities. As a group, they nearly doubled their credit commitments to emerging and developing countries between 2007 and 2010, and even more relative to previous levels (see Table 1). They also played an important role in the rapid provision of commercial credit services used by a wide range of private banks.[5] As indicated above, the WBG led this counter-cyclical response. Disbursements lagged, despite the measures adopted to accelerate them (loan advances and fast track facilities). Paradoxically, however, the MDBs responded more strongly to the needs of emerging economies than to those of low-income countries, generating a decrease in the share of credit commitments to the latter group, from 32% in 2007 to 22% in 2009 (Ocampo et al. 2012, Table 12).

[5]As indicated by the International Chamber of Commerce, 55% were utilizing trade facilitation programs implemented by MDBs by the summer of 2009 (ICC 2009).

The response of the MDBs was conditioned in part by the limits on their capital. For this reason, the G20 agreed to support their capitalization. Those of the ADB and the AfDB were rapid and massive: a 200% increase in 2009. That of the IADB, approved in 2010 for around 70%, was less ambitious, gradual, and less than the Latin American and Caribbean countries had proposed. That of the WBG also took place in 2010 but was more modest and formed part of a set of reforms to increase the participation of emerging and developing countries in the capital of the different institutions that are part of that Group.

In response to the COVID-19 crisis, MDBs adopted several support measures: special lines to address the crisis; increases in the scale of programs; streamlining credit approval processes; and, in some cases, the possibility of reassigning credits already approved to the needs of the emergency. The most extensive program was announced by the WBG at the end of March: a package of US$ 160 billion for the next 15 months, an amount that is larger than the total credits approved in the biennium 2009–10. An essential element of the package was the significant weight of resources destined for low-income countries, thus correcting one of the problems of the lending program adopted during the North Atlantic crisis.

The WBG significantly increases its lending in 2020. This is more remarkable if we look at annual data rather than at the fiscal years shown in Table 1: an increase from US$ 53.3 billion in 2019 to US$ 80.6 billion in 2020 — i.e., 51.4%. The strongest response was that of the new MDBs and partially of the ADB, which jointly increased their financing by 45.6%. In contrast, that of regional MDBs of Latin America and the Caribbean, Africa and the ERBD was small. Overall, the counter-cyclical response of MDBs was weaker than during the North Atlantic crisis (Table 1).

The WBG buily upon the capitalization of IBRD and IFC in 2018, and the 2019 replenishment of IDA. AfDB was also capitalized in 2019, and increased its disbursements but decided to rationalize its portfolio in terms of new commitments. ADB was able to significantly increase its leverage, and the new MDBs counted with their initial capital for their expansion. The lack of capitalization of Latin American and Caribbean banks was a major constraint in their capacity to increase their lending (Ocampo 2020a). Overall, the lack of commitments of the G20 to capitalize the MDBs was a significant omission during the COVID-19 crisis.

In terms of the long-term financing priorities, Table 3 summarizes the major destination of the resources from the WBG and the three major regional development banks (IADB, ADB, and AfDB). The details are presented in annual terms in Annex 1. Using a common classification is not easy because of the different criteria used by these institutions.

What strikes most clearly is the emphasis of all banks, but particularly AfDB and ADB, on infrastructure financing: half or more of total lending by these two institutions. Furthermore, given the rapid growth of these institutions, the increased resources they allocate for infrastructure have multiplied several times over the past decade. In this area, transport projects have the largest weight.

In the case of the WBG and IADB, social spending occupies second place. Commitments considered under this classification include mainly education and health. For the IADB, it was a priority when it was created, but has fallen as a share of lending. The low priority given to this area by AfDB and ADB is striking, though they also support several social programs.

Table 3. Multilateral Development Banks Commitments by Sector (%).

	World Bank		IADB		ADB		AfDB	
	2008/12	2013/19	2008/12	2013/19	2008/12	2013/19	2008/12	2013/19
Social	15.6%	19.0%	16.1%	17.3%	3.3%	6.8%	8.2%	6.4%
Agriculture	6.1%	7.5%	4.1%	2.5%	5.9%	7.9%	4.4%	11.3%
Industry and Trade	7.6%	8.8%	12.6%	7.1%	1.2%	2.5%	5.0%	1.1%
Infraestructure	35.4%	33.1%	31.5%	35.9%	56.7%	59.9%	50.9%	50.0%
Finance	18.9%	18.1%	13.0%	12.8%	5.0%	11.1%	11.9%	16.9%
Public Sector Management	16.2%	13.5%	10.6%	14.6%	15.8%	11.5%	-	-
Multisector and others*	0.1%	0.0%	12.2%	9.7%	12.0%	0.4%	19.6%	14.3%

*Multisector includes: in the IADB environment and natural disasters, science and technology, and urban development and housing; in ADB multisector and others; and in the AfDB multisector, urban development, and environment
Source: Banks' annual reports, various issues.

The finance category consists of a great diversity of projects with different goals. Collaborations with governments to strengthen regulatory institutions and support financial inclusion programs stand out. They also include projects to develop domestic capital markets.

Support for the production sectors is somewhat limited in all cases. Agriculture receives limited attention, although it has tended to increase as a priority for AfDB. Industry and trade used to receive significant support from IADB, but it has weakened. It receives minimal attention from ADB and AfDB.

Given the analysis of development banks' priority functions in the previous section, financing of innovation and the fight against climate change deserve special attention. In the first case, although the classification by sector does not allow to isolate the specific amount committed to this item, when analyzing each institution's annual reports, innovation, science, and technology are a cross-cutting issue in several sectors.

IADB is the only bank among those analyzed that includes a specific area of science and technology. In 2006–2019, it provided an average of 1.7% of its commitments to this area, with the highest percentage in 2017 (6.1%). However, some projects in other sectors positively impact the use of new technologies and innovation. In its *Update to the Institutional Strategy* (IADB 2015), it underscored the need to boost countries' domestic productivity and consolidate adequate knowledge innovation ecosystems.

In turn, ADB recognizes that Asia must base its growth on new engines that raise the quality of growth. It has emphasized that countries must foster technological innovation and new industries based on sustainability principles. Its *Strategy 2030* (ADB 2018) also includes monitoring digital transformation, knowledge, and innovations as part of a Digital Agenda 2030.

Regarding AfDB, the boost to technology and innovation focuses on the information and communication technology sector. In this regard, in its 2019 annual report (AfDB 2019), it identifies supporting e-government and innovation projects as priority issues. Also, it plans to continue supporting targeted interventions in broadband development and data infrastructure.

The WBG also recognizes the importance of boosting productivity and sustainable growth through technological improvements and innovation in the developing regions. In Africa, it seeks to accelerate digital transformation to guarantee that by 2030 governments, businesses, and people will be digitally enabled. The digital economy and the infrastructure it requires is also a priority for the WBG in East Asia

Table 4. Total MDB climate finance commitments with emerging and developing countries, 2011–2019 (US$ Billion).

Multilateral Development Banks	2011	2012	2013	2014	2015	2016	2017	2018	2019
PART A: Total reported MDB climate finance commitments (USD billion)									
World Bank (WBG)	10.7	12.7	9.4	11.8	10.7	11.5	13.2	21.3	18.4
Inter-American Development Bank (IADB)	2.2	1.9	1.2	2.5	1.7	2.7	4.3	5.0	4.4
African Development Bank (AfDB)	1.6	2.2	1.2	1.9	1.4	1.1	2.3	3.3	3.6
Asian Development Bank (ADB)	3.2	3.3	3.3	2.9	2.9	4.4	5.2	4.0	7.1
European Bank for Resconstruction and Development (EBRD)	3.7	3.1	3.5	4.1	3.2	3.5	4.6	3.8	3.9
European Investment Bank (EIB)*	5.6	3.7	5.2	5.2	5.1	4.3	5.5	5.7	3.6
Total	27.0	26.9	23.8	28.4	25.0	27.5	35.1	43.1	41.0
PART B: Total report MDB climate finance commitments as fraction of total loan commitments (%)									
World Bank (WB)	19%	25%	19%	20%	20%	20%	24%	36%	30%
Inter-American Development Bank (IADB)	21%	17%	9%	18%	15%	24%	32%	34%	34%
African Development Bank (AfDB)	18%	34%	18%	26%	16%	10%	26%	33%	36%
Asian Development Bank (ADB)	16%	16%	16%	13%	11%	17%	16%	11%	21%
European Bank for Resconstruction and Development (EBRD)	29%	27%	31%	35%	31%	34%	42%	34%	34%
European Investment Bank (EIB)*	31%	23%	29%	23%	26%	21%	27%	29%	37%

* The EIB climate finance figures included in this table do not represent EIB's total global climate finance. They include only a subset of EIB countries (emerging countries and economies in transition)

Source: Joint Report on Multilateral Development Banks Climate Finance 2011–2019 annual issues.

and the Pacific region. Again, there is interest in promoting the Digital Economy programs and a favorable environment for start-ups focused on digital technologies in the Middle East and North Africa. It has also worked with Latin American countries to improve public spending on science, technology, and innovation.

Concerning combating climate change, financing for mitigation and adaptation projects by MDBs has increased rapidly, though from low levels a decade ago. From 2011 to 2019, total commitments supporting climate change policies in emerging and developing countries grew from US$ 27 to 41 billion (Table 4). It should be underscored that EIB is also an important player but essentially supports its high-income members. Its climate change financing to these countries reached US$ 18 billion in 2019.

In terms of the proportion of climate financing in total commitments, the two European banks (EIB and EBRD) have the highest shares (including only emerging and transition economies in the case of EIB). The other banks show a significant increase in that share, with the WBG and IADB experiencing the strongest upward trend. Since 2017, AfDB registered a recovery after a declining trend between 2012 and 2016. The bank that lags is ADB.

Commitments on mitigation projects represented, on average, about three-fourths of the total climate finance commitments. According to the *2019 Joint Report on Multilateral Development Banks, Climate Finance*, the sectors that most benefited by mitigation commitments were transportation, renewable energy, and energy efficiency, with about one-fourth of commitments in each area. The main sectors to which adaptation financing has been allocated are energy, transport, and infrastructure, which jointly represented 26% of total commitments, followed by water and water-waste systems, and institutional capacity support, with 20% and 14%, respectively.

In the energy sector, the WBG has stopped supporting coal projects since 2010 and announced in 2017 that it would no longer finance upstream oil and gas after 2019. According to its analysis, the shift to a low-carbon economy will create a significant amount of new jobs: over 65 million globally by 2030. The development of climate-smart agricultural practices is also a priority. In has also set as an objective boosting adaptation financing with a whole-of-government approach, and develop a new rating system to improve the tracking of global progress on adaptation and resilience. Disaster management and resilience-building are clear priorities on this agenda. The strategy includes promoting resilient infrastructure. It estimates a $4 benefit for each dollar invested in resilience over the lifetime of a new infrastructure project (World Bank 2019 and 2020).

The major regional development banks serving emerging and developing countries have common elements on the agenda and strategies to combat climate change, though focusing on the specific problems and needs of the regions they support. The three banks include objectives such as reducing vulnerabilities, and promoting knowledge, climate resilience, capacity building, risk-sensitive land use management, climate- and disaster-resilient infrastructure design, and disaster response. A common problem is also how to increase resources for climate finance. To face this problem, they have adopted blended finance solutions such as first loss guarantees, local currency debt (senior, subordinated or contingent loans and bonds), equity and the issuance of green bonds.

Besides the direct role of the MDBs, the support of environmental funds — the Global Environmental Facility (GEF), the Green Climate Fund (GCF), and the Clean Technology Fund (CTF)[6] — is also crucial. The GEF, established in 1992, has awarded more than US$ 20 billion in grants and mobilized more than US$ 107 billion in co-financing for more than 4,700 projects in 170 countries. Its partner agencies include the WBG and the major regional MDBs. The GCF was established by the United Nations Framework Convention on Climate Change (UNFCCC) in 2010, and focuses on mitigation and adaptation activities in the Least Developed Countries and Africa, and includes as accredited entities some MDBs and NDBs. The fund has allocated more than US$ 1.3 billion of funding to Africa and US$ 4.1 billion of co-financing commitments. The CFT invests in projects and programs focused on transferring low-carbon technologies that help reduce GHG emissions. The beneficiary sectors are power, transport, and energy efficiency. It uses a diverse range of instruments, including grants, concessional loans, and guarantees. It has allocated resources from nine donor countries for US$ 5.7 billion to more than 150 projects, and works closely with several MDBs.

As suggested by Griffith-Jones, Attridge, and Gouett (2020), the NDBs are also essential to meet the financial commitments necessary to meet the climate change goals, working with the MDBs and global environmental funds. All of this means that the world has developed a financial network to support climate change mitigation and adaptation. The network has started to yield important results. However, the scale is limited, as current commitments are still very insufficient to reach the Paris Agreement's goals.

It should be finally highlighted that it is difficult to draw from the reports and data from MDBs how they support backward regions within countries. This should be a clear priority going forward.

[6]See the websites of the three institutions: https://www.thegef.org/, https://www.greenclimate.fund/ and https://www.climateinvestmentfunds.org/.

Table 5. The Architecture of National Development Banks.

Region	Number of Institutions	Assets (Billion USD)	Assets (% of Region GDP)	Commitments (Billion USD)	Commitments (% of Region GDP)
Sub-Saharan Africa	85	48.8	2.8%	9.8	0.6%
Middle East and North Africa	33	287.2	6.6%	57.4	1.3%
Central Asia	5	68.4	3.2%	13.7	0.6%
South Asia	26	129.3	3.6%	25.9	0.7%
East Asia and Pacific	79	4,908.7	18.7%	981.4	3.7%
Latin America and the Caribbean	81	486.9	9.2%	97.4	1.8%
North America	19	383.7	1.7%	76.7	0.3%
EU-15	66	3,224.0	19.3%	644.8	3.9%
Europe (Non EU-15)	31	113.0	3.6%	22.6	0.7%
TOTAL	**425**	**9,650**		**1,930**	

Source: Estimated from the database of the Agence Française de Développement and World Bank for GDPs.

4. The System of NDBs and Their Links to MDBs

The architecture of NDBs is more complex. It can be understood as made up of different state-owned financial institutions (some partially so), with varying objectives, business models, financing arrangements, and sizes. The Agence Française de Développement considers 'Development Financial Institutions' those with separate legal personality, government sponsorship and a public policy-oriented official mandate that manage financial instruments (loans, equity, guarantee, and insurance) and depend on funding sources that go beyond budgetary transfers. In turn, the most recent World Bank (2018, p. 12) report defines NDBs as 'any type of financial institution that a national government fully or partially owns or controls and has been given an explicit legal mandate to reach socioeconomic goals in a region, sector, or market segment'.

Table 5 indicates that there are over 400 institutions that meet the Agence Française criteria. Their regional coverage is quite different from those of the MDBs. The most remarkable feature is the significant importance in the core EU-15 countries and East Asia. Their assets are equivalent to around 19% of GDP in both cases. Some NDBs in these regions, notably the China Development Bank, are also active in international financing. Latin America and the Caribbean, and the Middle East and North Africa follow: the share of NDBs' assets in the regions' GDPs are 9% and close to 7%, respectively. In contrast, it is striking the low weight of NDBs in three regions that are well covered by MDBs: the two most impoverished regions, Sub-Saharan Africa and South Asia, as well as Central Asia. Non-EU 15 and North America also have relatively small NDBs.

As shown in Figure 2, although the creation of NDBs has been a process that has taken more than a century and speeded during Great Depression and the early post-World War II years, the creation of these institutions accelerated in recent decades. During the last two decades of the 20th century 120 new NDBs were created, and 143 during the first two decades of the 21st century. Although the Sub-Saharan Africa region has the highest number of NDBs, it is in the East Asia and Pacific region where more organisms have been established over the past two decades, followed by Latin America and the Caribbean and Sub-Saharan Africa itself.

Table 6 shows that the core EU-15 countries and East Asia also have the highest share in the total assets of NDBs at the world level — and by a large margin. It also shows that

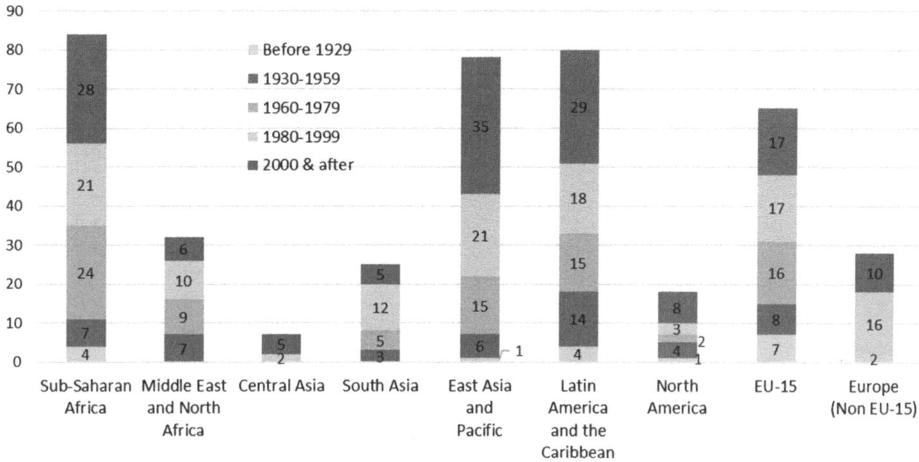

Figure 2. Creation of National Development Banks by region. Source: Own estimates based on data from the Agence Française de Développement. Eight NDBs without a precise date of creation were excluded.

the banks established in the 1990s have the highest amounts of assets. However, this is due to the China Development Bank, as it was established in 1994 and concentrates 48% of the East Asia and Pacific region's assets. The institutions created from the 1930s to the 1950s also have a high share of regional assets, particularly in the EU-15 and Latin America and the Caribbean. In contrast, the banks established during the first two decades of the 21st century concentrate only about 10% of total assets and includes a large number of small institutions.

It should be added that, as is the case of multilateral institutions, most NDBs are owned by the national or local governments, but some have partial private-sector ownership. The dominance of state ownership is confirmed in two World Bank's reports on NDBs: three-fourth in those surveyed in the first report (Luna-Martinez and Vicente 2012) and 85% in the second one (World Bank 2018).[7]

The views of the World Bank on NDBs played an important role in their history. Until the 1970s, the WBG supported, advised, and financed several NDBs — 'development finance companies,' as they were called by the institution (Diamond 1965; Diamond and Gulhati 1973). The analyses made by World Bank staff at the time underscored several strengths of the NDBs: their rapid growth, their contribution to the development of national capital markets, their capacity to promote profitable firms, the introduction of project evaluation and appraisal techniques, the stability of their management and staff, and their capacity to weather economic and political storms in the countries where they operated. At the same time, they expressed disappointment that some firms the NDBs supported were dependent on import substitution policies, that the promotion of small firms was minimal, and that some banks relied too much on official financing.

With the rise of the market reform agenda, the World Bank's views radically changed, and the NDBs were increasingly seen as the wrong type of institution. This was also a period in which several NDBs lost strong national support, and a few were privatized

[7]The first report surveyed 90, and the second one 64 institutions.

Table 6. National Development Banks: current assets and creation period.

	Current assets of NDB established in the following periods											Assets	
Region	Before 1900	1900–1929	1930s	1940s	1950s	1960s	1970s	1980s	1990s	200s	2010–2020	USD bn	% of total
Sub-Saharan Africa	0.0	5.8	0.0	10.2	4.8	2.5	3.7	9.2	2.4	3.9	6.2	48.6	0.5%
Middle East and North Africa	0.0	0.0	33.3	0.0	34.4	1.0	19.6	43.9	9.8	12.2	132.8	287.0	3.0%
Central Asia	0.0	0.0	0.0	0.0	0.0	0.0	0.0	51.9	5.9	10.8	2.9	71.5	0.7%
South Asia	0.0	0.0	0.0	3.8	0.3	2.8	0.4	97.3	22.7	1.7	0.0	129.0	1.3%
East Asia and Pacific	0.0	80.0	0.0	0.0	446.0	95.2	85.1	57.2	3,853.2	230.6	61.2	4,908.5	50.9%
Latin America and the Caribbean	19.1	0.5	86.8	6.1	298.3	12.7	4.9	0.6	34.3	13.8	9.4	486.6	5.0%
North America	0.0	7.2	21.1	73.8	0.0	257.4	0.0	1.9	0.9	0.1	21.2	383.6	4.0%
EU-15	802.3	181.8	0.0	668.0	256.2	42.0	437.5	97.8	288.9	267.6	181.2	3,223.3	33.4%
Europe (Non EU-15)	0.0	70.3	0.0	0.0	0.0	0.0	0.0	0.0	22.0	5.9	11.4	109.6	1.1%
Total	**821.4**	**345.6**	**141.2**	**761.9**	**1,040.1**	**413.5**	**551.2**	**359.9**	**4,240.0**	**546.6**	**426.3**	**9,647.8**	

Source: Own estimates based on data from the Agence Française de Développement. Eight NDBs without a precise date of creation were excluded.

or closed down. An important case is India, where the development banks had occupied an essential role in the financial system in the early decades of independence (Nayyar 2015).

In this context, the renewed interest of the World Bank on NDBs over the past two decades, and particularly after the North Atlantic financial crisis, has been a very positive step. This is reflected in two reports conducted in collaboration with the World Federation of Development Financial Institutions (WFDFI). The first one, prepared in 2012, concluded that 'DBs with clearly defined mandates, high corporate governance standards, strong risk management capability, proper regulation and supervision, and a strong management team have been successful' (Luna-Martinez and Vicente 2012, p. 24). Some did not meet those criteria. According to this and the most recent survey (World Bank 2018), they must clarify their mandates and strengthen their governance, monitoring and evaluation frameworks, and risk management strategies to reduce delinquent loans. In some cases, they must also reduce undue political interference in their activities.

The 2012 report indicated that they played an active counter-cyclical role during the North Atlantic crisis, increasing their lending by 36% between 2007 and 2009 vs. 10% in the case of private banks, and that they increased lending to old and new customers who faced difficulties in refinancing their loans or receiving new lines of credit. Both surveys confirmed that there has been an increased interest in creating NDBs in the 21st century.

As both reports indicate, the scope of their activities is diverse. Perhaps the most important role is in financial inclusion, reflecting their focus on SMEs and individuals not served by other financial institutions (World Bank 2018, p. 26). Nevertheless, they also support sectors and regions that private intermediaries do not serve sufficiently, and provide financing for infrastructure and environmentally friendly projects.

As several contributions of the volume on NDBs by Griffith-Jones and Ocampo (2018) show, NDBs have played a key role in fostering innovation and entrepreneurship in national economies. In particular, Mazzucato and Penna (2018) argue that there is mounting evidence that NDBs have fostered patient, long-term committed finance for mission-oriented investment in innovative activities. In fact, they are increasingly providing long-term committed venture capital for innovation projects. In several cases, private investors have joined NDBs in venture capital funds.

A large share of lending by NDBs is long term: 54% of loans according to the first World Bank survey (Luna-Martinez and Vicente 2012, Table 1.1). They mix first and second-tier operations, but only a few of them operate exclusively as second-tier institutions –and those are primarily located in Latin America. Their most important roles are mobilizing private sector investment, directly or through rediscounts in their second-tier windows, and providing counterpart private funds for public sector projects.

Their funding comes mainly from issuing bonds in the local markets and borrowing from other financial agents, including international capital markets and financial institutions. This includes borrowing from MDBs. According to the most recent World Bank survey, 77% of the NDBs declare that they can obtain official development funds provided by official agencies or multilateral institutions on a long-term basis. According to this report, NDBs have been among the main recipients of loans and grants that MDBs provide (World Bank 2018).

There is no doubt that the cooperation between MDBs and NDBs can be crucial for both types of institutions. However, this relation has not been systematically analyzed, and there is no regular information about how they work together.[8] Interestingly, even in the decades in which there was a conceptual rejection of NDBs, the WBG continued to work with them in several countries and sectors, including infrastructure, financial inclusion, energy efficiency, and traditional areas such as agriculture, housing, and export diversification. As the documents quoted indicate, the view of NDBs has become more pragmatic since the recent financial crises. This includes a clear recognition of the counter-cyclical role that NDBs should play alongside that which is now equally accepted in the case of MDBs.

However, broad implicit principles do apply in the relations between the WBG and the NDBs. The first one is that NDBs should not substitute private financing. Therefore, these institutions should have the explicit goals of offsetting market failures and gaps in domestic financing. Second-tier lending and guarantees may be preferable instruments, as they complement private financial activities. However, first-tier lending may be possible in sectors subject to high risks but also important social returns. There should be no interest rate subsidies in principle, but subsidized credit could be provided if financed with fiscal resources. Risk-management standards should be high. This is particularly important concerning the exchange rate risks that NDBs incur when financed in hard currencies by the MDBs. Those risks should be hedged if there are adequate future markets and can also be covered with bond issues in local currencies by MDBs; a third, and possibly common solution, is for the risks to be covered by the central government. Finally, corporate governance standards must be high, taking the OECD standards as a reference. Technical assistance from the World Bank is available in all of these areas.

An interesting alternative for NDBs is their capacity to organize by themselves to reach their development objectives. In this regard, an essential innovation is the International Development Finance Club (IDFC), created in 2011, which compromises 26 institutions, including national, some sub-regional development banks, and a regional one (CAF). Its principal focus is to promote and leverage sustainable development investment worldwide, contributing to implementing both the SDGs and the Paris Climate Agrement.[9]

5. Summary and Recommendations

This paper has analyzed the functions that development banks should play and the evolution and regional coverage of the system of MDBs and NDBs. It emphasizes the role of the WBG and the regional development banks that service emerging and developing countries. It also takes a look at the relations between MDBs and NDBs.

The paper starts by identifying the major market failures that development finance institutions must correct: (i) the pro-cyclical bias of private finance; (ii) the information imperfections that characterize financial markets, and the rationing of countries, regions, and economic agents that they generate; (iii) the reluctance to finance high-risk activities, which may hinder the development of innovative activities that are crucial for the

[8] The analysis in this and the following paragraphs is based with interviews with current and former World Bank officials working with NDBs: José de Luna Martinez, Eva Gutiérrez and Ana María Avila.

[9] https://www.idfc.org/

structural transformation of economies; and (iv) the underfinancing of activities with high externalities (social services and infrastructure) and public goods (the fight against climate change).

Based on this analysis, the paper proposes seven priority functions that the development bank architecture must fulfill: (i) providing counter-cyclical financing; (ii) supporting countries and regions within countries that lag in the development process; (iii) improving social development; (iv) enhancing financial inclusion; (v) promoting innovation and structural transformation; (vi) financing infrastructure investment; and (vii) supporting the provision of public goods, particularly combatting climate change. These functions are interrelated and involve both international and national objectives. It is, therefore, important to visualize them as integral tasks of the system of development banks.

Most MDBs were created from the mid-1950s until the 1970s, but there have been two new institutions in recent years, the NewDB and AIIB. The regional development banks supporting emerging and developing countries have grown faster than the WBG over the past two decades, reflecting the greater sense of 'ownership' of the regional institutions by these countries. In turn, EIB continues to be the largest MDB.

The coverage of MDBs in regional and sub-regional terms is very heterogeneous. They are particularly important in Sub-Saharan Africa, followed by South Asia and Latin America and the Caribbean. The next regions in terms of coverage are the Middle East and North Africa, Central Asia, and Europe. The region where MDBs are least important is East Asia and the Pacific. The WBG's support for the world's poorest regions (Sub-Saharan Africa and South Asia) stands out. The regional and sub-regional banks play an important role in all regions and the interregional banks in a few of them.

Although all MDBs have played a counter-cyclical function, the WBG — and IBRD in particular — is the most important institution in this area. However, there is a significant contrast between the role given to MDBs during the current COVID-19 turbulence vs. the North Atlantic financial crisis, as there has been no call by the G20 to capitalize them, as they did in 2009. So, although all MDBs have adopted relevant decisions to support their borrowing members during the current crisis, their response depended on their capital constraints and their capacity to leverage their existing capital. The WBG and Asian-based banks showed the strongest increase in financing in 2020.

In terms of other functions, ADB and AfDB have placed infrastructure financing on top of their agenda. Social spending plays an important role in the WBG and IADB. Enhancing financial inclusion is relevant for several of them. Support for the production sectors is limited, but innovation, science and technology play a role in several cases. There is also growing support by MDBs for action on climate change mitigation and adaptation, led again by the WBG, together with EIB in developed countries. Several international environmental funds also contribute to these objectives. This network has started to yield important results, but financing is still insufficient to reach the Paris Agreement's goals.

Although, as indicated, the WBG is particularly important in supporting the world's poorest regions, there is no reliable information about the extent to which MDBs support the development of backward regions in the countries they finance.

The creation of NDBs goes back to the 19th century but speeded up during Great Depression and the early post-World War II decades. The World Bank actively supported them until the 1970s but started to consider them as suboptimal institutions when it embraced the market reform agenda in the 1980s. Despite that, the creation of NDBs accelerated in the late 20th century and continued in recent decades, although mainly of smaller institutions. After the East Asian and North Atlantic financial crises, the support for NDBs has grown worldwide. This includes renewed support from the WBG.

The regional coverage of NDBs is quite different from those of the MDBs. The most remarkable feature is the significant importance they have in the core EU-15 countries and East Asia, followed by Latin America and the Caribbean, and the Middle East and North Africa. In contrast, it is striking the low weight of NDBs in the two most impoverished regions of the world, Sub-Saharan Africa and South Asia, as well as Central Asia, non-EU 15 countries and North America.

The cooperation between MDBs and NDBs can be crucial for both types of institutions. However, there has been no systematic analysis of this cooperation, and there is not even regular information about how they work together. In climate change, there is also growing support by the MDBs and global environmental funds to NDBs.

This analysis leads to four major recommendations. The first one is that the countercyclical role of MDBs should be a priority under current conditions, both to mitigate the COVID-19 crisis and to support the recovery of emerging and developing countries. This requires a capitalization of all MDBs, similar to that of 2009–10. The new MDBs can also play an important role in that process.

Secondly, the policies to support the recovery should be aligned with the SDGs and fulfill the other priority functions of MDBs. In particular, their role in promoting innovation and structural transformation and supporting climate change mitigation and adaptation should be enhanced. Their support in all the areas we have underscored should be better monitored, including how they contribute to the development of lagging regions in the countries they finance.

Thirdly, development banks should operate as a system. Cooperation between MDBs in all these areas is crucial, as well as networking better with the NDBs. The complementarity of the activities of MDBs is important, given the diversity of regional priorities. However, competition among them can help improve the programs they support. An additional priority is better cooperation between the MDBs and the international funds that finance climate change programs.

Finally, cooperation should be reflected in the support by MDBs to advance strong NDBs in the regions which lag behind in developing such national institutions, particularly sub-Saharan Africa and South Asia.

Disclosure Statement

No potential conflict of interest was reported by the author(s).

References

ADB (Asian Development Bank). 2018. *Strategy 2030: Achieving a Prosperous, Inclusive, Resilient, and Sustainable Asia and the Pacific*. https://www.adb.org/sites/default/files/institutional-document/435391/strategy-2030-main-document.pdf.

AfDB (African Development Bank). 2019. 2019 *Annual Report*, https://www.afdb.org/en/documents/annual-report-2019.

Bernal, J., and J. A. Ocampo. 2020. 'Climate Change: Policies to Manage its Macroeconomic and Financial Effects', *Background Paper 2-2020 for the Human Development Report*, United Nations Development Program.

Bhattacharya, A., J. Oppenheim, and N. Stern. 2015. *Building Sustainable Development through Better Infrastructure: Key Elements of a Transformation Program*, The New Climate Economy and Grantham Research Institute on Climate Change and the Environment, The Brookings Institution.

Calvo, G. A. 1998. 'Capital Flows and Capital-Market Crises: The Simple Economics of Sudden Stops.' *Journal of Applied Economics* 1 (1): 35–54.

Diamond, W. 1965. 'Development Finance Companies.' *The Fund and Bank Review* 2 (2): 97–102.

Diamond, W., and R. Gulhati. 1973. 'World Bank's Experience with Development Finance Companies.' *Economic and Political Weekly* 8 (23): M47 and M49–56.

Dikau, S., and U. Volz. 2019. 'Central Banking, Climate Change and Green Finance.' In *Handbook of Green Finance: Energy Security and Sustainable Development*, edited by J. Sachs, W. T. Woo, N. Yoshino, and F. Taghizadeh-Hezary, 81–102. Asian Development Bank Institute.

G20 (Group of 20). 2009. 'The Global Pact for Recovery and Reform', London, April 2nd.

G20 (Group of 20). 2020a. 'Extraordinary G20 Leaders' Summit Statement on COVID-19', March 26th.

G20 (Group of 20). 2020b. 'Communiqué G20 Finance Minister and Central Bank Governors', April 15th.

G20 (Group of 20). 2020c. 'Communiqué G20 Finance Minister and Central Bank Governors', October 14th.

Griffith-Jones, S., S. Attridge, and M. Gouett. 2020. *Securing Climate Finance Through National Development Banks*. Report, London: Overseas Development Institute, January.

Griffith-Jones, S., and J. A. Ocampo eds. 2018. *The Future of National Development Banks*. Oxford: Oxford University Press.

Helleiner, E. 2014. *Forgotten Foundations of Bretton Woods: International Development and the Making of the Postwar Order*. Ithaca, NY: Cornell University Press.

IADB (Inter American Development Bank). 2015. *Update to the Institutional Strategy 2010-2020 Partnering with Latin America and the Caribbean to Improve Lives*; Available on: https://publications.iadb.org/en/publication/17084/update-institutional-strategy-2010-2020.

ICC (International Chamber of Commerce). 2009. 'ICC Trade Finance Survey: An Interim Report - Summer 2009', Paris: International Chamber of Commerce, http://www.icc-portugal.com/images/documentos/comissao_bancaria/2009_ICC_Global_Report_on_TF_Interim_Report_(1).pdf.

IMF (International Monetary Fund). 2020. *Global Financial Stability Report*, April, Chapter 1.

Joint Report on Multilateral Development Banks Climate Finance. 2011-2019 Annual IssuES (These Reports can be Accessed from the Website of the Several Banks that Part of the Network; see, for Example, https://publications.iadb.org/en/2019-joint-report-on-multilateral-development-banks-climate-finance).

Kindleberger, C. P., and R. Z. Aliber. 2011. *Manias, Panics, and Crashes: A History of Financial Crises, 6th Edition*. Houndmills: Palgrave Macmillan.

Luna-Martinez, J. de, and C. L. Vicente. 2012. 'Global Survey of Development Banks.' In *World Bank Policy Research Working Paper, No. WPS 5969*. Washington, DC: World Bank.

Mazzucato, M. 2013. *The Entrepreneurial State: Debunking Public vs. Private Sector Myths*. London: Academic Press.

Mazzucato, M., and C. C. R. Penna. 2018. 'National Development Banks and Mission-Oriente Finance for Innovation', in Griffith-Jones and Ocampo (2018), chapter 10.

McKinnon, R. I. 1973. *Money and Capital in Economic Development*. Washington, D.C.: Brookings Institution.

Minsky, H. P. 1982. *Can "It" Happen Again?: Essays on Instability and Finance*. Armonk, New York: M.E. Sharpe.

Nayyar, D. 2015. 'Birth, Life and Death of Development Finance Institutions in India.' *Economic and Political Weekly* L (33): 51–60.

Ocampo, J. A. 2017. 'Dynamic Efficiency: Structural Dynamics and Structural Change in Developing Countries".' In *Efficiency, Finance, and Varieties of Industrial Policy*, edited by A. Noman, and J. E. Stiglitz. New York: Columbia University Press. chapter 3.

Ocampo, J. A. 2020a. 'International Financial Cooperation to Address the Latin American Economic Crisis.' *CEPAL Review*, 7–26.

Ocampo, J. A. 2020b. "Weak International Economic Cooperation in response to the COVID-19 Crisis", *Report*, Brussels: Foundation for European Progressive Studies (FEPS), September.

Ocampo, J. A., S. Griffith-Jones, A. Noman, A. Ortiz, J. Vallejo, and J. Tyson. 2012. 'The Great Recession and the Developing World.' In *Development Cooperation in Times of Crisis*, edited by J. A. Alonso, and J. A. Ocampo. New York: Columbia University Press. ch. 2.

Shaw, E. S. 1973. *Financial Deepening in Economic Development*. New York: Oxford University Press.

Stern, N. 2015. *Why Are We Waiting?: The Logic, Urgency, and Promise of Tackling Climate Change*. Cambridge: MIT Press.

Stiglitz, J. E. 1994. *The Role of the State in Financial Markets*. Washington, D.C.: World Bank.

Stiglitz, J. E., and B. Greenwald. 2014. *Creating a Learning Society: A New Approach to Growth, Development, and Social Progress*. New York: Columbia University Press.

Stiglitz, J. E., and A. Weiss. 1981. 'Credit Rationing in Markets with Imperfect Information.' *The American Economic Review* 71 (3): 393–410.

United Nations. 2002. '*The Monterrey Consensus*.' International Conference on Financing for Development. Monterrey, Mexico, http://www.un.org/esa/ffd/monterrey/MonterreyConsensus.pdf

United Nations. 2015a. *Addis Ababa Action Agenda*, Outcome Document of the Third International Conference on Financing for Development, July 15.

United Nations. 2015b. *Transforming Our World: the 2030 Agenda for Sustainable Development*, Annex to UN General Assembly Resolution A/69/L.85, August 12.

World Bank. 2018. 2017 *Survey of National Development Banks*, World Bank Group Global Knowledge and Research Hub in Malaysia, May.

World Bank. 2019. *The World Bank Annual Report 2019: Ending Poverty, Investing in Opportunity*. Washington, D.C.: World Bank. https://openknowledge.worldbank.org/handle/10986/32333.

World Bank. 2020. '3 Things You Need to Know About Adaptation and Resilience', https://www.worldbank.org/en/topic/climatechange/brief/3-things-you-need-to-know-about-adaptation-and-resilience.

Appendix 1. Development Bank Commitments by sector (Millon US dollars).

World Bank (IBRD, IDA, IFC)	2006	2007	2008	2009	2010	2011	2012	2013	2014	2015	2016	2017	2018	2019
Social	4,123	4,971	3,877	9,961	12,169	8,886	8,524	8,730	7,738	12,075	10,505	8,668	13,731	11,708
Agriculture	2,242	2,340	2,159	4,138	3,154	2,640	4,155	3,390	4,110	4,743	3,471	3,927	4,959	4,321
Industry and Trade	3,974	3,534	4,052	5,759	3,680	3,226	2,864	3,135	3,233	3,250	5,973	6,095	6,804	5,661
Infraestructure	9,749	11,278	14,163	19,437	25,215	21,661	14,905	13,583	21,263	17,748	22,348	19,211	18,379	15,231
Finance	5,383	5,222	6,443	8,455	16,199	9,073	11,623	13,069	12,925	9,299	8,109	9,324	7,566	8,693
Public Sector Management	5,858	5,468	5,296	9,492	10,828	9,673	8,729	7,991	8,838	5,922	6,611	6,708	7,203	8,436
Multisector**	614	82	46	105	166	35	0	0	0	0	0	0	0	0
TOTAL	**31,941**	**32,896**	**36,033**	**57,348**	**71,411**	**55,157**	**50,798**	**49,897**	**58,105**	**53,033**	**57,015**	**53,927**	**58,640**	**54,043**
IDB	**2006**	**2007**	**2008**	**2009**	**2010**	**2011**	**2012**	**2013**	**2014**	**2015**	**2016**	**2017**	**2018**	**2019**
Social	1,195	1,228	1,353	2,843	2,580	943	2,241	3,004	2,149	2,445	2,251	958	2,739	943
Agriculture	62	75	567	839	407	465	211	227	150	173	353	288	264	565
Industry and Trade	261	275	204	82	718	4,666	602	1,875	1,280	1,173	231	957	90	544
Infraestructure	2,465	5,414	4,987	6,443	3,601	183	4,691	4,113	4,603	3,435	2,777	4,272	4,977	5,677
Finance	444	365	2,199	2,352	1,033	1,226	1,024	1,614	2,547	1,479	1,650	1,146	1,540	707
Public Sector Management	1,464	407	707	1,719	2,738	94	1,473	2,319	2,227	907	1,470	1,880	2,307	1,226
Multisector**	491	1,206	1,209	1,230	1,629	1,788	1,182	747	588	1,652	532	1,884	1,285	1,251
TOTAL	**6,381**	**8,971**	**11,226**	**15,507**	**12,705**	**9,365**	**11,424**	**13,899**	**13,544**	**11,264**	**9,264**	**11,385**	**13,202**	**10,913**
ADB	**2006**	**2007**	**2008**	**2009**	**2010**	**2011**	**2012**	**2013**	**2014**	**2015**	**2016**	**2017**	**2018**	**2019**
Social	370	287	384	387	315	680	372	580	786	1,235	845	921	2,144	1,763
Agriculture	941	169	528	618	739	891	1,075	695	982	916	976	1,525	2,344	2,271
Industry and Trade	11	112	178	103	3	3	499	19	458	412	552	357	607	576
Infraestructure	3,577	6,090	6,087	5,843	7,599	9,595	7,802	8,733	8,034	9,147	7,519	12,873	12,231	11,929
Finance	1,859	1,160	119	514	1,289	209	1,143	1,246	1,060	2,392	1,607	2,761	1,992	2,160
Public Sector Management	228	1,196	2,067	5,363	932	622	1,508	1,520	1,559	2,084	1,755	1,250	2,258	2,945
Multisector**	950	1,764	1,943	1,516	1,638	2,021	624	372	0	0	0	0	0	0
TOTAL	**7,935**	**10,778**	**11,306**	**14,344**	**12,515**	**14,022**	**13,023**	**13,165**	**12,879**	**16,186**	**13,254**	**19,687**	**21,576**	**21,644**
AfDB	**2006**	**2007**	**2008**	**2009**	**2010**	**2011**	**2012**	**2013**	**2014**	**2015**	**2016**	**2017**	**2018**	**2019**
Social	368	189	345	358	298	693	807	516	532	826	720	397	245	436
Agriculture	362	282	252	342	105	224	474	660	708	713	1,002	1,159	1,057	1,524
Industry and Trade	84	257	423	175	289	451	150	0	57	4	0	211	352	122

(Continued)

Continued.

World Bank (IBRD, IDA, IFC)	2006	2007	2008	2009	2010	2011	2012	2013	2014	2015	2016	2017	2018	2019
Infraestructure	1,290	3,052	2,174	6,126	4,010	2,414	2,710	3,158	3,620	4,269	4,721	3,745	5,032	5,287
Finance	745	139	459	1,267	493	1,232	619	444	1,169	1,873	2,516	1,573	1,756	1,262
Public Sector Management	0	0	0	0	0	0	0	0	0	0	0	0	0	0
Multisector**	623	161	1,230	3,498	464	1,325	777	707	435	1,093	1,843	1,738	1,681	1,463
TOTAL	**3,472**	**4,081**	**4,883**	**11,767**	**5,659**	**6,338**	**5,537**	**5,484**	**6,520**	**8,778**	**10,802**	**8,824**	**10,123**	**10,095**

*Source:
-WB: Organizational Information and Lending Data Appendix, Anual Report 2019; Fiscal 2015 Lending Data; and World Bank Annual Report 2011. Also includes IFC (Annual Reports)
-IDB: Web Site, project details
-ADB: ADB Sovereign Projects, ADB Annual Reports, and ADB Annual Reports (volume 2)
-AfDB: Annual Reports
**Multisector:
-IDB: Environment and natural disasters, Science and Technology, and Urban Development and Housing
-ADB: Multisector, and Others
-AfDB: Multisector, Urban Development, and Environment
NOTE 1: Totals may not add because of rounding

OPEN ACCESS

Should National Development Banks be Subject to Basel III?

Ricardo Gottschalk, Lavinia B. Castro and Jiajun Xu

ABSTRACT

We address the question: What are the potential impacts of Basel III capital framework for National Development Banks (NDBs) upon their ability to fulfil their developmental mandate? We compare three large NDBs' experiences with Basel III implementation: Brazilian Development Bank, China Development Bank and Germany's KfW. We find that the biggest constraint from Basel III comes less from its levels of comprehensiveness and complexity and more from tightening the levels of capital requirements and demanding better capital quality. The disincentive to the use of internal models and changes in the method for the calculation of operational risks may result in a substantial increase in required capital. Meanwhile, the new large exposure rule may dilute the banks' focus on large, infrastructure projects; the high-risk weights for exposures to project finance and equity may hinder NDBs from using these financing modalities extensively to support large and complex projects and activities that involve innovation financing.

1. Introduction

The literature and policy analysis have addressed the possible impacts of the Basel Capital Accords on banks and their ability to provide development finance, especially in developing countries. However, limited systematic work has been undertaken on the potential impacts of Basel standards on National Development Banks (NDBs). This paper aims to fill in this research gap.

NDBs are different from commercial banks, in terms of funding, mandates and operational modalities. Given that, this paper focuses on the potential impacts of Basel III capital framework for large non-retail-deposit taking NDBs regarding their ability to fulfil their developmental mandates. Typically, large NDBs seeking to meet developmental mandates undertake concerted action that includes financing of large and complex projects, which are often long term, and supporting innovation, which, by its nature, involves above-average risks but also potentially very large developmental payoffs. These characteristics place them in a strong position to support the Sustainable Development Goals (SDGs) and provide climate finance — while setting them clearly apart from other profit-driven private banks and financial institutions. In addition, they undertake countercyclical actions during downturns and crises to protect incomes, jobs and the productive capacity for the next phase of economic expansion. Thus, Under Basel III, key standards to be considered for analysis are those that may constrain banks' ability to provide long-term finance, promote sustainability and operate countercyclically.

If compliance with certain Basel III standards can have an adverse impact on NDBs, the questions then are: Do these banks deserve special treatment? What can national regulators do to adapt Basel standards in order to reduce possible impacts? There is a substantial strand of the Basel literature that focuses on the political economy of the implementation of Basel standards, both in developed and developing countries.[1] This literature takes as a backdrop the fact that Basel standards have been designed by the Basel Committee on Banking Supervision, whose membership is dominated by developed countries and therefore with a focus on the characteristics of their own financial sectors. With this in mind, it argues that the decision-making process concerning their adoption across countries is both complex and political, with outcomes that can be quite varied. Indeed, recent empirical research covering over a hundred developing countries provides evidence that there is wide variation in how these countries are adopting Basel standards. That is, both regulatory convergence and divergence are found among these countries (Hohl et al. 2018). Several factors are driving countries towards regulatory convergence. These include desire to attract foreign capital, reputational concerns and peer pressure. Meanwhile, many other factors drive countries towards divergence instead. These latter include complexity of standards, constrained resources for effective implementation, desirability to develop a domestic financial sector that supports rapid development and domestic interest-group resistance to convergence (Jones 2020; Walter 2008).

NDBs are a particular sub-set category of banks. For them, the discussion that is relevant is not regulatory convergence or divergence in relation to standards designed internationally. Rather, what matters for these banks is compliance, or not, with the set of rules adopted by country regulators at the national level. That is, once international standards are incorporated in one form or another into a national financial regulatory framework, national regulators enjoy discretion to decide whether, or not, NDBs should comply with Basel standards and to what extent.

In related research, we conducted a survey among 50 NDBs to assess compliance with Basel III. For the purpose of NDB selection, the survey took into consideration the income level of their countries, asset sizes, and mandate representation. Of all the banks included in the survey, nearly 50 per cent have answered the questions. Among 24 banks, 16 banks explicitly acknowledge that they are subject to the same regulatory rules as commercial banks are in their jurisdictions and that these rules are very closely aligned with the Basel Accord. This means that, in that sample, about two-thirds of the NDBs are subject to Basel Accord. In addition, the three case studies undertaken in this paper shows that the NDBs analysed are subject to Basel standards. These results indicate that the concern raised by this paper, on possible Basel III impacts on NDBs, is not hypothetical but real instead. Although it is beyond the scope of this paper to examine why most national regulators decide to demand their NDBs to comply with Basel III, this issue is briefly discussed in the case study section of the paper and in conclusions. It will be

[1]See, inter alia, Jones (2020), Jones and Zatz (2017), Knaack (2017), Mosley (2010), Walter (2008).

argued that, in the process of adopting Basel standards for NDBs, little consultation between national regulators and NDBs has taken place.

The paper's focus is on mapping possible Basel III impacts. This topic choice is not necessarily a position against financial regulation for this category of banks. Like commercial and investment banks, large NDBs have the potential to create systemic risks (directly if they collect cash deposits and indirectly, if they do not) and generate credit crises, with significant economic and social impacts. The point is under what conditions NDBs deserve special treatment and how to grant such special treatment — through ad hoc waivers, or a tailored regulatory framework? Mapping possible impacts is important to inform regulators on how best to tailor regulation for this category of banks. Although Basel is not compulsory and national decision-makers have ample discretion, a wholesale Basel adoption could have sizeable real social and economic costs. These costs could take the form of less rapid growth and structural transformation, in case NDBs do not invest as much as they potentially could in transformative-inducing projects. The social impacts would be particularly large if the result is less investments in social infrastructures, which are so much needed to address the many SDGs and targets. In addition, there are the environmental and sustainability costs, if NDBs are deterred in their expected role in the coming years as major financing vehicles for innovation and the fostering of the green economy.

The remainder of this paper has five sections, besides this introduction. Section Two traces the theoretical underpinnings of banking regulation, which culminated in Basel III standards. Section Three examines what key characteristics make NDBs different, warranting regulatory divergence. Section Four provides an analytical discussion on how specific Basel III standards affect the ability of NDBs to fulfil their missions. Section Five explores the variation of Basel adoption across selected NDBs, drawing on in-depth case studies. Three case studies are conducted for the following NDBs: the Brazilian Development Bank- BNDES, China Development Bank (CDB) and Germany's KfW.[2] This selection implies that the paper focuses on large non-retail-deposit taking general purpose NDBs. Section Six concludes.

2. The Need for Regulating Financial Institutions

From the 1930s to the 1970s, having the US as a pioneer, prudential financial regulation focused on banks aimed at avoiding crises, with national supervision rules and special attention to liquidity risk (Carvalho 2003; Komai and Richardson 2011). This framework began to gradually change in the 1970s, a process that gained momentum from the 1980s onwards. It was in this context that the so-called Basel Capital Accords emerged and whose first milestone dates from 1988.[3] The main argument for justifying a change from national to international regulation was that, due to the lack of harmonized financial regulation across national jurisdictions, many internationally active banks were practicing regulatory arbitrage to gain a competitive advantage over other banks. The Basel framework aimed at creating a level playing field for these banks.[4]

[2]BNDES stands for *Banco Nacional de Desenvolvimento Econômico e Social* (The Brazilian Development Bank); CDB for 国家开发银行 (China Development Bank); and KfW for *Kreditanstalt für Wiederaufbau* (Credit Institute for Reconstruction)
[3]BCBS (1988).
[4]See, inter alia, King and Tarbert (2011).

Basel I proposed capital requirement standards to deal with credit risk and was supposed to apply only to internationally active banks. Like the previous regulatory framework, Basel I, therefore, focused on banks and maintained the prudential and tutelary nature of traditional financial regulation. Unlike the previous framework, however, liquidity risk controls, that were at the core of the 1930s reforms, were considered less important, since the view was that best risk management practices could avoid it (Kobrak and Troege 2015).

The development of the Basel standards since then reflects the incorporation of both external and internal criticisms.[5] As a result, the regulatory framework added capital requirements to face other risks: market risk and operational risk. In addition to the minimum capital requirement for these three risks (Pillar I), Basel II also established supervisory principles (Pillar II, whereby monetary national authorities can ask for complementary capital requirements) and market discipline (Pillar III).

Since Basel III, in addition to micro-prudential requirements, elements of macroprudential regulation have been incorporated into the regulatory framework. The attention to liquidity risk returned to the core of regulation and there was a recognition of the procyclical nature of credit markets. To address this type of procyclicality, additional capital cushions have been incorporated. Higher capital requirements for internationally active banks were also introduced. Finally, greater control over derivatives, back-testing, greater robustness in stress tests, as well as new capital requirements for counterpart risk and incremental risk have been proposed in response to the crisis.

From a theoretical perspective, prudential financial regulation is justified, ultimately, to address systemic risk[6] In its traditional form, systemic risk is related to three characteristics of the banking system: (a) the existence of fractional reserves, (b) the existence of interconnections between banks, leading to the problem of contagion and (c) the fact that banks are part of the national system of payments, which causes the financial crisis to spread throughout the economy. However, the concept of systemic risk, as well as financial regulation itself, has also evolved over time. Any event whose magnitude is significant is now considered 'systemic' — for example, if defaulted loans reach at least 10 per cent of total assets, or the cost of saving institutions reaches at least 2 per cent of GDP (Barth et al. 2006, p. 213; cited in Carvalho 2003, p. 10).

There are two main lines of justification for financial regulation: the approach to market failures and the Keynes-Schumpeter-Minsky approach.[7]

According to the market failure approach,[8] information on the solvency of financial institutions is a 'public good'. As such, the government must ensure its provision, imposing the disclosure of information by financial institutions. Stiglitz (1993) argues that financial markets are especially susceptible to sub-optimal outcomes as a result of

---

[5]External criticisms include tendency for standards to reinforce the pro-cyclical character of the financial system (especially before Basel III); risk of regulatory arbitrage between banks and other financial institutions; tendency to reinforce the portfolio bias towards government bonds (instead of loans); and tendency to reinforce bank concentration (e.g., Gottschalk 2010). Internal criticisms refer to model improvements, and improvements especially on the treatment of derivatives and market risk.

[6]For a discussion of the potential costs of financial regulation see, for example, Elliott, Salloy, and Santos (2012), who provide empirical estimates of Basel III costs.

[7]There are, in addition, the concerns with moral hazard as well as the emergence of too-big-to-fail dilemmas, as reasons for financial regulation.

[8]For a discussion of market failures in financial markets, see Stiglitz (1993, 1998).

information asymmetry. By monitoring banks, and requiring transparency on the data of financial institutions, governments can reduce the probability of insolvency of these institutions. But monitoring is not enough. Besides transparency, the government can contribute by imposing more efficient management of risks (risk-bearing) by banks, limiting opportunistic behaviour.[9]

A very different alternative for giving support to financial regulation is the one that emerges from a Keyenesian/Schumpeterian/Minskyan approach, KSM hereafter. According to this theoretical perspective, 'market failures' may exist, but they are not the most important problem to address. Unlike the market failure approach, public intervention in financial markets is called for as a rule and not as an exception. The concept of allocative efficiency, adopted in addressing market failures, is seen as poorly suited to address the problem of development finance and financial fragility. According to the KSM approach,[10] government intervention in financial markets is crucial, because they recognize financial markets' structural problems — and not only 'failures'. In short, the objectives of the intervention are: (1) to contain systemic risk; (2) to act in a counter-cyclical manner; and (3) to foster growth/development.

The first objective demands prudential regulation of the banking system, although the systemic risk is not necessarily entirely addressed by regulation of banks, due to the channels that link these institutions to others in the financial system. The second, counter-cyclical related, objective corresponds to the traditional defense of Keynesian intervention, which should be pursued in times of crises, not only through monetary and fiscal policies by governments and central banks but also by regulation. The third objective is to incentivize banks to provide long-term financing for development purposes. For that purpose, they may create public financial institutions (or, alternatively, foster the development of capital markets) since often long-term finance is not offered spontaneously by the markets due to greater risk. Development finance also involves the promotion of projects that reduce disparities (on income, among industries, or between different regions in the same country) and that support social inclusion, innovation and sustainable development. In these respects, development banks are seen as key financial institutions to meet such developmental objectives and that can contribute to the reduction of the fragility of the financial system.

At the same time, there might be a conflict between the first and the third objectives of the KSM approach. This is because prudential regulation (first objective) is general, thereby covering both commercial and development banks and thus potentially inhibiting the role the latter is expected to play (third objective). In practice, however, the adoption of financial regulation for NDBs implies not just possible costs but may also have its own reasoning as well — a main one being that it may guard NDBs against political intervention. Thus, the point is not just to exclude NDBs from the financial regulatory framework, given that the latter may help them be more sharply focused on their core mandates. Rather, it is to acknowledge that NDBs are different and may therefore require differentiated treatment.[11]

[9]In the literature of market failures, however, there is always a concern with the possibility of 'government failures', resulting from the costs of intervention surpassing those of the market.

[10]This approach combines many ideas presented in the seminal books of Keynes (1936 [1964]), Schumpeter (1912/1934 [1982]) and Minsky (1982).

[11]There might be the question as to whether differentiated treatment for NDBs could create the problem of uneven regulatory playing field among them. In fact, sometimes NDBs co-finance large and development-oriented projects. If it is the case that NDBs from different countries do compete for the same project, it is more likely that exchange rate risks and interest rate risk or interest rate levels will be more important than regulatory differences.

3. Key NDB Characteristics that Make Them Different from Other Banks

The key characteristics that set a typical NDB apart from other banks are as follows: First, instead of maximizing profits, NDBs are mandated to pursue public policy objectives. Second, rather than taking household deposits, typical NDBs generally are state-backed with more secure, long-term funding. Third, these banks are holders of accumulated technical expertise, especially in large, complex projects, and in assessing and monitoring risks that private banks do not. For large, general-purpose NDBs, these characteristics give them the capacity to lend at scale, provide long-term finance, and support a large variety of projects and activities. Examples include infrastructure projects in the areas of health, education, water and sanitation, logistics, urban mobility and energy; and activities to promote more and better jobs, to reduce regional inequalities and poverty, and for preparedness and adaptation to climate-related hazards, which are greatly needed for the achievement of the SDGs.

In addition, NDBs can be the financing arm of national governments taking strategic developmental choices that may include investments in innovation that, while implying risks, can yield formidable pay-offs in the very long term. In the macroeconomic area, they can act countercyclically protecting the economy from shocks and downturns, therefore reducing harmful deviations from the road towards sustainable development.

Besides these key characteristics and functions, NDBs do not play a major role in national payments systems, do not take profit-driven excessive risks, leverage less, do not engage in more complex forms of securitization that can imply financial and reputational risks, use derivatives not to speculate but to hedge their operations, and operate markedly less pro-cyclically than other banks. NDBs, therefore, do not engage in the sorts of activities or create the many risks Basel III seeks to address. The result is that an indiscriminate adoption of Basel III may have unnecessary and yet detrimental impacts on NDBs, especially the small ones due to the increased capital quality and new quantitative requirements.

Indeed, Basel III, through its wide-ranging measures, can affect significantly NDBs and the tasks they normally undertake to fulfil their missions. Summarizing the above, these tasks include: (a) lending at scale and long term; (b) lending counter-cyclically; (c) financing complex infrastructure projects; (d) supporting innovation, and (e) providing climate finance.

It is worth noting that NDBs may support projects and activities that embed all these tasks simultaneously and that involve sizeable risks. Long-term finance by NDBs is, in many instances, geared towards large-scale projects; large projects typically are infrastructure related and in most cases capital intensive, requiring substantial sums of frontloaded finance. Financing infrastructure and large projects can often require accepting temporarily the concentration of exposures: on economic groups, economic sectors and concentration on guarantors. Also, infrastructure projects are closely interdependent. If a national government goes for a big push, this may imply simultaneous execution of projects, which requires the availability of financial resources on a large scale. Moreover, some modalities of financing (e.g., project finance) can have higher risks in the pre-operational phase with high uncertainty and involve different types of risks. In the area of climate finance, many projects involve new technologies with little or no track records, making the task of risk assessment by banks harder. Thus, long-term finance may be provided for a development project that, at once, embeds all the traits and risks just mentioned.

4. How Can Basel III Affect the Ability of NDBs to Fulfil Their Missions? An Analytical Discussion[12]

This section examines how Basel III standards may affect NDBs. However, it does not discuss or highlight Basel III standards that, although important, are not central or pertinent to NDBs, such as the ones arising from banks' trading books or the use of derivatives.

4.1. Solvency and Liquidity Problems

(1) Capital requirements: Basel III demands banks to hold higher minimum capital requirements to reduce the risk of insolvency in situations of stress.[13] It has maintained the Basel II minimum capital requirements at 8 per cent of risk-weighted assets, but, to that, it has added the requirement of capital conservation buffers at 2.5 per cent of risk-weighted assets, to help banks withstand financial distress. When capital is drawn down, banks are expected to rebuild buffers by reducing the discretionary distribution of earnings. It has also created counter-cyclical capital buffers (see below). In addition, domestic systemically important banks (D-SIBs) and global systemically important banks (G-SIBs) are required to build additional capital buffers.[14] These are usually large institutions that can create systemic risk, not just due to their size but also because of high levels of interconnectedness with other financial institutions. Moreover, capital under Basel III should be of higher quality, with emphasis on Common Equity Tier 1 capital.[15] Finally, Basel III has adopted a 3 per cent leverage ratio — that is, a minimum level of capital against banks' unweighted assets. This is a non-risk backstop measure to reduce excessive leverage by banks — a problem that occurred during the 2007/2008 financial crisis, when capital proved to be not only insufficient but of low quality as well.

For NDBs under Basel III, such standards could also affect disproportionately the availability of credit to those exposures that require more capital (i.e., large and long-term projects, equity expositions and others). If permission is granted by the national regulator, NDBs with more technical resources and data availability may try to mitigate the quest by adopting internal models for risk assessment. These models permit banks to assign their own risk weights to their portfolio of assets and thereby potentially save capital. However, to avoid banks issuing too little capital due to the use of their own risk-assessment models, the Basel Committee has adopted measures that inhibit banks saving capital in this way. The first is the leverage ratio itself, the second is the

[12]This section starts from the analysis carried out in Castro (2018) and expands on it.

[13]For Basel standards discussed in this section, see BCBS (2011, 2017a, 2017b), unless otherwise indicated.

[14]D-SIBs are identified as such by national jurisdictions while G-SIBs are so by the Financial Stability Board (FSB) in consultation with the Basel Committee on Banking Supervision (BCBS 2012; BIS 2018a).

[15]Common shares and retained earnings should be the predominant forms of Tier 1 capital. In addition, common equity Tier 1 was raised from 2 per cent in Basel II to 4.5 per cent of risk-weighted assets. Moreover, the 2.5 per cent conservation buffers should be in the form of common equity Tier 1 capital.

prohibition of the use of internal models for certain exposures (see below) and the third is the adoption of an output floor. The purpose of the output floor is to ensure that banks using internal models have at least 72.5 per cent of capital compared with what the bank would if it used instead the standardized approach for capital determination. These measures are important to prevent major commercial banks from gaming the system. However, they removed, at least for several types of operations, the advantage of NDBs to use their own probability of default (PD), more suited to their own portfolio idiosyncrasies, and usually lower than the market.

(2) Liquidity (and funding) requirements: These are the Liquidity Coverage Ratio (LCR) and the Net Stable Funding Ratio (NSFR). The purpose of the LCR is to ensure that banks have enough high-quality liquid assets to cover net cash outflows over a 30-day time horizon in a stress scenario. It aims to avoid severe liquidity shortages as those that banks experienced during the global financial crisis. The NSFR intends to ensure that banks have enough funding with maturities that match those of their balance sheet assets and off-balance sheet commitments over a one-year horizon, avoiding significant maturity mismatches.

The introduction of internal models for credit risk by Basel II, and maintained (although discouraged), under Basel III, has in-built features that already require higher levels of capital for longer-term credit. The main concern is that the LCR and the NSFR may further inhibit long-term lending. The extent to which NDBs may be affected by these ratios depends on the structure of their liabilities — whether these are mainly short- or long term. These requirements are less binding for the NDBs under analysis in this paper, since these are non-household deposit taking institutions that rely predominantly on sources of funding such as national treasury resources, compulsory saving funds, the return of their own assets and capital markets.

4.2. Systemic Risks

(3) The large exposures framework: The large exposure risk was already addressed by the Basel Core Principles, and what the framework does is to clarify definition and measurement — and set upper limits. The limit set by Basel III is that banks' single exposures should not surpass 25 per cent of Tier 1 capital. If the exposure is from a G-SIB to another G-SIB, the upper limit is 15 per cent. A single large exposure is the sum of exposures to counterparties that are inter-connected, implying that the failure of one counterparty can lead to the failure of the other counterparties. Inter-connected counterparties can be both in terms of ownership and economic relations.

According to BCBS (2019, p. 15), all national supervisors adopt some sort of large exposure limit; and, in case such limits are breached, some of them suggest corrective measures or require additional capital. For NDBs, this rule restrains their ability to finance large projects, which usually are of infrastructure nature, but also some industrial projects. This new rule could be especially inapropriate for the smaller NDBs. The extent to which a bank is truly affected depends on how much national regulation is further tightened by adjusting to this new Basel standard. It is important to note that a few exposures, relevant to NDBs that are active internationally, as well NDBs operating domestically, are exempted from the single large exposure rule. These are exposures to sovereigns and their central banks, and public sector entities (in the latter case, according to the same rules that apply to them under credit risk for capital requirements) (BCBS 2014; BIS 2018b). The fact is that large exposures by NDBs, to public entities or, specifically to single large projects, should be guaranteed by their governments if such exposures are in the national interest — say, the undertaking of a large energy power project needed to eliminate bottlenecks to economic growth.

The large exposure rule addresses one type of concentration risk; other types of concentration risk such as those of sectoral and geographical nature, are addressed next.

(4) Other concentration risks: Concentration risk is dealt with under Pillar 2 of the Basel framework. Unlike Pillar 1, which is prescriptive, Pillar 2 is based on a set of principles that guide supervisors. This qualitative-based approach gives more leeway for national jurisdictions to decide what strategies and procedures to adopt to the successful fulfilment of Pillar 2 objectives (BCBS 2019). Consequently, the impacts of Basel III on NDBs depend, to an important extent, on what specific treatment NDBs' jurisdictions give to concentration risks. NDBs have, by design, a propensity to have concentrated portfolios in sectoral terms, since their activities target growth-related sectors, such as construction, infrastructure and manufacturing; and in geographical terms as well. It is important, then, that national regulators do take this reality into account, if they decide to target such risks, so that such banks do not face major restrictions on their developmental role.

4.3. The Pro-Cyclical Nature of Bank Credit

(5) Lending countercyclically: Basel acknowledges that bank credit operates pro-cyclically. To remedy this, the Basel Committee has introduced more rigorous stress tests, as these may help reduce excessive risk taking in the upside of the cycle; and, above all, capital buffers that should vary between 0 and 2.5 per cent of risk weighted assets. These buffers are expected to go up in good times and down in economic slowdowns (BCBS 2011).

Whilst these counter-cyclical buffers are welcome as they apply to commercial and investment banks, for NDBs their usefulness might be debatable. This is because NDB behaviour as regards cyclical lending is less clear. If their lending operations are mainly long term, this makes loan disbursements less variable over the business cycle, at least compared with other banks. In the downturn, such buffers may help, as NDBs do seem to scale up finance to help fight recession and unemployment. During phases of economic expansion, however, it is unlikely NDBs will slow down credit.

4.4. Market and Operational Risks (Some Also Systemic), and Those in Connection with Innovation

(6) Market risks: Basel addresses market risks with a focus on risks in trading books, which are treated under Pillar I. However, the most important sorts of market

risks NDBs face are interest rate and currency risks they have in their banking books. As regards interest rate risks in the banking books (IRRBB), Basel treats them all under Pillar II. If a bank IRRBB exposure reveals excessive risk, additional regulatory capital may apply (BCBS 2016). As regards currency risks, Basel addresses these under Pillar I, including trading and banking book exposures. Currency risks can be quite relevant for NDBs that borrow from abroad in foreign currency, which may cause a currency mismatch if their loans are extended to national borrowers in domestic currency — or an expensive hedge (if available) to be undertaken, due to the long term horizon of the loans. Also, some internationally active NDBs act as the financial arms of their countries' development agencies, and their operations may involve loans in currencies other than those in which they are funded. Moreover, a few other NDBs also engage in international operations, and lend in foreign currency to support the expansion of national corporates and other interests abroad.[16]

(7) Operational risks: Under Basel III, the use of internal models for operational risk — the advanced measurement approach (AMA) — has been removed. The Basel Committee recognized the inherent complexity of the AMA and the lack of comparability of methodologies among banks. NDBs that intended to use such models to save capital will no longer be able to do so, although they can use their information to meet new Pillar III information requirements.

Operational risks are hard to measure and may lead to double counting with other types of risks, such as credit and market risks. Moreover, NDBs often are more exposed to large, complex projects, which may involve legal risks, included in the operational risk concept, which, if materialized, can be quite severe. Project finance, which is a finance modality NDBs often deploy in large, complex projects, and which Basel already penalizes due to various risks, has the additional regulatory/legal risk to contend with. Guarantees may be offered by government agencies but, in general, these are to reduce losses related to credit risk, not legal and regulatory risks. This is an area in which the regulatory framework for NDBs may devote more attention.

(8) Risks in connection with innovation, including in climate finance: NDBs are keen to support innovation and do so with different instruments and practices. In this regard, two Basel III standards are discussed here: those that impinge on equity finance, an instrument NDBs use to support innovation, and climate finance, which, in many instances, involves betting on yet untested clean technologies.

Equity exposures (shares) classified in the trading book are submitted to market risk capital requirements; and the ones where there is no intention to frequently negotiate them (classified in the banking book) should be considered into credit risk capital requirements. The reason is that, if the stock price drops too much, it is like a default event, without guarantees to offset the losses.

For equity exposures not held in the trading book, investments are risk weighted at 100 per cent in the standardized approach for credit risk. In the IRB framework, depending on the method, the weights can vary from a minimum of 100 per cent to a

[16]BNDES is an example of a NDB providing foreign currency lending, but the bank has a source of funding in foreign currency (FAT Cambial) and hedges all its foreign currency exposures.

maximum of 1250 per cent. These risk weights penalize NDBs with a large share of equities in their total portfolio of assets.[17] Above all, the very high-risk weights disincentivizes NDB exposures to blue sky projects, which may fall under the category of speculative unlisted equity. Also, when shares are classified in the banking book, their counterparty is necessarily done on net equity, so total capital can go down or up significantly, according to market movements and the Basel capital ratio can be severely impacted, sometimes without any substantial credit event.

On climate finance, as economies transition to a low- or at least neutral-carbon growth model, NDBs will become increasingly engaged in climate finance to support such a transition. In terms of risks, this engagement can be beneficial to the extent that it will shift their portfolios away from high-emission sectors and thereby reduce their vulnerability to them. At the same time, supervisors are incorporating climate-related risks in their supervisory work, as they are concerned with banks' vulnerability to such sectors and with the ever more frequent weather events, which can cause losses to banks. Accordingly, they are asking banks to report their risk assessment and management practices in this area. According to BCBS (2019), climate risk assessment by supervisors has not translated yet into additional capital requirements. What needs further discussion is the overlooked fact that NDBs becoming increasingly engaged in low-carbon growth projects may be penalized if such projects are deemed as of higher risk by their supervisors, due to the fact that they often incorporate new — and thus hard to assess — green technologies. This is a problem that all banks face, but many NDBs have the promotion of sustainable investment as part of their mandates. Furthermore, in trying to find ways to support low-carbon growth, NDBs may feel impelled to create new lending practices and tools that supervisors may judge as idiosyncratic and thus require additional capital.

It is difficult to single out which of these standards are, in practice, the most important or binding for NDBs. It depends which NDB one might have in mind, since these banks are quite different amongst themselves. The next section highlights which ones are of greatest concern for the three NDBs it discusses.

5. The Challenges Basel III Poses for NDBs: An Empirical Discussion

This section compares three large non-retail-deposit-taking NDBs: BNDES of Brazil, CDB of China and KfW of Germany, by (1) identifying through secondary information key common and specific characteristics these banks hold; and (2) discussing Basel III adoption by the banks, drawing both on secondary information and interviews. The interviews were conducted with senior bank managers from BNDES and KfW departments of regulation and compliance and CDB's operational departments, and a senior regulator from China's national financial regulatory body in their personal capacity.[18]

[17]Of the three NDBs analysed in the next section, equity stakes for BNDES and KfW are quite important.

[18]Indeed, it should be noted that the views expressed do not necessarily represent the institutional views of the banks or China's regulatory body. The same applies for BNDES and KfW.

5.1. Banks' Key Characteristics

Both BNDES and KfW are NDBs created in the post-war II period. KfW was created in 1948 as part of the Marshall plan to help in the reconstruction of the German economy, following the destruction it suffered during the war. BNDES was established in 1952 to support Brazil's drive towards industrialization and to reduce infrastructure bottlenecks. CDB was established later, in 1994, but also as a policy bank to support the then ongoing process of economic transformation in China. All three are the largest NDBs in their respective countries and are fully owned by the state. None of them seeks profit maximization but all of them aim at reasonable levels of profitability, so that they can channel their profits to expand their capital base to be able to accomplish their developmental roles. All three banks have changed their main focus and expanded their roles over time.

KfW and CDB are fully backed by the State, in terms of guarantees. BNDES receives State guarantees in few operations. In terms of funding structure, all banks tap into long-term funding sources. This is what they need to be able to support large-scale infrastructure projects. BNDES's main source of funding is FAT,[19] a workers' compulsory savings fund; and, also, loans from the national treasury. In addition, BNDES has a small part of its funding coming from multilateral financial institutions, and national and international capital markets. For KfW, capital markets represent the near totality of its sources of funding. The bank taps such a source at low costs since it benefits from full German government guarantees. In addition, the bank counts on federal government transfers for DEG, the bank's arm specialized in development activities overseas.[20] CDB, in turn, raises resources by issuing long-term bonds, mainly in China's capital markets. The bank's bonds have large acceptance by local financial institutions, as the Chinese bank regulator grants CDB bonds as free-risk assets carrying zero-risk weight for capital allocation purposes. KfW bonds share the same privilege, but not BNDES.

In terms of the modality of operation and financing instruments, BNDES acts both directly and as a second-tier bank. Support to different projects and activities is given through direct loans and on-lending operations, equity, securities underwriting, and, in a small proportion, by private equity funds and provision of seed capital. KfW operates mainly through on-lending operations, equity participation, supporting venture capital, providing subsidized loans and engaging in equity acquisition abroad. CDB operates mainly through loans, extended both domestically and abroad, and acquisition and underwriting of corporate-issued bonds.

All three banks have comfortable levels of capital, which is reflected in their high total capital ratios (see Table 1).

5.2. Basel III Adoption and Challenges Going Forward

In a recent paper, Torres Filho and Xu (2020) propose four possible categories under which NDBs may fall, regarding bank standards. These are: (a) self-regulation, which means that NDBs are not subject to the supervision of national banks; (b) full compliance with Basel standards; (c) compliance with Basel standards, but with waivers and exemptions; and (d) the bank has a special and tailored regulatory framework.

---

[19]FAT stands for *Fundo de Amparo ao Trabalhador.*

[20]DEG stands for *Deutsche Investitions — und Entwicklungsgesellschaft, a subsidiary of KfW.*

Table 1. Banks' capital adequacy ratios (CARs).

Years	2014	2015	2016	2017	2018	2019
BNDES	15.9	14.7	21.7	27.5	29.0	36.8
CDB	11.9	10.1	11.6	11.6	11.8	
KfW[a]	14.1	18.3	22.3	20.6	20.1	21.3

Sources: BNDES website; KfW Financial Reports, various years; CDB Financial Reports, various years.
[a]KfW: Tier 1 Capital over risk-weighted assets.

All three NDBs are under the purview of national regulators,[21] so this excludes category (a). Both BNDES and KfW comply with Basel III standards, but with waivers and exemptions, thus falling under category (c). BNDES is exempted from Basel III compliance only with liquidity ratios, although it uses them for internal risk management and reports them to the Board. KfW is exempted from Basel III liquidity ratios as well. In addition, the bank is exempted from disclosure requirements (Pillar 3) and recovery resolution.[22] Unlike BNDES and KfW, CDB has been subject to a tailored regulatory framework.[23] In practice, however, the level of alignment with the Basel III framework seems high, at least regarding capital requirements. CDB's regulator requires the bank to establish financial discipline mechanisms with capital adequacy ratio (CAR) at its core. China's regulator has shown a more flexible approach to liquidity risk, as it recognizes that CDB is a bond-based bank and does not take household deposits.

5.2.1. What Are the Pros and Cons Regarding the Basel Framework and Basel III Adoption?

These banks do not directly create systemic risks — they are not household deposit-taking institutions and are not a major part of their country's payments system. Adherence to Basel, therefore, is perceived as a framework with excessive control systems (although this vision is not unanimous within some of them), given their specific characteristics and modus operandi. Moreover, the framework can affect their ability to play their developmental role, especially in fostering the SDGs.

Within BNDES, there has been also a view that Basel could provide an opportunity for the development of a culture of risk control, improve the quality of risk data and facilitate the adoption of integrated risk systems. A further potential advantage is that Basel compliance could help as BNDES turns to the capital markets. Moreover, as the Bank embarked on a continuous growth trajectory and portfolio diversification, new types of risk, such as market and operational risks, would gain a new dimension, requiring more sophisticated forms of risk management.

KfW, in turn, acknowledges that adherence to a supervisory authority and being subject to external audits help the bank become safer. The generation of data and data flows is also noted as positive. As a policy bank acting on behalf of the German State

[21]BNDES is under the purview of Brazil's Central Bank, the National Monetary Commission and the Securities Commission, and under the Basel framework since 1994. For the KfW, until 2013, the Basel capital framework applied for certain bank standards on a voluntary basis. From 2013, the bank became officially subject to supervision by the German Federal Financial Supervisory Authority (BaFin) in collaboration with the Bundesbank.

[22]Interview material.

[23]CDB is regulated by China Banking and Insurance Regulatory Commission (CBIRC), which is the same regulator for commercial banks. However, CBIRC has a so-called Policy Bank Supervision Department, which is responsible for the financial regulation of CDB.

to implement government policies, KfW can use the Basel compliance to have some degree of autonomy and shield itself from government pressure (see Moslener, Thiemann, and Volberding 2018). However, as KfW cautions, compliance efforts require more human resources, which is a cost to the bank, and which may drive critical resources away from their primary role, which is that of a promotional bank.

KfW reticence has also to do with the more strategic position the bank holds within the German banking system. This is the case particularly regarding the historical pivoting role it has played over the years by channelling resources to the country's SMEs, a mainstay of the economy, through Germany's commercial and regional banks. Thus, back in 2001, the bank was already expressing, in its Annual Report, concerns that the then under discussion Basel II could be a contributory factor to a deterioration in finance to SMEs. Since then, KfW has maintained its reticence in relation to the Basel framework, both in general terms and in what the framework affects it directly. For the bank, under Basel III, its type of business model — of a promotional bank — is not represented. Two areas have been particularly highlighted as of concern for the bank.

The first concerns KfW on-lending business model. KfW is a large bank — the third largest bank in Germany — with a big portfolio, but in most cases it can no longer (or will not be able to) use the A-IRB approach for credit risk, which could help mitigate the need for capital. Under the alternative approach, which is the foundation IRB approach, loss given default (LGD) is determined by the regulator. For KfW, calculating its own LGD was good as it could be of low value due to collateral.[24] The second concerns bank's equity exposures. Basel penalizes KfW significantly, as equity business (which includes venture capital) is a very important financing instrument for the bank. The DEG Unit of the bank, moreover, uses equity a great deal to support businesses in transition economies.

BNDES expresses similar concerns regarding the disincentive, or even outright prohibition, of the use of internal models for capital determination, although the use of internal models will not necessarily always save capital. In practice, internal models for credit risk under Basel III have their use restricted to a small number of operations, such as project finance. In the case of market risks, banks authorized to use internal models should also report the results from the use of the standard model, with the stipulation that capital gains with the use of the former should be limited to 20 per cent. Yet, despite these disincentives, BNDES does and will continue to use internal models, in order to provide the information requested by the national regulatory authorities and for managerial purposes.

Basel III's higher and stricter capital requirements with an emphasis on tier 1 capital, and additional backstops, such as the 2.5 per cent conservation cushion and the new leverage ratio, also affect all three banks. However, to date, these banks are doing well in terms of capital adequacy ratios (see above) and leverage ratio. The concern is that, when need arises for a counter-cyclical action or to expand investment in SDG investments, capital positions may erode quickly. Even without a crisis, Basel III new capital requirements may constrain their role in stepping up their development plans.

[24]According to (Lob, Schneider-May, and Kauffmann 2016, p. 8), KfW will be a disadvantage if the IRB approach is replaced by the standardized approach as the latter 'does not allow for any recognition of collaterals', despite the fact the latter is an inherent feature of the bank's on-lending business.

In terms of concentration risks, BNDES responded to the new large-scale exposures rule by selling shares. Other concentration issues for the bank include guarantor concentration and sectoral expositions, such as infrastructure sectors, State Governments and municipalities. Unlike BNDES, KfW does not have large exposures. In the case of CDB, given that the total assets are as large as $2 trillion, the concentration risks are less of a concern for the bank.

As discussed earlier, market risks in the trading books are not relevant for NDBs. IRRBB, treated under Pillar II, is considered a significant drawback for BNDES since it has a substantial banking portfolio. The method used is the standard model and may be subjected to new parameters by the Central Bank and thereby imply higher capital requirements. On operational risks, the proposed change, to be adopted from the year 2022, and which is based on banks' operational risk losses over the past ten years, may result in a substantial increase in required capital. However, both BNDES and KfW do not consider capital requirements for operational risk a major concern.

5.2.2. Going Forward: What Are Challenging Areas?

In the banks' views, development banks are expected to play a counter-cyclical role in times of recession/crises. This role implies a step change in their amount of lending and speed of disbursements, as other banks retreat in such times. Although all three banks are doing well in terms of total capital ratios, this is the case in normal times. In crisis times, when banks are expected to expand lending very rapidly, capital ratios can be eroded quickly.[25] Moreover, development banks are expected to play not just a countercyclical but a strategic role as well. A regulatory framework can be limiting and thus should allow for more flexibility, including in order to enable them to support investments for a green future.

Concentration exposures remain a concern for BNDES, due to Brazil's needs for infrastructure investments, although it has declined in the last years due to divestment strategies (sale of shares). Another significant challenge is how to treat environmental and climate risks. The bank has made progress in the creation of a policy for the management of socio-environmental responsibility and for an implementation plan that highlights the importance of managing associated risks. This is under an implementation phase. The quantitative assessment of environmental risk and, above all, climate risk, is still a challenging task for the bank. Important progress has been made with the definition of risk appetite of the institution and its limits. In contrast, little progress has been achieved on reputational risks, although a lot more on the treatment of strategic risk has been accomplished. All these risks fall under Pillar II.

For CDB, the key challenge is that the regulator and supervisor increasingly use the benchmark indicators similar to commercial banks to regulate and evaluate CDB. This tendency culminated in the adaptation of the Regulation of China Development Bank by China Banking Regulatory Commission (CBRC) — the predecessor of CBIRC formally unveiled in April 2018 — in 2017. Previously, CDB enjoyed much discretion and leeway in setting up the internal risk management system, which had enabled it to play a pivotal role in speeding up the industrialization and urbanization process in China.

[25] In the case of BNDES, during 2020, the capital adequacy ratio did not decline because the majority of the bank's response to the crisis came in the form of government operations, in which it was only the intermediary.

6. Conclusions

Our paper explores the potential impact of Basel III standards on the fulfilment of development functionalities of large NDBs. The empirical section, based on a combination of secondary information and interviews, brings together important elements and insights that support the view that Basel III may further constrain the ability of NDBs to fulfil their developmental missions, especially concerning the role they are expected to play in supporting the SDGs. The biggest constraint seems to come less from the levels of comprehensiveness and complexity of the framework, and more from the rather simple change towards tightening the levels of capital requirements and demanding better quality of capital. This is a concern shared not by small NDBs starved of capital, but by three large and well capitalized banks. Although the capital has not been a binding constraint for them in normal times, it can become so in times of crises. The counter-cyclical buffers the new framework has created do not seem to sufficiently address the problem.

A second area of contention for these big banks is the disincentive to the use of internal models, best suited to their own characteristics and which, again, may imply more capital requirements. A third area is the new large exposure rule, which is problematic for all three banks, given their focus on large, infrastructure projects. A fourth area refers to the high-risk weights required for exposures to project finance and equity. These are financing modality and tools NDBs use extensively, again, to support large and complex projects, and activities that involve innovation and risks. Essentially, these projects and activities require long-term finance. A final area which may have some impacts concerns changes in the method used for the calculation of operational risks. Liquidity and market risks, which are two areas Basel III targeted strongly in the aftermath of the global crisis, seem less relevant for the NDBs under analysis, given their funding structure based on longer-term liabilities, and the fact that they seldom engage in speculative activities.

Under Basel III, both BNDES and KfW benefit from some exemptions, whereas CDB has a tailored and separate regulatory framework. The adoption of such standards, designed having commercial and investment banks in mind, are not exactly suited to their own risk characteristics and can potentially have an impact on their future roles. What might be a better alternative is the possible adoption of separate standards, to be designed taking due account of their special forms of ownership, funding structure, business model and the strategic role they play on behalf of their national governments. Thus, what this paper suggests is that, in the case of BNDES and KfW, regulators move from the wavers'/exemptions approach adopted at present, towards a more tailored regulation for these banks, in order to ensure they are not constrained in their role to support rapid and transformative growth, especially concerning SDG goals. Ultimately, this is a political decision, of whether their governments really want these institutions to be key financing tools for supporting change and are prepared to underwrite their actions. As for CDB, although tailored regulation already exists, what it seems is that this is the case in formal terms but less so in practice.

Considering that having an international regulation can act as a protection or insurance against bad policies and decisions from administrations and governments, an alternative approach to tailored regulation for each NDB would be to have *a concerted regulatory framework at the international level for NDBs*, as the counterpart of Basel for commercial banks. A possible advantage of this latter approach might be that it would mitigate the downside or pitfall of a tailored approach, in terms of not sufficiently protecting NDBs against undue political intervention, if there are no hard regulatory rules to follow. This approach, of course, would still face the question of to what extent the diversity of NDBs would pose challenges for these concerted efforts.

Compliance with the Basel framework may also bring other palpable benefits, including better and integrated risk management systems, higher levels of bank safety, and the ability to tap capital markets at lower costs, although in the case of both CDB and KfW, low borrowing cost in capital markets has little to do with Basel compliance and more with government support. Despite possible benefits alongside costs, what transpires is that Basel adoption by these three banks was not the result of a dialogue or compromise between national regulators and banks. Rather, in each case decision on adoption was undertaken by national regulators, and only little consultation by regulators took place, though this has not been the case of CDB, which has a tailored regulatory framework. For all these banks, therefore, if an international alternative approach for development banks will not be possible, what seems needed is that more structured dialogue takes place between national policy makers, regulators and banks' senior management on how to build a regulatory framework that is more suitable to them and in line with national development priorities. To understand why this has not been the case to date, further research could throw light into decision-making process of Basel adoption for NDBs. This research could explore not only why Basel III was adopted in Brazil, China and Germany for their NDBs in the way it was, but also why, according to our own survey assessment, Basel standards were adopted by NDBs in other countries as well.

An area of clear concern relates to climate risks and climate finance. Despite the climate crisis, Basel III, a framework for capital determination based on a risk-based approach, still needs to appropriately factor in climate risks, remove the indirect forms in which it currently disincentivizes climate finance and go further by creating clear incentives instead, necessary both for bank stability and for the future of the world.

Finally, notwithstanding the insights the paper might provide by focusing on three large NDBs, the fact is that NDBs form a quite diverse group of banks. Many NDBs are just too small, are capital starved, lend too little, and lack the political support that banks such as BNDES, CDB and KfW have had over the years. In addition, many NDBs lack reliable funding sources and may be facing serious liquidity problems in their day-to-day operations. Therefore, future research is needed for an assessment of how the Basel framework affects these various other NDBs, as the policy recommendations might differ, possibly quite significantly, about what might be needed from the regulatory side to make these banks more effective tools to support the SDGs and the fight against climate change.

Disclosure Statement

No potential conflict of interest was reported by the author(s).

References

BCBS. 1988. 'International Convergence of Capital Measurement and Capital Standards.' https://www.bis.org/publ/bcbs04a.htm.

BCBS. 2011. *Basel III; A Global Regulatory Framework for More Resilient Banks and Banking Systems.* Basel Committee on Banking Supervision. Bank for International Settlements. Revised version, June. ISBN print: 92-9131-859-0.

BCBS. 2012. *A Framework for Dealing with Domestic Systemically Important Banks.* Basel Committee on Banking Supervision. Bank for International Settlements. October. ISBN 92-9131-141-3.

BCBS. 2014. *Standards. Supervisory Framework for Measuring and Controlling Large Exposures.* Basel Committee on Banking Supervision. Bank for International Settlements. April. ISBN 978-92-9197-987-5.

BCBS. 2016. *Standards. Interest Rate Risk in the Banking Book.* Basel Committee on Banking Supervision. Bank for International Settlements. April.

BCBS. 2017a. *Basel III: Finalising Post-Crisis Reforms.* Basel Committee on Banking Supervision. Bank for International Settlements. December.

BCBS. 2017b. *High-level Summary of Basel III Reforms.* Basel Committee on Banking Supervision. Bank for International Settlements. December.

BCBS. 2019. *Overview of Pillar 2 Supervisory Review Practices and Approaches.* Basel Committee on Banking Supervision Discussion Paper. Bank for International Settlements. June. ISBN 978-92-9259-279-0.

BIS. 2018a. 'The G-SIB Framework: Executive Summary.' FSI, Bank for International Settlements. 25 October. Accessed 13 April 2020. https://www.bis.org/fsi/fsisummaries/g-sib_framework.htm.

BIS. 2018b. 'The Treatment of Large Exposures in the Basel Capital Standards — Executive Summary.' FSI, Bank for International Settlements. 30 April. Accessed 10 April 2020. https://www.bis.org/fsi/fsisummaries/largeexpos.htm.

Carvalho, F. C. 2003. *Inovação Financeira e Regulação Prudencial: da Regulação da Liquidez aos Acordos da Basileia.* Rio de Janeiro: UFRJ: Texto para Discussão.

Castro, L. B. 2018. 'Financial Regulation and Risk Management in Development Banks.' In *The Future of National Development Banks*, edited by S. Griffith-Jones and J. A. Ocampo. Oxford, UK: Oxford University Press.

Elliott, D., S. Salloy, and A. Santos. 2012. 'Assessing the Cost of Financial Regulation.' IMF Working Paper WP/12/233. Washington, DC.

Gottschalk, R., ed. 2010. *The Basel Capital Accords in Developing Countries: Challenges for Development Finance.* London: Palgrave Macmillan.

Hohl, S., M. C. Sison, T. Sastny, and R. Zamil. 2018. 'The Basel Framework in 100 Jurisdictions: Implementation Status and Proportionality Practices.' FSI Insights on Policy Implementation, No. 11. Bank for International Settlements.

Jones, E., ed. 2020. *The Political Economy of Bank Regulation in Developing Countries: Risk and Reputation.* New York: Oxford University Press.

Jones, E., and A. Zatz. 2017. 'The Limits of Globalizing Basel Banking Standards.' *Journal of Financial Regulation* 3 (1): 89–124.

Keynes, J. M. 1936 [1964]. *The General Theory of Employment, Interest and Money.* New York: Harcourt, Brace, Jovanovich.

King, P., and H. Tarbert. 2011. 'Basel III: An Overview.' *Banking and Financial Services Policy Report* 30 (5): 1–18. May.

Knaack, P. 2017. 'An Unlikely Champion of Global Finance: Why is China Exceeding Global Banking Standards?' *Journal of Current Chinese Affairs* 46 (2): 41–79.

Kobrak, C., and M. Troege. 2015. 'From Basel to Bailouts: Forty Years of International Attempts to Bolster Bank Safety.' *Financial History Review* 22 (2): 133–156.

Komai, A., and G. Richardson. 2011. 'A Brief History of Regulations Regarding Financial Markets in the United States: 1789 to 2009' (No. w17443). National Bureau of Economic Research.

Lob, H., J. Schneider-May, and D. Kauffmann. 2016. 'Regulation of Promotional Banks and Potential Impacts.' KfW Research Papers and Proceedings on Economics. KfW Bankengruppe. November.

Minsky, H. P. 1982. *Can It Happen Again? Essays on Stability and Finance.* New York: M. E. Sharpe.

Moslener, U., M. Thiemann, and P. Volberding. 2018. 'National Development Banks as Active Financiers: The Case of KfW.' In *The Future of National Development Banks*, edited by S. Griffith-Jones and J. Ocampo. Oxford University Press. October.

Mosley, L. 2010. 'Regulating Globally, Implementing Locally: The Financial Codes and Standards Effort.' *Review of International Political Economy* 17 (4): 724–761.

Schumpeter, J. A. 1912/1934 [1982]. *The Theory of Economic Development: An Inquiry Into Profits, Capital, Credit, Interest, and the Business Cycle*. New Jersey: Transaction Publishers.

Stiglitz, J. 1993. 'The Role of the State in Financial Markets.' Proceedings of the World Bank Conference on Development Economics. Washington, DC: World Bank.

Stiglitz, J. 1998. 'The Role of Financial System in Development: The World Bank Group.' Presentation at the Fourth Annual Bank Conference on Development in Latin America and the Caribean (CAC- ABCDE). The World Bank (www.worldbank.org).

Torres Filho, E., and J. Xu. 2020. 'Regulating National Development Banks: The Historical Experiences of the Brazilian Development Bank (BNDES) since 1952.' Ford Foundation Visiting Fellowship Working Paper. Ford Foundation and Peking University (Institute of New Structural Economics). December.

Walter, A. 2008. *Governing Finance — East Asia's Adoption of International Standards*. Ithaca, NY: Cornell University Press.

Can Development Banks Step Up to the Challenge of Sustainable Development?

Régis Marodon

ABSTRACT
Public development banks (PDBs) — at sub-national, national, regional or international level — can cooperate and become central in the implementation of sustainable economic models. PDBs are over 500 globally. They are both providers of public funding and enablers to leverage private finance. PDBs need to acquire 'sustainable development analytical tools' to select operations on the basis of criteria other than purely financial ones. This paper explores why development banks can play a leading role. It proposes five recommendations for decision-makers: (1) Streamline into financing decisions the need to transition towards low-carbon and equitable economies. (2) Mobilise and encourage the private sector such that all stakeholders reach convergence on sustainable development. (3) Use development banks to channel funds for transition purposes into concrete projects, programmes consistent with international agreements signed by their governments. (4) Support emergence of a responsible demand, given that PDBs themselves are not originators of projects. (5) Build a global coalition of PDBs, to tackling global problems.

1. Introduction

There are some 520+ public development banks (DBFIs) across the globe, present on all continents and operating within an international, regional, national or sub-national perimeter. They are independently managed and ensure the financial implementation of the public mandate entrusted to them.

Their rationale has been heavily debated. Is a state-owned development bank better able than a private bank to optimally allocate its available resources? The economic literature raises questions on what role the state should play in finance. In what way are development banks different? Can their very existence be justified?

Clearly, certain market imperfections greatly harm social balances and the smooth running of the economy. Persistent poverty and inequality, the need for affordable social housing and financing for small farms or businesses all justify proactive public policies across the world. At international level, financing for low-income countries, who have only a limited access to financial markets, justifies resources should be channelled, at least partly, through development banks. The same holds true when it comes to financing for local authorities or support for international trade.

Yet, over the last twenty years, the nature of the problem has changed. Environmental and social awareness has brought to light the importance of externalities in investment and production processes. The United Nations' approval of the 'Sustainable Development' concept at the 1992 Rio Summit, then of the Sustainable Development Goals (SDGs) in 2015, concretely signals the need to think differently, with a universal and cross-cutting approach, instead of prioritising the sole path of economic development.

While the world remains preoccupied by the persistence of poverty and inequalities, by climate change and the loss of nature, the Covid-19 crisis is a reminder that the problems are interlinked and that, most often, they call for a combination of local and global actions.

We are entering a period of transition, during which we must chart the critical path to ensuring that consumption and production modes are compatible with sustainable growth. What are the possible modalities and who are the agents of change able not only to ensure a coherence between investment choices and the crucial need for sustainability but also to incite the international financial community to evolve?

This paper analyses the special role that development banks can play on this road to transition. It proposes that they take on greater responsibility and imagine their transformation through a mandate centred on the SDGs. It points up the societal responsibility of public development banks, currently insufficiently mobilised. It shows how the DBFIs have key advantages allowing them to broaden their operating procedures to include a cross-cutting vision of their activities and impacts, as the SDGs presume. It proposes five operational recommendations for development banks based on their purposes, their mandates, their governance, their financial tools and their sectors of operation. Lastly, it underscores the interest of having the DBFIs form a new global coalition.

2. Who Are the Development Banks?

2.1. Definition of a Development Bank

Despite their current global renaissance, we know quite little on Public Development Banks and Development Financing Institutions (DBFIs). Apart a few large and renowned ones standing at the front of the scene, such as the World Bank, The European Investment Banks or the China Development banks, DBFIs are a financial continent that remains largely unexplored. To that end, the Institute of New Structural Economics (INSE, Peking University) has initiated and then collaborated with the French Development Agency (AFD) to compute the first ever-exhaustive database on DBFIs (Xu, Ren, and Wu 2019; Xu, Marodon, and Ru 2021).

A first difficulty is to specificity the common characteristics of these institutions, in order to distinguish them from other official arrangements, including in particular government credit programmes, aid agencies, sovereign funds, grant-executing agencies, state-owned commercial banks with policy functions, cooperative banks or microfinance institutions. Five criteria need to be fulfilled at the same time to qualify as a DBFI:

(i) Government should play a steering role in setting the corporate strategy, the most common being holding the majority of the capital base.
(ii) It must have a separate legal status, dedicated personnel, financial statements and is not set up to achieve short-term goals;
(iii) Its mandate should focus on proactively implementing a public policy to fill a financing gap or market failure where private capital markets are unwilling or unable to offer financial support;
(iv) It should deploy financial instruments such as loans, equity investments, or guarantees that require some form of financial return as the main product and service;
(v) Without prejudice to its ability to receive grants, it must be in the capacity to finance itself beyond periodic budgetary transfers;

2.2. Panorama of Development Banks

According to the first database on DBFIs based on the definition stated above (Xu, Marodon, and Ru 2021), it has identified 527 institutions, totalling USD 13 trillion of assets in 2019 (excluding the two large US mortgage banks), representing 15 per cent of World GDP. Based on the first-hand data collection (Xu, Marodon, and Ru 2021), estimating the balance sheet rotation at an average of six years, DBFIs contributed to USD 2.3 trillion new financing in 2019. According to World Bank estimates, gross capital formation — a reasonable proxy of global investment — was USD 22.3 trillion USD in 2019, inducing that the annual financing of DBFIs is about 10 per cent of the world's investment.

However, these global figures hide major differences between DBFIs in terms of size, location, geographical operation and mandate.[1] Indeed, nine mega DBFIs, whose individual balance sheet exceeds USD 500 billion, concentrate 2/3 of total assets. At the other end of the spectrum, 166 micro DBFIs, whose assets is less than USD 500 million, account for merely 0.14 per cent of aggregate total assets.

Even though in absolute terms the vast majority of DBFIs appears to be modest in size, they carry a substantial weight in their respective countries or regions. They are indeed distributed across every region of the world, including in the least developed countries. As such, Africa and Southern Asia concentrate 25 and 20 per cent of national DBFIs respectively. National banks accounts for 70 per cent of the number of DBFIs worldwide, while multinationals account for only 9 per cent. An important feature of the base is also to reveal that 21 per cent of the DBFIs are sub-national DBFIs, created by local governments to compensate imbalances between various national territories.

Eventually, DBFIs differ in terms of ownership structure, geographical scope, asset size and mandate, constituting a rich and diverse financial system, heavily connected with the 2030 agenda. One could assume that virtually all large infrastructure projects or support programmes to SME investments around the world are connected to one or several DBFIs.

---

[1]For a detailed analysis, please refer to: Xu, Marodon, and Ru (2021).

3. Two Centuries of History

3.1. The Rationale for Development Banks

The appropriate scoping of the state's responsibilities in the financial and monetary realms is one of the subjects that sparks most debate among economists, though in-depth research on actual public development finance institutions has been fairly limited (Griffith-Jones and Ocampo 2018). Development banks have at times been stigmatised by free market advocates, while at other times, particularly during periods of crisis or war, there has been a call to reinforce them. Fortunately, we are now better able to understand that everything boils down to context and the moment in history.

Historically, the establishment of public financial institutions has targeted a twofold objective (Schmidt et al. 2011).

The first is to channel investments into infrastructure or sectors that the government considers a priority (Diamond 1957). This was notably the case during the industrial revolution and the 19th century was the cradle of national and specialised public banks. The driving idea was to support the construction of the infrastructure needed and rendered feasible by industrialisation (Mazzucato and Penna 2018). In this, the founding role played by public development banks was what forged their basic identity, as they invested in new sectors or organised financial pools that opened pioneering outlets for investment, most often partnered by the private sector. In 1850, the French Caisse des Dépôts invested massively in the capital of the newly created railway companies in France, permitting a rapid emergence of this quite new transport technology at the time.

The second objective aims to overcome market imperfections, especially those linked to the various economic, environmental and social impacts accompanying any development project, the so-called externalities. They are also questions of coordinating and implementing public policy, and information asymmetries, which leads this sectors to being underfinanced (Armendariz de Aghion 1999; Hausmann, Panizza, and Fernández-Arias 2020).

As a result, some projects judged to be economically, environmentally, or socially relevant by public authorities are not financed by private banks, as the rate of return is considered too low compared to the risk. This is the case when it comes to financing an industrial and innovation policy, or some infrastructure. These types of projects require long-term finance that the private sector is not always willing to provide, particularly when the risk involved stems from a governmental policy choice.[2] It is for example the case for the small family farms that make up the economic and social bedrock of many countries, particularly low-income countries.

The role of the public sector in the financial system intensified during the reconstruction in the wake of World War II. These years were marked by the state's growing role in regulating the economy both in the near term (Keynesian policies) and long term (planning). The International Bank for Reconstruction and Development (IBRD), later known as the World Bank, was created at this time and emerged as the financial pillar of a multilateral system that needed rebuilding, notably to assist those countries that had been ravaged by war. The German KfW was also established during this period (1948)

[2]The French Caisse des Dépôts provided its first financing in support of territorial development in 1822 to the Port of Dunkerque.

funded by the Marshall Plan. In the post-war years, development banks were bolstered or created so that they could take over, at local level, the drive for industrial investment (Diamond 1957). This was the case of the Industrial Development Bank of Turkey (TSKB), which the country set up in 1950 in partnership with the World Bank.

Another reason for creating development banks emerged in the 1950s and 1960s, as governments were eager to foster regional integration. Solidarity between countries holding stakes in the same financial institution unlocked powerful political and financial leverage. The existence of these banks enabled states to jointly raise capital, giving them the possibility to finance structural projects in a given sub-region. The objective of economic integration dovetailed with political ambitions, and proved to be a contributing factor to peace and security between neighbouring countries within the same geographical region.

This is the moment when regional banks appeared on the scene. The European Investment Bank (EIB — 1958) illustrates the success of this shared vision between European governments. The pooling of European debt is operational for quite some time yet through the EIB's bond issuance, and the bank is still one of the world's best-rated signature. It has played a major role in funding European infrastructure and innovation, as well as European SMEs through lines of credit to national banking systems. The Council of Europe Bank (CEB — 1956), the Corporación Andina de Fomento (CAF — 1970), the West African Development Bank (WADB — 1973), and more recently the Black Sea Trade and Development Bank (BSTDB — 1997) also exemplify this reality. The European Bank for Reconstruction and Development (EBRD), established to facilitate the integration of Eastern Europe, extended its mandate southwards because of the absence of a full-fledged Mediterranean development bank, that would be a great signal that peace and prosperity are a feasible and suited future for that sub-region.

Mention should also be made of the years following the African independencies, when the need for national financial institutions independent of the former colonial powers was to be met by the newly established governments (Duchaussoy 2017). The local financial sector was embryonic, having very few national institutions. In these circumstances, development banks had to support the autonomy of the newly constituted nations and fully contribute to promoting the drive for economic growth.

3.2. DBFIs' Decline and Revival as Public Policy Instruments

After many years of a more Keynesian and plan-based vision, the 1970s and 1980s were marked by a challenge to government intervention in the economy. The political issues of the Cold War divided the world and ideological clashes often prevailed over economic considerations.

In the realm of finance, the general trend was towards liberalisation (cf. John Williamson and the Washington Consensus). The recommendations of the structural adjustment programmes implemented by the International Monetary Fund and World Bank pointed in this direction, although paradoxically the World Bank is itself a large Public Development Bank. The shortcomings, real or perceived, in the management of public institutions, be it governments, state-owned enterprises or public banks, brought on widespread distrust of public sector effectiveness (Scott 2007), not only on account of suspected corruption but also because it was seen as a systemic failure. The private sector and rules of free competition were called on to take over. Financial regulations were revised and relaxed, and the move towards the privatisation of public banks, facilitated by management irregularities in some institutions (La Porta, Lopez-De-Silanes, and Shleifer 2002; Smallridge and de Olloqui 2011), became common in many countries.[3]

Public development banks were caught up in this movement and many were liquidated, restructured or privatised, particularly in Latin America and Africa. Poor governance was a major obstacle in weak institutional environments. In less developed countries, in particular, a consensus emerged that the context in these countries was not conducive to reaping the potential benefits of development banks.

At the same time, in Europe and particularly in France, Germany and Italy, the picture was less clear-cut. Certainly, in France, the experience of the Sociétés Locales de Développement (local development agencies) had ended in failure, bar a few exceptions. Yet, although state-owned commercial banks were privatised, some public development banks escaped this trend and their potentially structuring role continued to receive support and recognition. Several countries that had recently left the Soviet bloc created their own development banks in the 1990s, more often than not successfully.

In the wake of discussions on the new institutional economy during the 1990s and evidence that the private sector was blind to certain risks, it was effectively the 2000s and especially the major 2008 financial crisis that gradually shone the spotlight on the positive state's regulatory role (Griffith-Jones and Ocampo 2018; Thorne and du Toit 2009).

The possibility of mobilising public development banks in this countercyclical role hangs on two specific features that universal banks do not have (Brei and Schclarek 2015):

- The first is institutional: as the state is the shareholder of development banks, the need to safeguard the economy stands as a priority. The bank can be used to transfer resources to economic agents who can justify their need. The risk of moral hazard is lower than when private intermediation is involved, and the signal is useful for restoring market confidence.
- The second characteristic is structural: public development banks have balance sheets based on long-term resources (De Luna-Martinez and Vicente 2012), which limits the risk of a maturity mismatch. Fanny Mae and Freddie Mac as well as Dexia,[4] privatised institutions that were DBFIs at their inception, were caught in the crossfire of the 2008 financial crisis for this reason. By contrast, the business model of DBFIs does not require a fast turnover of assets. They lend over a duration that matches their resources and thus have no great need for short-term refinancing. In the event of market volatility, they are less exposed than others to the risk of illiquidity. This more stable balance sheet structure (Macfarlane and Mazzucato 2018) is clearly an advantage in periods of crisis, as it allows them to step in until market tensions ease.

All in all, development banks' business model positions them very differently from private banks. They have, of course, to factor in banking margins and risks that affect

[3]The World Bank's 2013 report on financial development is symptomatic of this view (Global Financial Development Report: Rethinking the Role of the State in Finance).

[4]The case of Dexia bank, a former public development bank, now privatised, that specialised in local government financing, is interesting on this count. Its liquidation (by orderly resolution) in 2009 owed nothing to the quality of its portfolio, which was excellent, but rather to the maturity mismatch of its refinancing.

their financial equilibrium and sustainability. They remain governed by banking law or similar standards but, on top of this, they also have to meet the requirement of fulfilling their government mandate. They are expected to strike the right balance between operating equilibrium, risk management and allocation of their resources with a view to maximising the economic, social and environmental impacts of their financing. This robust financial stability and investment thesis fashions them into specific instruments able to play a government-defined role which differs from that of commercial banks across all financial systems. Redefining and amplifying this role in line with the Sustainable Development Goals could constitute a fresh rationale for their continuing and expanding trajectory.

3.3. The Covid-19 Crisis and Sustainable Development

In peacetime years, there is almost no history of a decision leading to the lockdown of all 'non-essential' economic activities in less than 24 hours, except for health services and distribution of food supply (Marodon 2020). Neither is there any prior example of the recipe that can ensure a successful recovery, given the magnitude and depth of the crisis. Governments and central banks, especially in developed economies, which have more fiscal space, have put in place large-scale financing measures and blown the cap on fiscal deficit ratios.

In these unprecedented circumstances, the mobilisation of governments, both in terms of speed and scale,[5] much more so than in 2008 when a wait-and-see approach had prevailed for several months. This attitude was, in fact, justifiable given that the 2008 crisis was endogenous to the financial system and spurred financial institutions, whatever their level of exposure, to relevant caution. In 2020 and 2021, the crisis is purely exogenous and affects first and foremost the real economy. It stems from the policy decision to close borders, restrict economic activity and even confine whole countries. The consequences and risks are thus of a very different nature, and rebooting economic activities that were healthy pre-crisis depends over-archingly on the recovery of world trade, with each actor seeking to return to the pre-crisis situation as soon as possible. Unlike 2008, the current revival requires above all a particularly agile and dynamic financial system capable of generating the necessary liquidity. The public component, including DBFIs, has thus been particularly in demand since March 2020, as confirmed by the numerous cases observed within the International Development Finance Club (IDFC Response to COVID-19 Crisis — IDFC). This is also because the private financial sector has been unwilling to lend, unless strong public guarantees or co-financing with DBFIs was available, due to widespread uncertainty.

The urgent need for a swift reboot of the economy has also opened the debate on the nature and quality of this reboot. Is it a matter of returning to the previous situation as quickly as possible? Before the Covid-19 crisis, many development banks had already engaged at enhancing the compatibility of their financing with the international agreements on climate and the SDGs, which their own governments had signed in 2015.

[5]According to the International Monetary Fund, the G20 countries had already mobilised USD 10 trillion in July 2020, twice the amount that they had announced in March. Source: https://www.imf.org/en/Topics/imf-and-covid19/Fiscal-Policies-Database-in-Response-to-COVID-19.

In a context of climate change, loss of nature and social inequalities, questions are being raised on the extent to which operations, albeit cost-effective, are really of benefit in the long run. Certainly, assessing investment opportunities goes hand in hand with identifying related externalities. Whether these are positive or negative, considering them can quite radically change the view on a project. Good examples of this are given by projects that are justified economically but whose realisation nonetheless implies the destruction of a landscape or a natural area. The INELFE project for the electrical interconnection between France and Spain is interesting from this standpoint. Heated debates took place between nature conservationists and those defending the economic priority of interconnecting electric networks between France and Spain. The need to strike a balance between these two stances led to justifiable interventions by the EIB (EUR 350 Million) and the European Commission, permitting that most of the cable link was laid underground, at a higher cost, but with limited damage to the natural landscape.

Many are hoping that the economic recovery and the monies spent on it will provide the opportunity for a fresh start on new foundations. The DBFIs should be at the forefront of a 'new finance' aimed at reconciling financial equilibrium, risk coverage and a resolute step in the direction of a sustainable and inclusive development model.

4. Development Banks for Sustainable Finance

One prerequisite is, of course, the setting-up of a governance system and effective regulation of the activities of development banks. Here, no one-size-fits-all model exists, but the economic literature reminds us that, if directors are not relatively free from political interference in the financial and operational management of their institution, the risk of nepotism and abuses is high (see particularly Smallridge and de Olloqui 2011). It is equally crucial that regulatory and supervisory banking practices be aligned on industry standards. In some cases, exceptions to Basel III standards may be envisaged, to help DBFIs fulfil their mandates better, provided they are justified and proportionate.

Once these fundamentals are clearly and firmly established, five structuring recommendations can be proposed, which could give development banks a leadership role in financing the transition without crowding out private financing.

- Mainstream the imperative to transition in financing decisions
- Mobilise and redirect private finance
- Use development banks to channel transition funds
- Promote the emergence of a responsible demand
- Build a new global financing architecture

4.1. Mainstream the Imperative to Transition in Financing Decisions

For governments that engage in the multilateralism dynamic and participate in the ongoing transition, two points tend to gather consensus:

- The United Nations agreements of 2015 on the SDGs and the Paris Climate Agreements represent a unified strategic horizon for all countries.
- The SDGs are a matter for all economic actors, at all levels, in all countries, all sectors, whatever their level of income. The private sector needs to become part of this dynamic. This is a requisite for the transition to take place.

This new imperative for sustainable development requires a thorough rethink of the mandate and functioning of development banks (Attridge, te Velde, and Soren 2019; Clark et al. 2019; Griffith-Jones, Attridge, and Gouett 2020).

Since 2015, a growing number of development banks have already integrated into their evaluations the issue of the carbon emissions linked to the projects they fund. The multilateral banks and IDFC members have committed to ensuring that their activities are compatible with the Paris Agreement objectives. Many of these institutions are setting up criteria and metrics to guide their strategies, their analysis of counterparties and transactions, and to proactively management climate risks.

Yet, much remains to be done. Although the climate question is pivotal, it is only part of the problem. Strictly speaking, no 'climate project' exists independently of its social and economic impacts. The relative failure of current policies to fight global warming — given that emissions continue to rise — is because they have not adequately integrated the diverse dimensions of sustainable development.

Moreover, when crafting pro-poor policies, the questions of climate and nature are essential and must not be viewed as secondary (OECD 2019), not only because the impact of global warming is felt worldwide but also because this warming, as well as natural resource depletion, is exacerbating the fragility of the most vulnerable populations. The challenge lies in ensuring consistency between investment choices and the imperative of sustainability — which is a major responsibility for development banks. This issue is particularly challenging in low-income countries, which have relatively low CO_2 emissions and high poverty rates. They are compelled to make trade-offs to ensure the investments crucial to their economic growth while, at the same time, giving utmost importance to climate change.

The Covid-19 crisis reveals just how devastating the great planetary issues of climate and the loss of nature can be in a world that fails to prepare for them. It also shows that the economic and social consequences (resurgence of poverty, unemployment, exploding debt, bankruptcies, etc.) of a transition involving an annual 7 per cent reduction in carbon emissions, for instance, have been vastly underestimated, where this drop in emissions is achieved through a proportional drop in growth.

There is also a lesson to learn from the last twenty years of climate finance (Buchner et al. 2019): the multiplication of commitments made in good faith, no matter who the actors may be, are unable to move the needle on the necessary scale. During the Covid-19 lockdowns, we saw increasing declarations to the effect that the 'world after' would not be as before, that lessons would be drawn from the crisis, that we would have to 'reinvent ourselves'. Yet, the stimulus measures implemented are primarily aimed at boosting consumption and pushing production back up to its former levels. Reconstitute the 'world before' — basically the only world that we know — as quickly as possible.

One of the challenges of the 21st century is to give a new direction to all financial flows to ensure their compatibility with the SDGs, include climate. A first step is doubtless for development banks: to have a simple and credible analytical tool to qualify the compatibility of their business with sustainability.

The main difficulty is linked to the multi-faceted character of the SDGs and their mutual coherence. It is indeed very difficult to determine whether an investment project or public policy programme is comprehensively positive for all 17 SDGs, but also and more importantly, assess to what extent the negative impact on one of the goals should be disqualifying. Their interactions are too numerous and often still largely unknown. Research work plays a decisive role in shedding light on this. Further questions arise concerning priorities, and these are not identical for Mauritania and for Germany. The magnitude of the social or environmental damage potentially caused by an investment compared to the expected economic and financial benefits is highly specific to each investment, each context, each country.

Development banks are on the front line regarding these questions.

Each development bank needs to address these questions to make sure that its own constraints and the social structure and economic level of the country in which it operates are tailored in its approach. But all of them must ensure that each project includes an assessment of the externalities of the investment under consideration and clarify what it could achieve or has to avoid, in any related aspects. This is the only way to justify unlocking an emissive investment or harming a natural area, if the achievement of vital social progress is truly is the balance.

In fact, there is hardly any other means to ensure that financing initiatives prioritise activities with direct or indirect co-benefits for climate or nature. Innovative operations must be identified and hold top priority when the projects are able to trigger structural changes, be it on a small scale (pilots) or large scale.

Governments should ask all public development banks, to develop such methodologies, use them as concrete 'echo chambers' able to mobilise research resources, and then catalyse other financial flows. The myth of market self-regulation has reached its limits. Setting a new course for the financial system can only be achieved through the alignment of financing with their measured impacts, under the eye of regulators likely to impose the precise and demanding standard to set the pace of the transition.

4.2. Mobilise and Redirect Private Finance

Among the needs to redirect global investment, the vast bulk of which is private, is the need to finance the various transitions. Today, this requires changing scale, especially when it comes to climate. Some preliminary remarks are useful:

- Markets are not efficient when it comes to giving the signals needed to channel private resources in the direction of the SDGs. In fact, markets pay little attention to the long term, sending no price signals on externalities and encouraging 'free-rider' behaviour, particularly in fragile political and economic contexts.
- Private finance continues to invest heavily in the industries it knows well, even though some of these are contributing to climate change and the loss of nature. Investments in oil-related sectors are still very high, representing around USD 500 billion globally

each year,[6] that is, triple the total annual amount of official development assistance (UDS 152 billion in 2019).[7]

- On the other hand, the flows of private resources required to finance the costs of transitioning towards sustainable and inclusive economies are far higher than current flows. The International Energy Agency estimates the energy transition alone will cost USD 44 trillion. This is beyond the reach of public financing alone, be it domestic or international. What's more, it would prove ineffective should private investors continue to pull in the opposite direction by financing investments detrimental to the SDGs.
- The 47 least developed countries, in particular, run a serious risk of being unable to finance this transition even though their populations are the furthest away from the SDGs. Even if financing is doubled, the amount of official development assistance mobilised would be incommensurate with their needs, estimated minimally at one trillion dollars a year.[8]
- Public debt levels, already elevated before the Covid-19 crisis, leave no leeway for the conjecture that governments will be able to implement the necessary transition infrastructure without a major redirection of private capital and adapted financial packages. One of the priorities that the Tharman report[9] underlines in its proposed reform of the international financial architecture is the mobilisation of vastly greater private investment.

These arguments are not new (Gössinger and Raza 2011). The creation of many development banks in the mid-1970s, including Proparco, was based on this rationale. With the mobilisation of the international community around the SDGs, this line of reasoning is gaining strength and everyone agrees that what is crucial is for all stakeholders to fully take on board the pressing need for transition.

This means that potentially available private sector funds must be channelled into sustainable development. Development banks are well-placed to help this redirecting of private financial flows (Griffith-Jones, Attridge, and Gouett 2020). They are already often present in most of the financing rounds for large infrastructure projects and are in a position to bring their influence to bear. They need to strengthen their catalytic role through well-adapted financing methods and channels, in order to drive up SDG-compatible financing. In other words, what counts is not only that their own financing be in line with the requirements of the transition, but also that they try to bring all financial actors on board, so that a project that fails to adequately account for its social and environmental consequences finds no takers. More importantly, it is essential that projects contributing to a low carbon economy find sufficient funding.

To facilitate the mobilisation of private funds, the most common financial instrument is blended finance, which involves subsidising part of a private investment through grants or low-interest loans (Eslava and Freixas 2018). Other frequent arrangements rely on

[6]IEA (2019).

[7]https://www.oecd.org/fr/cad/financementpourledeveloppementdurable/normes-financement-developpement/aide-publique-au-developpement.htm.

[8]https://www.brookings.edu/blog/future-development/2019/07/29/how-much-does-the-world-spend-on-the-sustainable-development-goals/.

[9]Making the Global Financial System Work for All, Report of the G20 Eminent Persons Group on Global Financial Governance, October 2018.

trust funds, or ad-hoc mechanisms such as first-loss guarantees (e.g., for mezzanine finance). To be effective, development banks need to establish precise rules to prevent blending from introducing a competitive bias or, more importantly, from creating moral hazard by generating unjustified profit for private players.

Moreover, it is very difficult to put a figure on the level of subsidy that an investment requires to enable it to integrate a positive externality or cover a risk. This same question was raised by states with respect to the unfair use of Overseas Development Assistance for commercial purposes. The rules of the OECD's 1978 Arrangement — which has since been regularly added to and updated — had attempted to establish a common framework to allay this concern. Different international actors have endeavoured to establish rules of conduct for blended finance (particularly the IFC and more recently the OECD via the Tri Hata Karana Roadmap) to limit possible criticism of moral hazard. The international debate is focusing on this question: beyond standards and regulations, how can investments be steered towards sustainability and, during an intermediary transition stage, how can those who take this direction be encouraged by financial incentives?

Given their knowledge of the economic realities of each sector, their experience gained from different operations and their close ties to government, development banks are probably the financial actors best positioned to move this debate forward and systematise this type of intermediation. To do so, they must be able to make substantive financial commitments by having their capital increased by governments and leveraging their balance sheets,[10] in line with objectives that their shareholders need to set for them much more precisely and ambitiously.

4.3. Use Development Banks to Channel Transition Funds

To accomplish their mission, development banks need to have a level of capital commensurate with their counterparty-risk-bearing capacity, while also ensuring that liabilities are backed by long-term resources. The failure of some development banks, regardless of the quality of their management, often stems from the conjunction between an unbalanced liability structure and an inadequately collateralised activity.

A prerequisite for their missions to succeed is government support, be it through loan guarantees, subsidised interest rates, tax breaks or maintaining a sound capital adequacy ratio. A mission broadened to include sustainable development financing presupposes extending the term of loans, as is often the case in the social housing sector. Loans with maturities of 30, 40 or even 50 years are justified if they promote solutions that prevent investments from being locked into highly emissive activities.

The question then arises of development banks' having sufficient capital, as well as access to grants or subsidies to support virtuous projects, or transform non-virtuous projects to become so.

- Ethically and economically speaking, the neo-classical rationale would suggest that companies pay and factor into their product the pricing of all related costs: not

[10]The leverage effect is the amount of additional lending permitted either by increasing equity capital or by receiving budget allocations from government.

only the direct costs of inputs to production, such as labour and capital, but also the costs of all externalities, particularly if they cause environmental damage. Social responsibility and ethical treatment of employees also exist in most labour legislations and should be imposed as a standard to be met.

- Another vision, less market-oriented, would justify providing a subsidy to a private company, as long as it yields a benefit for the community as a whole. The subsidy in a way 'buys' a positive externality. This is the approach adopted, for example, by the Global Environment Facility, the Green Climate Fund or the European Commission. These grants supplement and bolster an operation financed at near-market rates, thus ensuring its feasibility via specific financing for the environmental component.

Having no market value, the fair 'purchase price' for a social or environmental benefit is hard to determine. Assessing the appropriate level of a grant or subsidised interest rate that can be optimally given to a private enterprise for a specific operation thus remains complex.

It requires having the capabilities to distinguish between limitations that can be overcome and those that are in any event unsurpassable. When this involves subsidising an environmental or social externality, it also requires being able to put a 'price' on what the subsidy makes it possible to offset. Currently, the fact is that very few quantitative methods dispose of the necessary elements for calculating the right level of subsidies to apply. One important and valuable exception is using the shadow price of carbon to evaluate projects, as the European Investment Bank does; such a practice could be generalised to other DBFIs.

In light of this, there is a certain consensus around the idea that a subsidy backed by market financing can 'buy' three types of services:

- Promoting an 'inclusive service' component, such as opening up access to a service that is unaffordable for poor consumers at a market price.
- Gaining a collective advantage for the community by preserving a common good that has no market price (climate, nature, conservation of a landscape, etc.). This may involve promoting an SDG that is difficult to operationalise in a specific context.
- Enabling the implementation of an investment offering high economic and social utility, but whose risk/return profile is unacceptable to private investors, particularly in fragile or crisis countries.

These questions are crucial for a successful transition. Development banks, operating in close contact with the economic realities of their country, provide some evidences on whether or not it is justifiable to grant subsidies or reduced interest rates through their intermediation:

- Their mandate relies on the fact that market imperfection exists, whether they affect social housing, SMEs or financing for the poorest countries. If an additional dimension relating to the environment or climate is integrated, this is but another brick in an edifice already designed with this imperfection in mind, and is thus relatively easy to integrate.

- Although providing a grant to a company may raise questions of moral hazard, it is less so for a public entity not driven by profit. Certainly, it is financially healthy and necessary for development banks to balance their accounts. It is just as healthy and necessary that government or the international community give them the means to support positive externalities resulting from their clients' operations. If this involves creating a market bias in favour of sustainability, development banks are effective tools, wielded by the state and suited to acting as executing agencies, at least to inspire an initial phase before such mechanisms can be extended to the private sector.
- All countries and sectors have their own specificities. Faced with the very different economic realities of countries, national or sub-national development banks know better than anyone does what constraints apply to local economic agents. A 'tailor-made' response is possible, if the bank itself has access to the necessary support funding.

In exchange for this government support, development banks must stand accountable. Their contribution to sustainable development must be auditable. Financial innovation must also step up to the mark, particularly through investments in impact funds, results-based aid or guarantees.

4.4. Promote the Emergence of Responsible Demand

Development banks do not originate projects, they finance them. This means that they count on the capacity and motivation of project sponsors and owners to design sustainable projects. However, DBFIs can provide technical assistance or funding to generate desirable projects, or even help in the design of key projects for a sustainable economy, which will prioritise particular areas of investment.

In reality, there is a relatively broad spectrum of initiatives ranging from private enterprises following a 'traditional' model to those working to integrate their externalities into their business model. For some, the prime objective remains financial profitability and factoring in the transition, or even simple CSR criteria, is a constraint.[11] For others — ground-breakers that need to be identified and supported — an investment project must be designed with the whole gamut of impacts, and profitability is but one factor among many.

- Innovations, whatever qualities they may have, are still 'laboratories'. They are certainly relevant, but very few go to scale.
- For many countries, catching up the infrastructure deficit remains a non-negotiable priority, as it is their prime lever for development. The 'silk road' promoted by China is based on this premise. Social externalities, such as environmental impacts, of this type of large-scale investment are systematically underestimated, especially with regard to more emotional or political concerns.
- Even though things are slowly changing, many small businesses still continue to perceive the reconciliation of financial, social and environmental agendas as purely theoretical, costly and far-removed from their everyday reality.

[11] Added to this are questions of taxation and distortions to competition linked to the diversity of social and environmental standards across the world.

Sustainable development is a complicated, cross-cutting notion that is hard to mainstream in financing decisions. It is even more so for entrepreneurs, who are focused on product design and their market trends. In the current context, is there a critical mass of businesses and projects ready to take up the challenge of sustainable production? In the vast global fabric of SMEs, how can we kindle and support the motivation required to ensure that investments take sustainability issues into account?

This key question runs up against the fact that the support tools, advisory assistance and 'non-banking' services that development banks could offer to their clients are insufficient to generate this type of demand on a massive scale. Considerable progress has been made, but purely and simply abandoning certain economic activities sparks the fear of social chaos. Such is the case of coal production in countries like South Africa and Poland since their energy mix and employment are closely tied to this sector.

This implies that investors must build up their capacity to identify possible options, clarify and spell out long-term objectives, then translate these into investments that underpin concrete steps in the right direction. Admittedly, entrepreneurs' motivation alone will not suffice. Failing public financial support and without technical and financial assistance, the transition will remain problematic.

Disseminating good practices, 'show-casing' and funding projects with positive environmental externalities and supporting clients to change their approach should come with the responsibility of 21st-century development banks much more clearly and ambitiously. The current Overseas Development Assistance rules, based on volumes more than impacts, should be reviewed to incentivise financial flows toward sustainable development. The momentum for such change could come from the national DBFIs that do not abide by these rules and through which concessional resources could be usefully channelled.

4.5. Build a New Global Financing Architecture

The current political climate is marked by the resurgence of nationalism and questions of immigration and security. Several elections, including those in the world's largest democracies, have shown that, unfortunately, inter-governmental cooperation is not granted and that an inward-looking attitude based on nationalism and denial of science is an option. This would hardly be compatible with building global cooperation on the various transitions, as this presupposes trust, cooperation and time.

Global governance of the transitions is not yet stabilised; the example of climate and the United States' withdrawing and then re-joining the Paris Agreement under two different administrations prompt caution as to the possibility of building on a long term consensus. Apart from citizen mobilisation, the political thrust must come from actionable solutions concretely financed and implemented. This is the field of the public development banks, and first and foremost the national DBFIs.

SDG financing necessarily means rethinking the international finance landscape and perhaps even its very architecture. Currently, this system locks the actors into fixed roles, each acting according to their own logic. Yet, multilateral banks, special international funds (e.g., Green Climate Fund, Global Partnership for Education), national development banks, aid agencies, foundations, ONGs, cities, regions or federal states, private firms must share a common 'radar screen', in the form of the SDGs, to guide their financing decisions.

Development banks can collectively organise themselves to act as this powerful new vector for financing the transition. They need to build an offer that can link up the great planetary questions and their operational responses.

To do so, the development banks need to form a coalition, a global platform on which they can collaborate and coordinate their efforts internationally. Basically, this means doing things differently and in a more collaborative way.

- The first priority is to develop a service to governments in order to channel towards transition solutions the resources injected by the monetary authorities in the wake of the Covid-19 crisis. These resources must translate into sustainable projects, distributed fairly across countries. A coalition of development banks can create this actionable plan linking the decisions taken in international fora with local solutions
- Bank staff must be trained on the issues, methods and analyses required to integrate a larger range of impacts when assessing an operation. A coalition can organise these types of exchange, scale them up and finance them. The processes for discussion, experience-sharing and cross-comparing situations are perhaps some of the most powerful drivers of change.
- Development banks operating in low-income countries with shallow financial systems, particularly in Africa, must benefit of a special solidarity from the larger, older and more financially sound banks. For those whose mandate is to finance international development, they must set up specific financial tools to strengthen the paid-in capital of the smaller and more vulnerable banks. Long-term credit lines, Tier 2 funding (i.e., included in the bank's regulatory capital under Basel III see Bolton et al. 2020), bond issue guarantees, grants for technical assistance and training, and equity investments are some of the solutions.

5. Conclusion

The magnitude of the changes needed to bring a solution to sustainability sometimes has us believe that 'we will never make it', given the necessary step change in our habits, efforts, and even in what we have to give up. Tocqueville, although he lived before this period of climate change, considered democracies to be short-sighted and incapable of averting long-term dangers (https://jancovici.com/recension-de-lectures/societes/de-la-democratie-en-amerique-alexis-de-tocqueville-1840/). Could it be that this grim future is unstoppable?

A great many surveys, however, indicate that a new roadmap for the transitions is mustering broad grassroots support from the general public, and that the Covid-19 health crisis has further bolstered the learning process and raised conceptual awareness and forward-looking attitudes.

Based on the above and on the latest expert reports, various conclusions can be drawn.

- Governments must make sure that their DBFIs meet four key conditions to ensure the effectiveness of the financings they mobilise: a credible 'sustainable' development

strategy; independent high-quality governance to be carefully respected as this is a guarantee of the institution's financial sustainability; a level of capital aligned with increases in their risk-taking, and new challenges; and alignment with their national climate plan.
- The imperative to transition plunges us into a world that is no longer unequivocal, a world that has to deal with the complex impacts of any investment project. Mainstreaming criteria and analytical tools based on the SDG roadmap in the project appraisal cycle is a prerequisite for success.
- Public development banks can amplify their dual function as a provider of public funding and an enabler of private financing through blended finance or support for impact investments. Their leverage effect must be scaled up and maximised.
- At international level, the global and regional DBFIs must support and strengthen national DBFIs through a better understanding of how the latter operate. They must use their intermediation more systematically to give these national DBFIs easier access to local markets and concessional financing, provided that this delivers benefits for the climate and the other SDGs. They must also transfer their expertise so that these national development banks can act as effective relays for the implementation of the key agreements signed between governments.

By synergising international, multilateral, regional and national levels and by highlighting how the interests of countries — and their citizens — dovetail with the preservation of the planet, development banks can make a difference. They have the potential to form an alliance that, at scale, will make it possible to finance the economic actors and actions of the transition.

Disclosure Statement

No potential conflict of interest was reported by the author(s).

Funding

The author(s) reported there is no funding associated with the work featured in this article.

References

Armendariz de Aghion, B. 1999. 'Development Banking.' *Journal of Development Economics* 58: 83–100.

Attridge, S., D. W. te Velde, and P. A. Soren. 2019. *Impact of Development Finance Institutions on Sustainable Development: An Essay Series*. London: Overseas Development Institute.

Bolton, P., M. Despres, L. A. Pereira Da Silva, F. Samana, and R. Svartzman. 2020. *The Green Swan — Central Banking and Financial Stability in the Age of Climate Change*. Basel: BIS — Banque de France.

Brei, M., and A. Schclarek. 2015. 'A Theoretical Model of Bank Lending: Does Ownership Matter in Times of Crisis?' *Journal of Banking & Finance* 50: 298–307.

Buchner, B., A. Clark, A. Falconer, R. Macquarie, C. Meattle, R. Tolentino, and C. Wetherbee. 2019. 'Global Landscape of Climate Finance 2019.' Climate Policy Initiative Report.

Clark, A., J. Choi, B. Tonkonogy, V. Micale, and C. Wetherbee. 2019. 'Implementing Alignment with the Paris Agreement: Recommendations for the Members of the International Development Finance Club.' Climate Policy Initiative &I4CE.

De Luna-Martinez, J., and C. L. Vicente. 2012. 'Global Survey of Development Banks.' World Bank Policy Research Working Paper 5969.

Diamond, W. 1957. *Development Banks*, xiv, 128, Economic Development Institute, International Bank for Reconstruction and Development. Baltimore: The Johns Hopkins Press.

Duchaussoy, V. 2017. Les filiales bancaires de la Caisse Centrale en Afrique, in '75 ans au service du développement, l'Agence Française de Développement des origines à nos jours' AFD.

Eslava, M., and X. Freixas. 2018. 'Public Development Banks and Credit Market Imperfections.' CEPR Discussion Paper DP11160.

Gössinger, A., and W. Raza. 2011. 'Bilateral Development Finance Institutions in Europe.' OFSE Working Paper 29, 1–48.

Griffith-Jones, S., S. Attridge, and M. Gouett. 2020. 'Securing Climate Finance Through National Development Banks.' ODI Report.

Griffith-Jones, S., and J. A. Ocampo. 2018. *The Future of National Development Banks*. Oxford: Oxford University Press.

Hausmann, R., U. Panizza, and E. Fernández-Arias. 2020. 'Smart Development Banks.' *Journal of Industry Competition and Trade* 20: 395–420.

IEA. 2019. *Oil 2019*. Paris: IEA. https://www.iea.org/reports/oil-2019.

La Porta, R., F. Lopez-De-Silanes, and A. Shleifer. 2002. 'Government Ownership of Banks.' *Journal of Finance* 57: 265–301.

Macfarlane, L., and M. Mazzucato. 2018. 'State Investment Banks and Patient Finance: An International Comparison.' IIPP Working Paper 2018-01.

Marodon, R. 2020. *Financing Our Common Future*. A Book Illustrated by Ruedi Bauer. Zurich: Lars Müller Edition.

Mazzucato, M., and C. C. Penna. 2018. 'National Development Banks and Mission-Oriented Finance for Innovation.' In *The Future of National Development Banks*, edited by UCL Institute for Innovation and Public Purpose. Oxford: Oxford University Press.

OECD. 2019. *Aligning Development Co-Operation and Climate Action: The Only Way Forward, the Development Dimension*. Paris: OECD Publishing.

Schmit, M., L. Gheeraert, T. Denuit, and C. Warny. 2011. *Public Finance Institutions in Europe*. Brussels: European Association of Public Banks.

Scott, D. 2007. 'Strengthening the Governance and Performance of State-Owned Financial Institutions.' World Bank Policy Research Working Paper 4321.

Smallridge, D., and F. de Olloqui. 2011. 'A Health Diagnostic Tool for Public Development Banks.' Tech. Notes IDB-TN-225.

Thorne, J., and C. du Toit. 2009. 'A Macro-Framework for Successful Development Banks.' *Development Southern Africa* 26: 677–694.

Xu, J., R. Marodon, and X. Ru. 2021. 'Qualifying and Classifying Public Development Banks and Development Financing Institutions.' New Structural Economics Development Financing Research Report No. 2/AFD Working Paper to be Published for the 2nd edition of the Finance in Common Summit.

Xu, J., X. Ren, and X. Wu. 2019. 'Mapping Development Finance Institutions Worldwide: Definitions, Rationales, and Diversity.' New Structural Economics Development Financing Research Report No. 1.

Scaling Up Public Development Banks' Transformative Alignment with the 2030 Agenda for Sustainable Development†

Maria Alejandra Riaño, Jihane Boutaybi, Damien Barchiche and Sébastien Treyer

ABSTRACT
Public development banks (PDBs) can accelerate SDGs implementation, by coupling their leverage capacity with systemic and cross-cutting 2030 Agenda alignment practices that catalyse real transformations in their behaviours and investments. This new research assesses how PDBs — from different sizes and geographies — have interpreted and are including sustainable development priorities in their day-to-day discussions, processes and operations. It shows that most PDBs have the interest and willingness to take the necessary steps to mainstream SDG priorities into their strategies and operations. Nonetheless, findings suggest that both strategic and operational endeavours are at the early stages of alignment. Identified innovative practices by PDBs leading the way, should now be shared among their peers in a view of harmonisation and coherence, as a crucial prerequisite to a scaled-up alignment. As for governments, shareholders and other stakeholders, they should also contribute to this alignment endeavour by an enhanced political backing and support to PDBs.

1. Introduction

1.1. Setting the Scene: 2030 Agenda and Its Promises — Why the Concept of Alignment with Agenda 2030 Is Important?

The UN 2030 Agenda for Sustainable Development (United Nations 2020) continues to be the widely endorsed reference framework to bring about the necessary social, economic and environmental transformations for communities to recover and thrive. Public development banks (PDBs) around the world can play a vital role not only in minimising economic decline and supporting recovery, but also in financing structural transformations. Fulfilling this role requires that these institutions are able to fully capture the interconnected and transversal nature of the 2030 Agenda and therefore align their practices, operations and investments accordingly.

The 2030 Agenda promised integrated solutions and contributions from all countries and the different actors. Thanks to its 17 specific objectives and 169 indicators,

---

†This article is an overview of the study: *Riaño, M.-A., Boutaybi, J., Barchiche, D., Treyer, S. (2020). Scaling up public development banks' transformative alignment with the 2030 Agenda for Sustainable Development. IDDRI, Study N°05/20.*

it also promised to make the abstract concept of sustainable development more operational. Furthermore, this project for structural change is grounded on key promises and principles to stand for a holistic and integrated Agenda; an Agenda for all that leaves no one behind and; a transformative Agenda that can help tackle and reduce the structural causes of vulnerabilities that the world currently faces (Hege et al. 2019).

The SDGs are thus presented as a 'transformative project' (Koehler 2016), leading ideally to a 'systemic change'. The 2030 Agenda can be considered as transformative agenda BUT under certain conditions such as respecting Leave No One behind and the integrated character of the Agenda (Hege and Barchiche 2019). Among the goals with high transformative potential, we can identify SDGs 5 (gender equality), 10 (reducing inequality), 12 (transforming production and consumption patterns) and 16 (institutions, justice, peace) (Bhattacharya, Khan, and Salma 2014). Nonetheless, the SDGs were not designed as targets to be met independently, but as a mutually supportive package (Korosi 2015).

This is what makes the 2030 Agenda transformative, since no current development pathway can achieve all of the SDGs together. The true transformative potential of the 2030 Agenda lies in its integrated and indivisible nature, which can help tackle and reduce the structural causes of vulnerabilities that the world currently faces.

In this regard, there is a need to develop a clear vision of what does or does not contribute to the SDGs, and to prevent the SDGs from falling victim to an overly vague game of interpretation that everyone can join without questioning the real impact of their actions on the agenda as a whole. PDBs can play a critical role in this regard.

1.2. What Do These Promises Mean for PDBs — The Specific Role of PDBs for the Implementation of 2030 Agenda, Particularly on the Example of the Covid 19 Crisis?

1.2.1. PDBs at the Forefront of the Implementation of the 2030 Agenda?

PDBs have certain advantages that enable them to position themselves at the forefront of this movement. With a clear knowledge of the specific context in each region or country where they operate, and unequalled flexibility in the design of concessional loan programmes, in recent years these banks have positioned themselves as an essential and complementary voice for traditional Official Development Assistance (ODA) and commercial investors (Xu, Ren, and Wu 2019).

Both academics and policymakers are recognising the importance of PDBs in playing countercyclical roles, bridging financing gaps in key development sectors, addressing defects in capital markets, and enhancing structural transformation. Thus, PDBs are not only better suited for carrying out countercyclical lending during a crisis but are also particularly suited to reignite growth after a crisis.

It is clear that Multilateral and regional PDBs are important sources of financing, especially for emerging and developing countries. By making use of their credit and lending instruments — concessional and non-concessional — and by providing non-reimbursable technical cooperation resources, they allow governments to access new funding at preferential rates and terms. Given that PDBs can borrow from other financial institutions or issue debt, these guarantees allow them to borrow at a relatively lower cost and eventually transfer that lower cost to final borrowers.[1]

In this regard, the more than 400 PDBs around the world can play a vital role not only in economic decline and supporting recovery, but also in financing structural transformation, helping to lay the foundations for a financial model that is conducive to an equitable and sustainable growth, in line with the SDGs.

1.2.2. What Does 'Financing the 2030 Agenda' Really Mean?

Financing the 2030 Agenda entails ensuring investments are not contradictory to environmental and social goals like climate and biodiversity, but also inequalities and food security. A significant proportion of financial flows — in both the public and private sectors — are still not aligned or even compatible, with the SDGs (Rain Forest Action Network et al. 2020). Investing to fulfil certain SDGs, without simultaneously ensuring that other areas of their own activities do not counteract those objectives, evidently undermines efforts to achieve sustainable development at large (Riaño and Barchiche 2020).

For PDBs, aligning with the 2030 Agenda would mean that the design/implementation of project and strategies, the structuring/financing of projects, as well as monitoring of its effects, should focus on maximising synergies and co-benefits, while reducing possible trade-offs. In other words, the successful implementation of this paradigm shift would rely upon disentangling complex interactions between the goals and their targets.

If PDBs are to play a transformational role to redirect, mobilise and unlock the necessary funding to attain the 2030 Agenda while helping countries out of the crises, standalone, 'cherry picking' approaches are definitely not enough.

Stepping up and undertaking transformative changes is certainly challenging, especially for National Development Banks (NDBs) — given the fact that in many countries, the national PDB is either 'forgotten' or takes an intentionally low profile. Furthermore, moving from strategic intent to true ownership implies high-level commitment together with profound governance and, probably business model restructurings.

By making sustainability an integral part of their DNA, PDBs can easily create socially and environmentally sustainable economic opportunities that are now more urgently needed than prior to the coronavirus crisis.

1.3. The Choice of the PDBs Nomenclature

PDBs are financial institutions with an independent legal status that are supported, owned and administered by central or local governments and with an aim to promote economic development and address market inconsistences (Finance in common, Eurodad).[2] They can operate at a sub-national (SDBs), national (NDBs) regional (RDBs) or multinational level (MDBs) and each PDB has a defined mandate that will describe the sector(s), the beneficiaries or activities that the institution is expected to support (Luna-Martinez and Vicente 2012).

---

[1] https://www.iddri.org/en/publications-and-events/blog-post/role-public-development-banks-supporting-post-covid-19-crisis.

[2] https://financeincommon.org/wp-content/uploads/2020/04/Booklet-Finance-in-Common-Summit.pdf and Public development banks: towards a better model April 2017 by Eurodad.

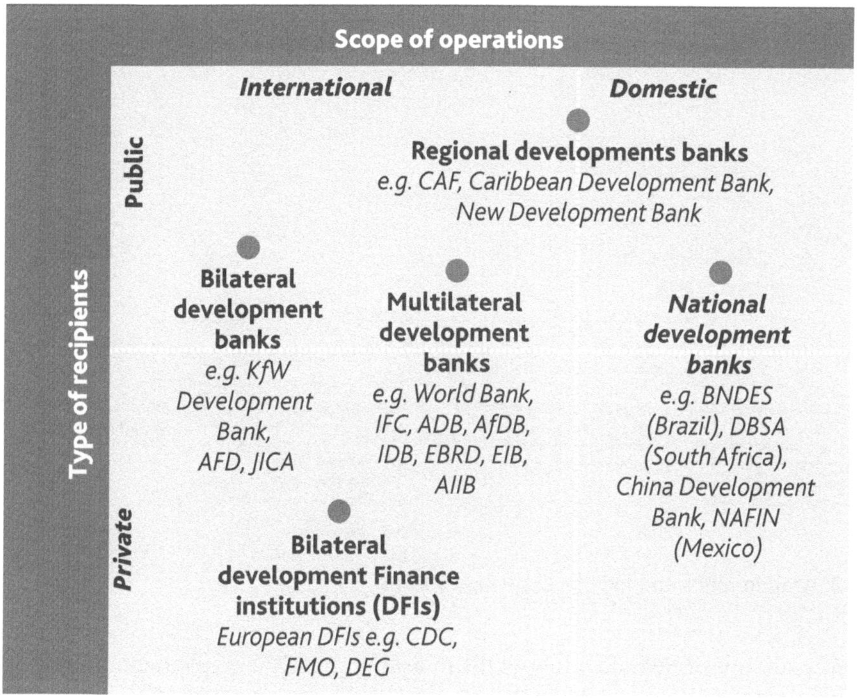

Figure 1. Main categories of public development banks (PDBs).

This paper focuses on the broader definition for development banks, the so-called PDBs. Our choice is based on the diversity of the PDBs' interviewed sample. The aim was to assess PDBs in different continents with different mandates and acting in different economic contexts and sectors, in order to find solutions and innovative practices to achieve the SDGs for the global community of PDBs. However, in some cases we differentiate between NDBs or SDBs from the broader term of PDBs, because as said above, their mandate and geographical scope of operations will determine the bank's activity and effectiveness to achieve its goals (Figure 1).

2. An Overview of Public Development Banks' Lending and Leverage in the Last Decade[3]

In our study, we discussed which has been PDBs behaviour scaling up loans over last decade and reflect on their potential to contribute even more to the SDGs' implementation. To do that, we looked at leverage and loan-to-equity ratios of a sample of PDBs,[4] most of them interviewed and whose results are presented in the study. Making use of

[3]Note: This section has been substantially reduced due to length limitations. For more detail refer to the original publication.

[4]The financial statements' information was gathered for the following PDBs: Bancoldex, Bancomext, BDE, BDMG, BNA, BNCR, BNDES, BRDE, COFIDE, DBSA, FINAGRO, FMO, NAFIN, SIDBI, EXIM, CDG, DPB, DFCC, FDB and BancoEstado. In addition, some selected multilateral, bilateral and regional development banks were included: AfDB, IADB, ADB, AFD, KFW, TDB and BCIE. See Appendix 1 for more detailed information on each abbreviation.

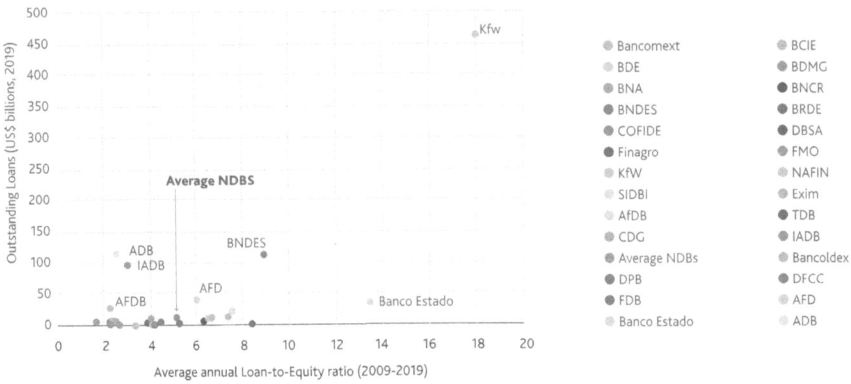

Source: Authors' elaboration based on respective banks' annual reports and financial statements. Nominal exchange rate at the end of the period was used in each case. Loans levels correspond to gross levels before provision for impairment.

Information available at December of each year or at march of the following year. It depends on the fiscal year used by each country.

Average between 2009-2019 includes information for 2009, 2013, 2018 and 2019. Average of NDBs excludes IADB, ADB, AfDB, AFD, KFW, BCIE, TDB. Outstanding loans include direct lending to customers and intermediated by credit institutions.

AfDB and ADB includes ordinary capital resources. It excludes the Fund for Special Operations and other funds.

Figure 2. Gearing ratios and loan levels, selected PDBs.

their leverage capacity would allow PDBs to accelerate SDGs implementation, as long as this is accompanied by good practices of alignment with the 2030 Agenda.

It is important to state that although we are aware that PDBs have at their disposal other financial instruments, like guarantees, loans are still the main instrument used by these banks and it is their main asset. In our sample loans represent the 69 per cent of their total assets.

This work points out two important results:

(1) We see that there is a large heterogeneity between NDBs, some of them with loans to equity ratio close to 2, which means that for every dollar in equity, the bank has lended 2 dollars. But there are other banks, with gearing ratios close to 6 and 8. This means that these banks are being more ambitious and are extending loans 6 or 8 times more than their equity. In average we see that NDBs are being less conservative than MDBs (Figure 2).

(2) It is quite clear that this indicator has not improved substantially during the last decade. Once the values registered in 2009 and 2019 are compared, just some banks have really improved the loans disbursed in relation to their shareholders capital. A remarkable percentage of them, have reduced or kept unchanged this ratio and still remain at very conservative levels.

Given the commitment of countries worldwide to the Sustainable Development Goals, they should foster their PDBs to push their financing within the threshold imposed by financial markets and credit rating agencies. PDBs have spare lending capacity (Humphrey 2017, 2018, 2020). Shifting PDBs policy and expanding lending to face the current crisis should be done with the explicit support of the shareholders (Studart and Gallagher 2016). For instance, not all PDBs benefit from an explicit sovereign guarantee that would allow them preferred access to softer financing terms. It is mandatory to find mechanisms to bridge the financing gap.

Making use of their leverage capacity will allow PDBs to accelerate SDGs implementation, as long as this is accompanied by good practices of alignment with the 2030 Agenda as we will further describe in the upcoming sections of the study.

3. What Practices Are PDBs implementing to Align Their Behaviours, Lending Practices and Actions with the 2030 Agenda?

Scaling up lending has to come hand in hand with transformative behaviours and investment practices. It is not just a question of encouraging banks to leverage their capital to grant more loans. It is about making use of this underutilised potential — as seen from data in the section below — in order to contribute more deeply and strategically to sustainable development (Riaño et al. 2020).

It is precisely by assuming a more active role, not only as financers but also as mobilisers of investments (Griffith-Jones, Attridge, and Gouet 2020) that PDBs will be able to support truly transformative changes in the countries or regions in which they operate. Changes that will hopefully lead to the attainment of the 2030 Agenda and its SDGs, with the sufficient impact and scale to generate real change in the territories and communities that they seek to support.

Thus, what are the best practices and innovative solutions developed by PDBs and in particular NDBs in order to align all their functioning, processes and practices with the 2030 Agenda in order to have a transformative effect, at a desired scale? Here lies the need to provide empirical information on how these institutions have interpreted and included sustainable development priorities in their day-to-day discussions and operations.

Drawing on interviews with high-level officials and creditors from a number of PDBs that cover the Latin-American, African, European and Asian regions (Appendix 3), together with the analysis of year-end/sustainability reports, strategy and policy documents, the following sections will characterise the main SDG alignment efforts observed at both inner and external levels.

3.1. Strategic Level

Regardless of their size or nature, most PDBs are aware of the existence and relevance of the 2030 Agenda and its SDGs. Mainstreaming the 2030 Agenda into the banks' strategic vision is one way to ensure that the different actions, programmes and initiatives promoted by the entity will be carried out under an SDG lens.

Not every bank has in place strategies that make reference to the 2030 Agenda or mention a certain number of SDGs. In fact, a recurring concern expressed by respondents was their limited capacity to translate this Agenda into their priorities and being able to find a way to turn its promises into practice. Most reviewed banks are in what we could call an 'initial phase of alignment', in which they have started to link and assign certain SDGs to their current sectors of focus, existing programmes or projects (BRDE 2017). In the words of one of the banks interviewed, PDBs have understood SDG issues gradually or in a segmented way — showing a higher degree of relevance of SDGs in their existing operations, but a lower evidence of their use to drive strategy (Authors Interviews 2020). In occasions, the window of opportunity that has been presented to kick-start the incorporation of the 2030 Agenda at a strategic level has been the green growth or climate change issues. From there on, it has been possible for some banks to go further and engage into discussions on how to incorporate sustainability criteria in their current lines of credit or on the disposition of SDG credit lines.

Being a fully fledged SDG PDB is not necessarily tied to the bank's given mandate and sector of focus. Both banks with a broad mandate and banks with defined sectors are implementing actions to align their strategies with the 2030 Agenda.

However, in order to speak of a true integration of the 2030 Agenda at a strategic level, more is required. Until they deliberately embed SDG considerations into existing mission and vision statements, as well as in definitions of strategies and policies, banks will unlikely be able to strategically and systemically align themselves with the 2030 Agenda as a whole.

3.1.1. Including or Making the 2030 Agenda Part of the PDBs' Multiannual or Long-Term Strategy

Something worth noting is that many PDBs have taken the opportunity of updating their long-term strategies or annual corporate goals to intensify actions in support of the 2030 Agenda or even, as some stated during the interviews, place it at the core of their strategies. By doing so, PDBs are reflecting upon how to develop suitable courses of action for enhancing their management from a sustainability perspective. Concrete actions that we were able to identify both in interviews and in annual reports range from rearranging their sectors of intervention, defining new dimensions to frame their strategies, or establishing drivers that will ensure financial sustainability, while maximising impact and development, to generate value for the society at large.

A key aspect that should be kept in mind while establishing the strategic objectives within the multi-year plans of a PDB is to assess where the market gaps are, why they exist and whether and how they can be addressed by them (Smallridge et al. 2019). This analysis should encompass the nature of existing opportunities and potential customer demand, so that the gap between supply and demand for financial services can be quantified and their relevance determined. Based on this, the types of projects to be financed and the instruments — financial and non-financial — that can be used can be better defined. In this way, PDBs will be able to concentrate on addressing market weaknesses without encumbering or crowding out other local financial institutions, investors or private enterprises. PDBs, especially NDBs, should act as partners and not as competitors of the other private financial institutions and commercial banks that are present in the countries or regions where they operate.

On the other hand, our research shows that PDBs are deliberately embedding SDG considerations into their strategies either by selecting certain SDGs as focus for action or defining cross-cutting dimensions to guide their portfolio. This practice also appears useful for banks to have clarity of their value creation and even propose a holistic approach that can define how they will internalise and systematically apply this agenda throughout every operation.

Regarding SDGs alignment efforts, AFD and KFW, two of the major European bilateral development banks, have interesting approaches at strategic level, which can serve as examples even for smaller PDBs. AFD's strategy is grounded on six transitions,[5] five engagements and two commitments and links (100 per cent Paris agreement and 100 per cent social links). Their thematic strategies are periodically revised and renewed and together with their SDG Assessment Framework (AADD), they are building a bold strategic framework oriented to financing only SDG projects. Furthermore, their efforts are focusing on trying to move away from pure sectoral projects and support projects that will contribute to the alignment with the long-term SDG trajectories prioritised by the different countries. In the case of KFW, besides having a new mission statement that incorporates the SDGs, business is managed on the basis of 'key megatrends', aligned with the German Sustainable Development Strategy and thus with the core messages of 2030 Agenda.

Therefore, although interesting things are being done to align long-term strategies, commitments and missions, it would be interesting to propose as a future discussion to structure PDBs strategies around the six transformations[6] proposed by the 2019 *Global Sustainable Development Report* (Independent Group of Scientists appointed by the Secretary-General 2019), which points out that co-benefits, trade-offs and tough choices are at the heart of sustainable development, but have not always been appreciated as such. Indeed, early interpretations that focused on the three dimensions of sustainability (economic, environmental and social) tended to reinforce decision-making in thematic silos, often prioritising immediate economic benefits over the social and environmental costs that would materialise in the longer term. At the same time, this approach has also consistently deferred consideration of the hard choices that need to be made. Within this framework, objectives and targets are useful, but above all, the interactions between them need to be optimised. GSDR's systemic entry points are a way to exploit important synergies, multiplier effects and trade-offs between several objectives, but also to identify levers and actors that can help achieve these objectives.

3.1.2. Establishing a Sustainability Policy with Some Priority SDGs

PDBs are also making use of additional policies or frameworks, such as their sustainability policies. Many PDBs are developing independent sustainability policies to serve as frameworks and guidelines for their investments at all different scales (project, sector, and portfolio).

In some cases, we see these sustainability policies becoming the cornerstone of the banks' SDG alignment. Whereas in other cases, sustainability policies are being drafted to reinforce and strengthen banks' commitments towards mainstreaming the SDGs into their strategies and operations. Having both strategies and additional policies in line with sustainable development priorities serves to anchor the 2030 Agenda at the heat of banks' decision-making processes.

---

[5]Demographic and Social Transition, Energy Transition, Territorial and Ecological Transition, Digital and Technological Transition, Political and Civic Transition, Economic and Financial Transition.

[6]The six transformations are: human well-being and capabilities; sustainable and just economies; food systems and nutrition patterns; energy decarbonisation and universal access; urban and peri-urban development; and global environment commons.

It is worth mentioning that in some cases, banks are devoting their SDGs implementing efforts solely in their sustainability policy, with no reference or mention whatsoever within their main strategies. Hence, despite being consecrated in a guiding policy, it is not always embraced as a central and determinant part of the banks' financial decision-making.

3.1.3. Constituting SDG-Focused Pipelines of Projects

Most of the revised PDBs are still in a stage where alignment efforts are mostly seen at a project level. It is uncommon to find banks that are using the 2030 Agenda as a driving force to comprehensively build and assess new and existing projects, programmes, areas of intervention, desired impacts, etc. Most banks have yet to realise that having a systemic analysis at the project level may come with many advantages, but that if they do not widen their scope of analysis to the portfolio scale, they will certainly fall in wrongful assumptions, e.g., facing the temptation to say that any project can solve all challenges of sustainable development (Authors Interviews 2020). This sometimes leads PDBs to overload a project; initially destined for a sector, the bank tries to have positive effects on the governance of the sector, effects of maximising economic benefits and also a concrete effect for poor recipients, all-in-all to comply with the SDGs' cross-cutting issues related to the social inclusion and reduction of inequalities.

Building a project pipeline and ensuring bankability is a key first step in the investment cycle and a crucial hurdle to further investment (Griffith-Jones, Attridge, and Gouet 2020). While this theme is critical if banks are to fulfil their potential as 2030 Agenda transformative financers, our interviews revealed that there are still many pitfalls in the development of project pipelines able to meet the needs and demands related to the SDGs. One of the key challenges is to not just develop a pipeline of good individual projects, but to try to develop a comprehensive portfolio. A portfolio with an SDG lens that aims at reallocating capital flows towards critical sustainable development priorities, instead of allocating available funds to invest in projects/programmes that tend to deplete natural capital or reinforce the low environmental sustainability of economic activities.

It is no longer a matter of acting as mere financers, but also taking the time to reflect upon building bankable projects (DBSA 2019a, 2019b) and an entire portfolio that offers integral responses to sustainability challenges on the ground (FMO 2019). Hence, dedicating efforts to better understand the territories, communities and countries where PDBs operate is absolutely essential. Regardless of their business model — 1 tier or 2nd tier PDB — these institutions need to know the true challenges and necessities that their end-beneficiaries are facing, in order to be more effective and have a greater impact with the products and services they provide.

In the end, what is important for PDBs to take into account when reflecting upon how to better structure their new project pipelines and align themselves with the 2030 Agenda is the sustainable development challenges that the region/country faces, which are not the same for every country. And thus, try to build a portfolio that is well oriented in relation to these key issues and with the trajectories that the country wants to pursue the attainment of the 2030 Agenda and its SDGs.

3.2. Operational Level

At the operational level, alignment requires changes in how investments are assessed and how capital is deployed.

3.2.1. Mapping Operations with Different SDGs

The most common mechanism that PDBs use for analysing and measuring the contribution of their activities with the SDGs is what we call 'Mapping'. This practice consists in linking the bank's activities with one or more of the 17 goals. The interviewed banks using this practice explained that this approach to characterise their operations proves useful as it allows them to have a general picture about the bank's input for SDGs. Furthermore, it facilitates the communication between stakeholders about the importance of their activities to achieve SDGs and it raises a general understanding and a commitment to the 2030 Agenda.

An innovative practice we found is meant to allow the PDB to monitor SDG alignment throughout the entire cycle — from instruction to project evaluation — and distinguish between: (i) 'problematic projects' in terms of sustainable development; (ii) good avant-garde projects and; (iii) 'New Frontier' sustainable development projects.

Other banks have developed different methodologies to align with SDGs. Certain align their annual disbursements, others their total portfolio. Since there is not a unique methodology for mapping, PDBs create their own approaches. This entails different interpretations of alignment and therefore, different results. The majority of the interviewed banks have several questions and difficulties to understand what it means to be aligned with the SDGs. Does contributing to one or few SDGs already mean that they are aligned? Do they need to prioritise one SDG over the others? Or are still considered an SDG-aligned PDB when they contribute to an SDG but harm another one.

No matter how important these efforts are, if PDBs want to take advantage of their potential as strong and leading contributors to the 2030 Agenda implementation, they have to go beyond mapping their operations at project level. Practising this alignment approach leaves behind a much deeper comprehension of the 2030 Agenda, one that reflects upon capitalising on synergies among objectives and targets, while deploying strategies on alleviating trade-offs.

3.2.2. Ex-ante Verification

Establishing assessment methodologies before investments are disbursed is fundamental. Ex-ante verification practices comprise actions undertaken by PDBs to run initial scans and discard proposals that might not decisively contribute to sustainable development or that will bring negative impacts to prioritised SDGs. During interviews, we identified that PDBs have different mechanisms to prevent a negative impact on social or environmental dimensions. The most used are the following ones:

3.2.2.1. Screening for SDGs. As reported by the OECD in its study on scaling up climate-compatible infrastructure, 'several MDBs have started rolling out climate risk-screening measures to support the climate-proofing of projects' (OECD, UN-Environment, and WBG 2019). Regarding SDG-related screening approaches, we observe that PDBs — equally MDBs, NDBs and SDBs — are beginning to include at early stages of project preparations and assessment, practices that help them to carefully research the financing opportunity and assess its impact on the environment, employees and workers, communities and other stakeholders.

Other banks such as KfW or AFD have developed stringent eligibility criteria within their screening processes to be able to analyse potential projects with an eye of finding out if they are likely to have an unacceptable environmental or social impact that cannot be prevented or mitigated by suitable measures and therefore, will not be eligible for funding.

3.2.2.2. Environmental Social Governance (ESG) criteria — Environmental and Social Risk Analysis System (SARAS). Most PDBs have developed frameworks to identify and evaluate the social and environmental risks of credit operation (SARAS) and to establish mitigation measures to minimise the losses. These systems also include standards verification (Environmental, Social and Governance-ESGs) of practices that PDBs are implementing at project, sector, portfolio or country level (depending on their degree of alignment to the 2030 Agenda and their scope of action) that takes place before investment decisions. These tools serve as a mechanism to avoid or exclude areas of investment that are not compatible with SDG goals or priorities that might have been traced at the strategic level.

During the interviews, the greater part of PDBs claimed to have a system to assess social and environmental impacts and risks. Risk assessment and standards verification performed by PDBs is still very narrow; inability to identify and quantify environmental and social risk is still the norm. Although is a good start, approaches still lack a comprehensive understanding of the 2030 Agenda multidimensional nature. Likewise, not all PDBs use these mechanisms for both their 1st tier and 2nd tier operations, hence, actual knowledge of impacts and risks of their total portfolio is still very poor. Lastly, it would be important that more PDBs, throughout the lifetime of their financing, monitor client's progress on meeting the requirements of the environmental and social risks mitigation plan, and support them in building a sustainable business for the long-term.

3.2.2.3. Exclusion Criteria. BDMG uses the ESG risk assessment to identify sectors of exclusion. This practice is very common, and it consists in developing a list of sectors that PDBs refuse to finance.

The sectors or activities normally identified as ineligible for investment include gambling, arms trade, tobacco, mining etc. However, a robust taxonomy that will helpfully avoid sectors with negative sustainable development impacts — do no harm approach — is still inexistent for the majority of PDBs. There should be a careful evaluation of the destination of the funds when reflecting upon exclusion lists. At the top of mind should be for instance, avoiding that investments accentuate the lock-in in carbon intensive technologies, the financing of activities aimed at the production of fossil fuels, or the production of goods with a high unfavourable impact on the environment or that, for example, still indirectly drive deforestation (Carlino et al. 2017).

Lastly, interesting learning opportunities may arise when refusing applications. It can create awareness to the refused part and can yield valuable information about the conditions under which the project would have been approved (Fernández-Arias, Ricardo, and

Panizza 2019). PDBs have to take advantage of this and open a window of opportunity for possible guidance to their clients. The bank can provide feedback and accompany the client to make better decisions in the future; nudging upcoming proposals towards sustainable related sectors. During interviews, some banks shared their practices of helping clients to change their mindset and adapt their businesses to sustainable development.

3.2.3. Ex-Post Impact Assessment

Ex-post assessment is required to evaluate the impact and the progress towards the 2030 Agenda. It is key for PDBs to discern impact from exposure. Most of the interviewed PDBs include in their annual reports — sometimes they even have individual sustainability reports — the results related to the attainment of certain SDG targets. However, the majority of these reports still focus a lot on volume of flows — loans provided — rather than on outcomes and qualitative impacts of their portfolio as a whole. There is a lack in quality performance indicators, segmentation of end-beneficiaries, estimated lifetime results of projects to measure how much the various flows actually contribute to sustainable development. The assessment of direct results as number of companies served, credits granted or disbursements are insufficient due to the fact that it does not reflect the additionality achieved by PDBs for SDGs.

PDBs must translate their goals into performance indicators that will be later included within lending conditions and monitored to verify ex post results. A few NDBs are making efforts to develop methodologies and indicators for impact evaluation but report having obstacles such as lack of consistent information, costs related to data collection and lack of follow up capacity.

For PDBs to have a more comprehensive ex post impact assessment of their operations and accurate knowledge of their SDG contributions, more systematic integration of monitoring and evaluation components at early stages of project preparation are required. Lessons learned after evaluation should be introduced into subsequent strategic plans and turn them into criteria for credit allocation.

In addition, PDBs can build commitments on environmental or social impact, as complementary to their financial impact, to address the issue of trade-offs between SDGs. The annual performance results and commitments need to be discussed at the Board level or with key stakeholders to give more weight to the commitment in the bank orientation.

Finally, PDBs should standardise their indicators and evaluation systems, as well as their other practices at the operational level, with the aim to simplify the development of a comprehensive assessment of their contribution to SDGs implementation.

3.3. External Engagement

When analysing how PDBs are approaching and implementing the 2030 Agenda in their daily operations, it is important not only to assess their practices at internal level, as we have done so far, but also at external level. Alignment efforts are permeating and defining how PDBs relate and engage with their beneficiaries and other stakeholders. Thus, it is important to review: (i) how these institutions are engaging with their clients, beneficiaries of their funding, (ii) if they are actively taking part in any dialogues or partnerships with other stakeholders in which the 2030 Agenda is used as a lever for scaling up their impact and efforts and, (iii) if they are making use of the different investment instruments at their disposal — besides their loans — to mobilise additional funding, catalyse sustainable development transformations and scale up their efforts — at national, regional or global level, depending on their scope of action-.

3.3.1. Understanding and Engaging with Beneficiaries

An important practice in order to facilitate an SDG alignment is to ensure long and permanent dialogue with PDBs' beneficiaries (governments, local authorities, communities, private commercial banks that serve as intermediaries).

Thus, incorporating these practices into the bank's engagement culture allows them not only to have a better understanding of their context, but also to become more strategically involved with stakeholders that will benefit from their financial and non-financial support. As mentioned in a previous section, some directors and managers said during the interviews that their banks are trying to have a better grasp of what is happening on the ground, by holding regional consultations and by having more technical experts in the field. Accompaniment programmes for structuring sustainable development projects are also something that are being done by PDBs in order to support clients to have the necessary specialised technical equipment to conduct the technical and financial assessment of markets and evaluate their projects' viability. NDBs, who are closer to national contexts than MDBs might be, are starting to realise that is vital to engage with its customers before and during the lifetime of an investment to understand their context and risks. This enables them to offer products and services that suit the specific needs of its customers.

On the other hand, banks expressed their interest in devoting additional efforts to educate their beneficiaries on the shared benefits that come along with promoting and financing projects that contribute to sustainable development. It is important that both PDBs and beneficiaries see SDG-related priorities as strategic investments, rather than as costs. Therefore, educating and communicating the importance of SDG's when talking to clients is a key practice that should be grounded on PDBs' daily activities. This applies both for 1st tier banks as well as for 2nd tier banks, where the challenges are even tougher and of even more relevance: these PDBs need to ensure that private commercial banks and institutions that serve as their intermediaries have the awareness, knowledge and capacity to assess if a project proposal positively contributes to the attainment of SDGs or not. This is an area where, to date, we see there is still a lot to be done.

Therefore, providing capacity building and follow-up support from the side of PDBs seems as a key practice to prepare and accompany its beneficiaries. As highlighted by one bilateral DB manager, 'including a capacity building component in all our projects make us more attractive than a private bank; is not only about providing concessional financing, but also offering within the package technical assistance' (Authors Interviews 2020).

3.3.2. Stakeholders Dialogue

PDBs are also paying attention to how they can build up a strong network with the array of actors with which they work. Engaging with relevant stakeholders (Government institutions, shareholders, NGOs, Investors, Partner DFIs, and Think Tanks) is proving to be key for PDBs to ensure their strategy and business are better aligned with the 2030 Agenda. Actively participating in dialogues on the Bank's priorities and strategy for sustainable development with these diverse actors is allowing PDBs to gain visibility of their sustainable development contributions, receive feedback on their impact and even engage in discussions related on how to better drive countries towards transformative sustainable development trajectories.

Several interviewees noted that they see themselves as conveners of all main actors within the system; acting as bridges, local anchors, articulators. Certainly, PDBs, especially NDBs or subnational banks, are able to perform as neutral bodies between the private and public sector to bring them together and exchange on their perception of sustainable development, existing challenges that hinder SDGs implementation in the country/region. PDBs are beginning to play a pivotal role acting as policy leaders and innovators, becoming strategic first-hand implementers of the 2030 Agenda and its SDGs.

Given their in-house technical expertise, governments should more openly welcome PDBs, especially NDBs, to the policy table. By holding on their both economic and technological knowledge, PDBs are taking bolder steps to provide policy advice, help shape new national development policies and, in some cases, even support governments revise legislation proposals (refer to Moslener, Thiemann, and Volberding 2018 for KFW's example). However, bank officials expressed that there is still not an active invitation from governments' side to integrate them in the policy process and this has undermined their ability to truly become a government partner in supporting SDGs implementation.

Therefore, if PDBs are to engage in proactive discussions with government authorities to feed in sustainable development implementation efforts, clear lines of communication need to be established. On one side, the government has to be clear on the policies and sectors being prioritised to achieve the SDGs and thus, the bank will provide the funding to incentivise new behaviours or help fund projects on key SDG sectors that may be underfunded. On the other side, achieving this policy synergy with the government will certainly place the PDB in a strategic position, whereby it will start to be perceived by other stakeholders — government included — as facilitating the sustainable development agenda and contributing to the attainment of specific SDG priorities.

Some PDBs are also devoting an important part of their efforts to actively engage with their key stakeholders with the purpose of receiving feedback on their performance, as a tool to identify the topics that are most material to them and assess how these engagements contribute to realising the bank's long-term sustainable development objectives.

Existing well-established PDBs are hence playing a significant role within their own ecosystems — either regional, national or subnational depending on their nature and scope of action — as catalysts of change and most importantly, as conveners of other relevant stakeholders that can also contribute to the financing and implementation of the 2030 Agenda. Hence, these institutions need to start taking advantage of this privileged position and see themselves as instruments for the formulation — not only the execution — of public policies aimed at promoting sustainable development.

3.3.3. New Financial Instruments

PDBs are certainly strategic actors that can help bridge the financial gap of this international agenda by performing different catalytic roles — financers, mobilisers, intermediaries, policy influencers, niche levers of sustainable transformations (Griffith-Jones, Attridge, and Gouet 2020; Mazzucato and Penna 2016). However, thus far, PDBs haven't made use of the wider range of financial products at their disposal and we believe that is one of the largest limitations for unlocking their SDGs investment potential.

Since PDBs still favour loans as their primary financial product, they have dedicated limited structuring efforts towards maximising potential of guarantees, bonds, or direct capital injections.

Nonetheless, the interview and research process allowed us to identify successful examples of innovative approaches to financing that a number of PDBs are starting to use. Although there is still a long way ahead, these first attempts can serve to stimulate a more accelerated diversification on the part of its other Peers.

3.3.3.1. Guarantees. Guarantees possess an interesting potential to unlock private investment in countries, sectors and segments that traditionally these financers will avoid since risk levels are deemed higher. Backing up the financial operation serves as an incentive for private investors since the development bank will assume all or part of the project's credit risk. Governments can also serve as sovereign guarantors of their NDBs, thus supporting them to scale up their lending, have more appetite to innovate and engage in transactions of higher financial additionality.

This financial instrument has a great leverage potential. In fact, between 2012 and 2017 44 per cent of the capital mobilised for the energy sector was in the form of guarantees (Sangare and Hos 2019). Surprisingly, despite its leverage capacity, conversations with banks lead us to think that not all PDBs are using guarantees and if they do, they represent a small portion of their portfolios. The last green finance survey of the IDFC — a global network of PDBs and finance institutions based in OECD and non-OECD countries — states that only 1 per cent of the commitments for green energy and mitigation activities came from guarantees (IDFC 2019).

Reasons for why PDBs are not availing guarantees as a tool might lie in the complexity for setting them up and the capacity required to do a proper monitoring of the ongoing project (Griffith-Jones, Attridge, and Gouet 2020). Furthermore, they require good management of liabilities and large provisions in order to preserve financial indicators. This can at the same time limit the lending capacities and henceforth, the development impact. PDBs need to keep working on strengthening their selection schemes to determine those cases in which guarantees represent the best risk / benefit option and at the same time, catalyse the finest behaviours concerning sustainable development.

3.3.3.2. Venture Capital. An interesting novel practice that we observe PDBs are beginning to explore in order to contribute to sustainable development comprises investing through acquiring equity in innovative start-ups that have a major financial risk. Acting as direct investors allows banks to develop new markets or strengthen nascent industries that can catalyse sustainable development transformations. Moreover, bank's participation in such ventures renders useful in two ways: (i) as part of the venture's internal decision structures, the bank is able to share its expertise and provide guidance to safeguard the project delivers sustainable development impacts; (ii) by taking this stake, it sends a signal of reliance to other potential investors that thereafter will be interested in investing as well (Fernández-Arias, Ricardo, and Panizza 2019).

This financial instrument is very interesting as it can be led towards catalysing sustainable development by economically helping innovative ventures that need more capital to develop. Moreover, PDBs can capitalise on those that can potentially have a good impact on key SDG-related sectors. Though, as the guarantees, venture capital is an instrument that can be risky and needs a good selection process to opt for the opportunities with a potential of financial success. Coupling direct investment together with technical assistance, for those ventures still lacking adequate conditions for investment, is also a good practice that PDBs should foster.

3.3.3.3. Labelled Bonds. PDBs are exploring new ways of generating income and are designing specialised bond frameworks. Although issuing debt in international or domestic financial markets is not something new for these institutions, what is noteworthy in this case is ongoing efforts of PDBs to shape issuance and investment conditions in order to channel obtained funds towards green or sustainable development priorities.

Green bonds are the most developed ones but there is a growing trend to define frameworks for social bonds, blue bonds and SDG bonds. In the case of green bonds, many NDBs such as Bancóldex, BNCR, PT SMI, NAFIN report being first or early movers in the issuance of these types of bonds for their countries or regions (Authors Interviews 2020; Morris 2018b)

However, there are still many unresolved questions regarding green or SDG bonds: Do they really bring additionality? What is their added-value? Do they attract capital into investments that are more novel? Are bonds an important innovation for sustainability or just the same business-as-usual with a new cover?

Some reflections can be gleaned from the conversations with the interviewees. On one hand, NDBs mentioned that once they issue their bonds on local capital markets, MDBs usually support them by leveraging the bond and thus, allowing them to get credit enhancement. This enables them to tap the market without paying costly interest rates and using spare funds to invest in SDG-related priorities. Besides, bonds can be in themselves transformative instruments since they imply following international standards and undertaking profound internal reforms at all levels — strategy, operations, interaction with other stakeholders — in order to structure, issue and monitor the instrument.

On the other hand, NDBs and SDBs noted that they face many challenges at all different stages of labelled bonds issuance and follow up: (i) issuing labelled bonds entails many additional costs which represent an expensive overhead for the bank. These types of bonds tend to have higher transaction costs than traditional bonds and on the contrary, they may limit bank's flexibility (Maltais and Björn 2020); (ii) pricing green/SDG bonds can be a difficult task because domestic investors are still not aware of the importance of sustainable development and on the benefits of complying with additional conditions to access these financial instruments. In most markets, acquisition prices between traditional and labelled bonds are almost the same, which makes the issuance of these bonds more expensive for the NDB. During an interview, the idea of thinking about creating exchange insurance for national and subnational banks came up as a suggestion; (iii) reporting and assessing projects to allocate bonds is very expensive because it requires a specialised team and consistent data collection; (iv) lastly, NDBs say inability to obtain good credit ratings represents a barrier to increasing labelled bond issuance on capital markets.

3.3.4. Partnerships

In their efforts to align and implement the 2030 Agenda, PDBs are actively participating and fostering the rise of partnerships with an SDG focus. Harnessing the potential of partnerships is paving the way for PDBs to provide practical results and catalyse sustainable development transformations. In our interviews, we came across different ways in which these banks are working together with other DFIs, private investors, governments and regional banks' associations with the aim to find the path to a sustainable finance and achieve the SDGs.

Interesting practices in this domain are: (i) joining forces to develop common methodologies and standardise existing approaches; (ii) fostering alliances that will allow PDBs to learn how their peers are adapting to the Global Agenda and; (iii) establishing partnerships seeking to crowd in technical and financial support from other stakeholders also willing to contribute to the attainment of the 2030 Agenda.

3.3.4.1. Harmonisation of Standards and Practices. Respondents expressed that one of their main concerns is to understand the best path to accomplish SDG alignment. The 2030 Agenda is multisectoral and interconnected in nature, meaning an integrated approach is needed to maximise the impact of investments. Thus, one of the main challenges of achieving true alignment lies in understanding how synergies and trade-offs among goals play out in a particular setting. For that reason, providing common frameworks and standards that facilitate the task of understanding which investments are sustainable is of the outmost importance.

PDBs are fostering agreements between their peers who are in similar geographies or conditions (country, economic context) in order to spread the awareness of SDG's and define common principles and methodologies for SDG interpretation and alignment (Authors Interviews 2020). In this regard, regional national banks associations and wider organisations such as the IDFC are starting to play an active role creating common grounds for discussion and support their associates harmonise their alignment efforts.

3.3.4.2. Partnerships for Research. PDBs need to invest in research on SDG alignment, financial instruments for sustainable development, how to deal with trade-offs between SDGs, on blocking factors, etc. Alliances where PDBs can learn from other stakeholders and from their peers facing the same challenges can help the emergence of new financial instruments and practices to align operations with SDGs.

Over the interviews, we identified some examples of scientific research for the design of financial instruments and SDG projects. For instance, ABDE together with IDB, the Securities and Exchange Commission of Brazil (CVM) and the GIZ launched a couple of years ago a financial innovation laboratory (LAB).[7] MDBs, DFIs and international organisations are playing a key role in building capacities and providing technical support to scale up the funding and improve internal capacity to align with SDGs.

---

[7]http://www.labinovacaofinanceira.com/.

Coalitions for research between development institutions can spread the knowledge about different sectors, practices or financial solutions and demonstrate by the experience of others the success of certain exercises. This can also attract private investors that will be more aware about the benefits of investing in some underserved sectors and successful practices used for SDGs (Olloqui et al. 2013).

3.3.4.3. Create Incentives to Change Behaviour. This type of partnership encourages and incentivises PDBs to enhance the sustainable performance within the institution. In the course of interviews, we came upon some experiences between NDBs and MDBs, whereby the latter establishes certain impact indicators or socio-environmental criteria as a prerequisite to deploy the capital. By doing so, MDBs are accelerating in certain cases the alignment of PDBs with the 2030 Agenda. However, in most cases, the aforementioned conditions are still focusing mainly on ESG standards or climate change goals. Thus, it is important that PDBs, in their different levels of engagement, are more accurate in the inclusion of SDG-related conditionalities that comprise the integrated and cross-cutting dimensions the 2030 Agenda stands for.

The Green Climate Fund and some European Funds also ask for improvements in some indicators depending on the project — such as energy efficiency, social inclusion, gender equality. The stringent accreditation process to access these international funds — GEF, GCF, EU DEVCO — obliges PDBs to improve their internal systems, increase transparency and tighten reporting standards (Smallridge et al. 2019). Therefore, since PDBs are highly interested in fulfilling the terms and conditions of these funds, it operates as an incentive to develop and set up internal indicators to evaluate their impact and contribution to sustainable development.

3.3.4.4. Blended Finance Partnerships. PDBs are engaging, and in some cases, leading or administering platforms where private investors, businesses, philanthropists and other public entities are investing to fund SDG-aligned projects. The aim of these platforms is to blend the PDBs finance with concessional resources from governments and public finance in order to improve the terms and conditions of their funding and attract the private capital.

Some SDG-related investments such as financing sustainable infrastructure require large initial investments and long maturity financing; commercial viability takes longer and thus, these projects have in most cases long payback periods (Griffith-Jones, Attridge, and Gouet 2020). Moreover, most financial markets are weak or still immature in developing countries, making it harder to find loans with long-term repayment (Authors Interviews 2020). This is partly why PDBs are devoting important efforts to strengthen their role as mobilisers of investments and co-financing these types of projects with other lenders, in order to share risks and maximise the positive impact on SDGs.

We were able to identify some innovative examples on how PDBs are making use of blended finance instruments to assure they have a greater collective impact with the funding they provide. However, to get international investors to shift their portfolio towards a long-term SDG investment it is necessary to have the capacity to assess and supervise the long-term risks. For this purpose, PDBs still need to develop expertise in project design, evaluation and follow-up in order to pave the way for private investment.

Although blended finance mechanisms are an innovative way for public and private investors to work together, they not always contribute to financing the 2030 Agenda. Harnessing the potential of those tools demands real commitment to invest in areas critical to sustainable development and overcome the short-term approaches and aversion to invest in fragile settings that has characterised private investors so far (Riaño and Barchiche 2020). PDBs need to take the lead when structuring bending platforms and be assertive when determining areas of focus — cross-cutting transitions that catalyse sustainable development — since in the end, they are the ones assuming the largest part of the risk compared to their private partners.

4. Conditions for Success

Achieving the SDGs is not only dependent on internal adjustments and alignment from PDBs, but also on complementary effective actions from governments, the international financial system and the private sector, in addition to collaboration among all stakeholders. Furthermore, as pointed out by Thorne and du Toit (2009), PDBs are unlikely to be successful and accomplish their developmental objectives if certain conditions — both internal and external — are not also in place. Most NDBs and SDBs operate in countries or contexts where public institutions are still weak and provide no clear guidance on governments' priorities; internal staff has some but not all skills or qualifications that allow them to catalyse sustainable development priorities; or they find it harder to access international financial markets that could support their efforts in leveraging funds and scaling up their impact.

4.1. Internal Conditions

Undertaking structural governance and culture reforms is an indispensable requirement for these institutions to move from strategic intent to actual 2030 Agenda alignment and implementation. Ownership of this agenda needs to come from the very inside, from the core of the bank. In other words, it has to become part of its DNA, meaning that from top to bottom — from the high-level directives to those who hold the positions of planning, reviewing and approving credits — the 2030 Agenda is used as a cornerstone for action.

However, catalysing the desired internal adjustments is not always easy for PDBs and can become a challenging task, due to lack of resources, capacity, time constraints, among others. As mentioned by some interviewees, mainstreaming sustainable development within their structures requires the existence of bold high-level commitment towards SDGs implementation. Otherwise, the bank's business-as-usual will absorb any isolated effort to encourage the use of the 2030 Agenda as a framework for action.

- *Qualified board and employees who are standard-bearers of the SDGs and have the determination and interest to permeate the strategy, operations and external engagements with the promises of the 2030 Agenda.* The above will definitely serve as a lever for PDBs to foster breakthrough thinking capacity and capability, especially amongst management and leadership.

- *Strengthening existing governance structures and internal restructuring with an SDG focus.* PDBs should engage in internal discussions to identify their governance gaps, in view of their efforts to align with the 2030 Agenda. In this regard, conducted interviews and performed research point out that some PDBs are devoting important efforts to undertake significant internal reforms with the purpose of better embedding sustainable development within their structures (Box 1).

Box 1.

BOX 1. OBSERVED SDG-RELATED GOVERNANCE STRUCTURES WITHIN PDBS

— Position of Chief Sustainability Officer
— Environmental committees/Inclusion & Sustainability Department attached to the President's office
— Impact & ESG governance structures
— Specialised divisions (energy, carbon neutrality, human rights, gender and diversity)
— Planning Department with SDG focus
— Decentralised sustainable development specialists in every agency of the bank, central departments and core business sectors

- *Expanding culture of sustainable development across the employees.* PDBs need to have adequate internal capacity and skills to scale up transformational action on SDGs. To do this effectively, the staff — especially those working on designing, approving, following up and assessing investments — needs to have sufficient training and access to information to be able to factor SDGs into their decision-making and analysis throughout each stage of the investment process.

4.2. External Conditions

4.2.1. Public Policies and National Context

4.2.1.1. Allowing PDBs to Assume More Risks and be Contra-Cyclical in Time of Crisis. Political instability and economic vulnerability have always been seen as a constraint for efficacy in economic development. This applies also to social and environmental development. Countries at global level and governments at national and local level need to create a financial, economic and political environment that will allow PDBs to assume more risks and be contra-cyclical in time of crisis.

PDBs have extended both short and long-term credits to existing and new customers who were facing difficulties in debt refinancing and in receiving new lines of credit.

With the support of their government, National PDBs can act as a 'financial arm' of many countries, using a full range of instruments including the moratorium and rescheduling of existing loan obligations, working capital loans, and portfolio insurance policies.

4.2.1.2. Sending the Right 'SDG Signals' for Investments. An adequate financing of the 2030 Agenda should imply putting in place policies and regulations that send the right signals to catalyse the desired behaviours and investments. PDBs have a leadership role to play but cannot succeed on their own as they are usually working under governments priorities. They often depend on the orientation and priorities established by their governments or local authorities. To be really effective in aligning with and financing SDGs, PDBs need to intervene in national or regional context with cleared and identified priorities related to SDGs. In some cases, it seems that the PDB is more advanced in its alignment with the 2030 Agenda than the domestic government or local authorities.

On the other hand, PDBs are often assessed and measured by the same standards as commercial banks or conventional financial institutions. Thus, regulatory incentives tailored for their specific nature are imperative for PDBs to have more room for action.

4.2.1.3. Financing Sustainable Development Strategies. There is a clear lack of national financing strategies to implement the 2030 Agenda. Although some countries have set up policy frameworks for SDG implementation, as observed from the Voluntary National Reviews (VNRs), only very few have presented an associated financing plan.

According to the UN Report on Financing for Sustainable Development (2019, 2020), Integrated National Financing Frameworks INFFs could help define financing strategies that are grounded in the country's specific context.

These powerful planning tools, still overlooked by countries, can definitely help overcome many of the existing impediments to financing sustainable development. Once countries know what needs to be funded — laid out in their sustainable development strategy — INFFs will map how this plan ought to be financed and implemented.

Such a process will allow stakeholders and financial actors, in particular PDBs, concerned at the local, national and global levels to target their investment efforts with the needed clarity on where their funds could provide effective results. And it will clarify the leading role of PDBs in supporting investment and financing of SDGs within a country and identify where PDBs can make a real difference. PDBs will be in a better position and scenario to assume more risks and become strong enablers of SDGs financing.

4.2.2. Credit Rating Agencies

Credit rating agencies definitely have an impact on how PDBs take decisions in terms of where to invest and what to finance. 'We are told to be careful in fragile markets so how can we invest in down-rated countries?' (Authors Interviews 2020). Therefore, credit rating agencies might represent an obstacle not only for PDBs to be less risk averse and invest in areas or regions most in need, but also affect their ability to raise additional funds, since investors will base their decisions on existing ratings. In the end, PDBs end up being conservative and pro-cyclical.

Taking into account that market conditions and scores given by credit rating agencies might have an important impact on PDBs contribution to SDGs implementation, future research could focus on how these institutions should consider impact as a return of investment. During interviews, the idea of creating an SDG credit score emerged, which would be a major step to support the job of PDBs and DFIs in allowing financial actors to include in their investment considerations SDG-related criteria, beyond plain market assessments.

5. Recommendations[8]

PDBs' strategies should lead to a complete, comprehensive and systemic integration of the SDGs, percolating all of their activities, instead of classifying existing projects with individual SDGs. In order to integrate SDGs in all actions and processes of their banks, the 2030 Agenda needs to be solidly anchored within PDBs' organisational culture, backed by adequate incentives and capacity building. PDBs should also place more emphasis on support for early stage project preparation and for facilitating the structuring of SDG bankable projects.

PDBs need to take ownership and leadership in their roles as enablers and catalysers of sustainable finance. It is crucial that they seize opportunities offered by the SDGs to work side-by-side with other stakeholders — underpinned by strategic partnerships, blended finance or other financial mechanisms like guarantees or Green/SDG bonds — to play a larger and potentially transformational role in scaling up finance to achieve the SDGs.

PDBs' actions need to be upheld by a clear SDG national policy and budget — through an Integrated National Financing Framework (INFF) for instance — and tailor made regulations that increase their appetite for risks and invest in non-traditional sectors or poor/fragile settings. Establishing an 'SDG Credit Score' would also be a major step to encourage and support PDBs to drive sustainable development transformations.

Expanding lending capacities. PDBs, particularly NDBs should bet on being less conservative with their lending practices. They have a wide margin of opportunity to leverage new resources and increase the amount of loans granted.

Disclosure Statement

No potential conflict of interest was reported by the author(s).

References

Bhattacharya, D., T. Khan, and U. Salma. 2014. 'A Commentary on the Final Outcome Document of the Open Working Group on SDGs.' *SAIS Review of International Affairs* 34 (2): 165–177.

BNDES. 2017. *Social and Environmental Performance in the Financial Sector: Benchmarking of Development Finance Institutions.* Brasilia: BNDES.

BRDE. 2017. 'Relatório de administração e socioambiental 2018.'

Brei, M., and A. Schclarek. 2018. 'The Countercyclical Behaviour of National Development Banks of Latin America and the Caribbean.' In *The Future of Development Banks*, edited by S. Griffith-Jones and J. A. Ocampo. Oxford University Press.

Carlino, H., M. Netto, E. Suarez, and A. Vasa. 2017. *La contribución de la banca pública de desarrollo a los Objetivos de Desarrollo Sostenible en los países de América Latina y el Caribe.* Inter-American Development Bank.

Clark, A., J. Choi, B. Tonkonogy, V. Micale, and C. Wetherbee. 2019. *Implementing Alignment with the Paris Agreement: Recommendations for the Members of the International Development Finance Club. Climate Policy Initiative (CPI).* https://www.climatepolicy

[8]Note: For a complete analysis on conclusions and recommendations refer to the original study.

initiative.org/wp-content/uploads/2019/09/Implementing-alignment-recommendations-for-the-International-Development-Finance-Club-_-Full-Report.pdf.
Cochran, I., and A. Pauthier. 2019. *A Framework for Alignment with the Paris Agreement: Why, What and How for Financial Institutions?* Paris: I4CE.
DBSA. 2019a. '2019 Integrated Annual Report Performance Highlights.'
DBSA. 2019b. '2019 Sustainability Review.' https://assets.ctfassets.net/f7tuyt85vtoa/4MJVhRWWstldLyyNHt1dFY/93a8af747a3b66089efbbed118f42af7/Sustainability_Review_V11_AW_Digital.pdf.
Engen, L., and A. Prizzon. 2018. *A Guide to Multilateral Development Banks.* Overseas Development Institute. 1–92. https://www.odi.org/sites/odi.org.uk/files/resource-documents/12274.pdf.
Fernández-Arias, E., H. Ricardo, and U. Panizza. 2019. 'Smart Development Banks.' IDB Working Paper.
FMO. 2019. '2019 Annual Report.'
Griffith-Jones, S., S. Attridge, and M. Gouet. 2020. *Securing Climate Finance Through National Development Banks.* ODI.
Griffith-Jones, S., and J. A. Ocampo. 2018. *The Future of National Development Banks.* Oxford University Press.
Hege, E., and D. Barchiche. 2019. 'Assessment and Conditions for Success of the 2030 Agenda for Sustainable Development.' IDDRI, Issue Brief N°15/19.
Hege, E., D. Barchiche, J. Rochette, L. Chabason, and P. Barthélemy. 2019. 'Initial Assessment and Conditions for Success of the 2030 Agenda for Sustainable Development.' IDDRI, Study N°07/19.
Humphrey, C. 2017. 'Six Proposals to Strengthen the Finances of Multilateral Development Banks.' Overseas Development Institute, Working Paper, 509 .
Humphrey, C. 2018. 'The Role of Credit Rating Agencies in Shaping Multilateral Finance: Recent Developments and Policy Options.' Inter-Governmental Group of 24, Washington DC: G24.
Humphrey, C. 2020. *All Hands on Deck – How to Scale up Multilateral Financing to Face the Covid-19 Crisis.* Overseas Development Institute.
IDFC. 2019. 'Green Finance Mapping Report 2019.'
Independent Group of Scientists Appointed by the Secretary-General. 2019. 'Global Sustainable Development Report 2019: The Future Is Now – Science for Achieving Sustainable Development.' United Nations.
Koehler, G. 2016. 'Assessing the SDGs from the Standpoint of Ecosocial Policy: Using the SDGs Subversively.' *Journal of International and Comparative Social Policy* 32 (2): 149–164.
Korosi, C. 2015. 'Négocier un avenir commun : ce que nous ont appris les Objectifs de développement durable.' Regards Sur La Terre 2015.
Luna-Martinez, J., and C. L. Vicente. 2012. 'Global Survey of Development Banks.' World Bank, Policy Research Working Paper, 5969.
Maltais, A., and N. Björn. 2020. 'Understanding the Role of Green Bonds in Advancing Sustainability.' *Journal of Sustainable Finance & Investment*, 1–20. https://doi.org/10.1080/20430795.2020.1724864
Mazzucato, M. 2015. 'Building the Entrepreneurial State: A New Framework for Envisioning and Evaluating a Mission-Oriented Public Sector.' SSRN Electronic Journal.
Mazzucato, M., and C. C. Penna. 2016. 'Beyond Market Failures: The Market Creating and Shaping Roles of State Investment Banks.' *Journal of Economic Policy Reform* 19 (4): 305–326.
Morris, S. 2018a. *Rising to the SDG Challenge: The Unique Contribution of the International Development Finance Club.* Center for Global Development. https://www.idfc.org/Who-We-Are/who-we-.
Morris, S. 2018b. *The International Development Finance Club and the Sustainable Development Goals: Impacts, Opportunities and Challenges.* Center for Global Development.
Moslener, U., M. Thiemann, and P. Volberding. 2018. 'National Development Banks as Active Financiers: The Case of KfW.' In *The Future of Development Banks*, edited by S. Griffith-Jones and J. A. Ocampo. Oxford University Press.

OECD. 2018. *Development Co-Operation Report 2018: Joining Forces to Leave No One Behind.* Paris: OECD.

OECD. 2019. 'Aligning Development Co-operation and Climate Action: The Only Way Forward.'

OECD, UN-Environment, and WBG. 2018. *The Financing Climate Futures: Rethinking Infrastructure.* OECD.

OECD, UN-Environment, and WBG. 2019. 'Scaling Up Climate-Compatible Infrastructure: Insights from National Development Banks in Brazil and South Africa.' OECD Environment Policy Papers, Financing Climate Futures: Rethinking Infrastructure, 18.

Olloqui, F. d., M. Chrisney, J. J. Gómez Lorenzo, A. Maffioli, R. Monge-González, M. Netto, F. Nieder, A. Palma, and C. M. Rodríguez. 2013. *Public Development Banks: Toward a New Paradigm?* Inter-American Development Bank.

Rain Forest Action Network, BankTrack, International Indigenous Environmental Network, Oil Change International, Reclaim Finance, and Sierra Club. 2020. 'Fossil Fuel Finance Report.'

Riaño, M., and D. Barchiche. 2020. 'Financing the 2030 Agenda for Sustainable Development: Prerequisites, and Opportunities for the Post-Covid-19 Crisis.' IDDRI, Issue Brief N°03/20.

Riaño, M.-A., J. Boutaybi, D. Barchiche, and S. Treyer. 2020. 'Scaling up Public Development Banks' Transformative Alignment with the 2030 Agenda for Sustainable Development.' IDDRI, Study N°05/20 .

Sangare, C., and T. Hos. 2019. *Amounts Mobilised from the Private Sector for Development.* OECD Publishing.

Sedemund, J., N. Crishna Morgado, B. Lasfargues, and O. Taskin. 2018. *Financing Climate Futures: The Role of National Development Banks in Brazil and South Africa.* OECD Case Study. http://www.oecd.org/environment/environment-development/Financing-Climate-Futures-NDB-Brazil-South-Africa.pdf.

Smallridge, D., M. Becker, J. Henderson, and M. Sider. 2019. *Build or Renovate? The Decision to Establish a new Green Bank, or 'Green' an Existing National Development Bank.* Edited by Maria Netto, Enrique Nieto, and Alexander Vasa, May. Inter-American Development Bank. https://www.greenfinancelac.org/wp-content/uploads/2019/05/Paper_establishing-a-Green-Bank-or-Greening-of-Existing-Bank_vertical_vs4_web.pdf.

Spratt, S., and S. Griffith-Jones. 2013. *Mobilising Investment for Inclusive Green Growth in Low-Income Countries.* GIZ.

Studart, R., and K. Gallagher. 2016. 'Infrastructure for Sustainable Development: The Role of National Development Banks.' Global Economic Governance Initiative Policy Brief 007.

Thorne, J., and C. du Toit. 2009. 'A Macro-Framework for Successful Development Banks.' *Development Southern Africa* 26 (5): 677–694.

Thwing Eastman, M., P. Horrocks, T. Singh, and N. Kumar. 2018. 'Institutional Investing for the SDGS: A Joint Discussion Paper from MSCI and the OECD.'

UNCTAD. 2018. 'Scaling Up Finance for the Sustainable Development Goals: Experimenting with Models of Multilateral Development Banking.' United Nations Conference on Trade and Development.

United Nations. 2020. 'Sustainable Development Goals Report.'

World Bank. 2018. '2017 Survey of National Development Banks.'

Xu, J., X. Ren, and X. Wu. 2019. *Mapping Development Finance Institutions Worldwide: Definitions, Rationales, and Varieties.* Peking University, Institute of New Structural Economics.

Appendices

Appendix 1. Sample of PDBs reviewed in Section Two

Bank abbreviation	English name	Name in original language	Country/ region
America			
Bancoldex	The Bank of Foreign Trade	Bancoldex S.A.	Colombia
Bancomext	National Foreign Trade Bank	Banco Nacional de Comercio Exterior	México
Finagro	Fund for the Financing of the Agricultural Sector	Fondo para el Financiamiento del Sector Agropecuario	Colombia
BNDES	Brazilian Development Bank	Banco Nacional de Desenvolvimento Econômico e Social	Brazil
COFIDE	Finance Development Corporation S.A.	Corporación Financiera de Desarrollo S.A.	Peru
BRDE	Far South regional Development Bank	Banco Regional de Desenvolvimento do Extremo Sul	Brazil
NAFIN	National Development Bank	Nacional Financiera	Mexico
BDMG	The Development Bank of Minas Gerais S.A.	Banco de Desenvolvimento de Minas Gerais	Brazil
BNCR	National Bank of Costa Rica	Banco Nacional de Costa Rica	Costa Rica
BNA	Bank of the Argentine Nation	Banco de la Nación Argentina	Argentina
BancoEstado	Bank of the State of Chile	Banco Estado	Chile
BDE	The Development Bank of Republic of Ecuador	Banco de Desarrollo del Ecuador	Ecuador
BCIE	Central American Bank for Economic Integration	Banco Centroamericano de Integración Económica	Americas
IADB	Inter-American Development Bank	Inter-American Development Bank	Americas
Asia			
Exim	Export-Import Bank of India	Export-Import Bank of India	India
FDB	Fiji Development Bank	Fiji Development Bank	Fiji
SIDBI	Small Industries Development Bank of India	Small Industries Development Bank of India	India
DPB	Development Bank of the Philippines	Development Bank of the Philippines	Philippines
DFCC	DFCC Bank PLC	Development Finance Corporation of Ceylon	Sri Lanka
FDB	Fiji Development Bank	Fiji Development Bank	Fiji
ADB	Asian Development Bank	Asian Development Bank	Asia/Oceania
Africa			
DBSA	Development Bank of Southern Africa	Development Bank of Southern Africa	South Africa
CDG	Deposit and Management Fund	Caisse de Dépôt et de Gestion	Morroco
AFDB	African Development Bank	African Development Bank	Africa
TDB	The Eastern and Southern African Trade and Development Bank	The Eastern and Southern African Trade and Development Bank	Africa
Europe			
FMO	Netherlands Development Finance Company	Nederlandse Financierings- Maatschappij voor Ontwikkelingslanden	Netherlands
KFW	KFW Banking Group	KFW Bankengruppe	Germany
AFD	French Development Agency	Agence Française de Développement	France

Appendix 2. Interview guide

Questions related to inner aspects of PDBs' practices

(1) *Awareness*:
   (a) The 2030 Agenda and the SDGs have often been presented as a 'paradigm shift', and as a 'transformative project', leading ideally to a 'systemic change'. What do you think about the transformative role that has been given to the 2030 Agenda and its SDG?
   (b) What is the bank's understanding of sustainable development and of the 2030 Agenda?

(c) What particular role do you think DBs are poised to play in the implementation of the 2030 Agenda?
(d) How do you think your bank, through its business, can contribute to its implementation?
(e) Do you consider that DBs may play a key role to promote projects, and leverage and crowd-in private capital to transformational investments that sum up to the achievement of the 2030 Agenda?
(f) What is the place of the SDGs in the bank's strategy or goals?
(g) Which year did the bank start developing sustainable strategies in its operations?
(h) Do the concepts of indivisibility, interconnectedness, crosscutting resonate to you? How do you think the banks' SDG strategy contributes to the 2030 Agenda promises?

(2) *Alignment Efforts*:
(a) Has your bank developed an explicit SDG framework to help drive operational strategy or to track 2030 Agenda related financing activities?
(b) If the SDGs are integrated into the bank's strategy, is there any prioritisation among the objectives of the Agenda 2030? If so, what are the objectives that are prioritised, and why?
(c) Does the Bank make any analysis of synergies and trade-offs throughout the stages of the investment process? (product/service development and capital allocation decisions: plan, design, implement the investments, assess results) If so, how does the Bank cope with the conflicts/incompatibilities that may arise?
(d) How could the synergies and trade-offs between SDG targets be reconciled/tackled when structuring projects or defining investment priorities?
(e) What methodology/approach would you implement within the Bank to promote building pipelines of technically sound and bankable projects that focus on cross-cutting sectors?
(f) Regarding synergies and trade-offs between SDGs, how is the Bank translating that insight into practical action across its different financial and non-financial operations?

(3) *Governance and Culture*
(a) Has the Bank assigned clear and specific roles and responsibilities at the Board level and across all functions of your bank regarding your bank's sustainability agenda and provided adequate resource allocation to implement these roles?
(b) Is the Bank working to build internal expertise on the environmental, social and economic topics relevant to your bank's context, such as climate change, deforestation, pollution, biodiversity, human rights, gender equality. And if so, which strategies have you put in place to inform, educate and train your staff regarding the 2030 Agenda?
(c) Since the adoption of the SDGs, have you set up a dedicated, specialised team of sustainability experts (e.g., a corporate sustainability department) with strong leadership and clear roles and responsibilities, to facilitate sustainable finance and the implementation of the SDGs across all functions of your bank? If yes, how has this worked out?
(d) Would you consider useful for the Bank to put in place incentives for board members, directives and staff to act accordingly the SDGs and 2030 Agenda objectives? If yes, which sort of incentives?
(e) Do you believe that it could be feasible to formally include sustainability criteria into the Terms of Reference or charter for your Board's nomination, remuneration and audit committees or create a dedicated Board Committee focused on sustainability and responsible banking? How do you think this strategy could enhance the Banks' ability to actively contribute to SDGs implementation?
(f) Would pursuing a broader SDG mandate for DBs be a plausible option to move from strategic intend to a more effective implementation of the 2030 Agenda?

(4) *Impact Assessment, Accountability*
(a) Besides measuring the volume of flows that the Bank allocates annually, does the Bank has monitoring and evaluation frameworks to measure how much the various flows actually

contribute to sustainable development?, Can you share how are they structured and what results they are providing?

(b) Has the focus of annual reporting changed (annual report, sustainability report) since the adoption of the SDGs in 2015? Is the Bank focusing on outcomes and impacts, rather than process?, Do you include for example, an analysis in relation to the expected environmental and social benefits, do you use quality performance indicators, any segmentation of end-beneficiaries, estimated lifetime results/economic lifespan of projects?

(c) During the analysis of the development banks' sustainability reports, we have observed that several banks conduct *a posteriori* analyses of their alignment with the SDG's. Banks are trying to align their year-end results with various SDG's. Do you consider this as an effective practice or an obstacle? Why?

(d) How do you demonstrate that your bank has, through consistent processes linked to its own governance mechanisms, identified where it can have the most impact in terms of contribution to the SDGs and the targets it has set in this regard?

(5) *Undertaking Transformative Changes*

(a) What practices of the bank are aligned with the 2030 Agenda or the bank's understanding of sustainable development? And Why?

(b) Since the 2030 Agenda adoption, has the bank restructured the types of subsidies, credits or other financial instruments given to align with the SDG? Can you recount if there has been an evolution?

(c) Does your bank commercialise, or has it commercialised 'green financial products'? Could you cite some of them? Is there a mechanism for analysing the environmental, social and economic impact of these products? If so, what is the tangible impact of these products in terms of sustainable development?

(d) During the process of project development and implementation, is there a method for assessing environmental risk or alignment with SDG/sustainable development?

(e) Can you describe how does the Bank builds the pod of 'sustainable development bankable projects'? Are there any exclusion or screening criteria to avoid certain incompatible sectors or impacts?

(f) Have you structured metrics to deliver palpable impacts through investments and projects? For example: For every investment you do, do you thinking about the theory of change and the pathway to impact, and then define metrics around those?

(g) During our analyses of sustainability reports, we have highlighted that there are several common practices among banks. These are:
- Green energy financial products
- SARAS
- Green Bonds

Does your bank use any of them? If so, why do you consider them as an innovative approach to comply with the 2030 Agenda?

(h) Are there any initiatives, projects or practices currently underway that you consider innovative for implementing SDGs? How do you think they can bring the transformative changes the 2030 Agenda is expecting to achieve?

Questions Related to external engagements, drivers, pathways

(1) *Beneficiaries and Customers*

(a) Are you a first tier — second tier development bank?

(b) Does the Bank have any geospatial eligibility criteria in your credit lines or portfolio to target end-beneficiaries in vulnerable population groups? (for example groups living in extreme poverty, indigenous, elderly, children)

(c) Is the Bank developing new products and services that encourage and support more sustainable business models, technologies, practices, and lifestyles? Which ones will you highlight and why?

(d) Do you offer 'sustainability-linked loans' or 'positive impact loans', where some of the terms could be linked to corporate progress on sustainability? (e.g., discounts could be provided based on the use of the funds or the achievement of certain sustainability-related targets).
(e) Is the Bank providing specialised financial products and services to social enterprises and social entrepreneurs making a positive contribution to sustainable development, for example through innovation hubs, incubators, and supplier development programmes?, Could you share an example?
(f) Under the non-financial activities that the Bank offers, do you have any that encourages/builds capacity of clients to improve their own social and environmental impacts and adopt robust sustainability standards?, Can you share an example where the Bank has provided technical expertise to undertake a long-term sustainable development project?
(g) For the year 2018, what is the amount of disbursements granted for projects aligned with the 2030 Agenda and in how much do you estimate the corresponding to non-financial services, such as technical assistance, monitoring, etc.?
(h) Is the Banks' lending capacity, due to limited capital base, a constrain for scaling up lending to support the 2030 Agenda? What implications does it have?

(2) *Stakeholders Engagement*
(a) What initiatives or partnerships does the bank support or endorse that aim at sustainable development?
(b) Why do you think these multi-stakeholder partnerships or coalitions are an innovative example to deliver on the 2030 Agenda?
(c) Does the Bank engage actively in ESG discussions with shareholders, investors, private companies, beneficiaries? Do you see ESG criteria as a tool to implement the SDGs, or do you think it falls short?
(d) What is the role of 'blended finance' in attracting investment aimed at the implementation and achievement of the 2030 Agenda? What are valuable experiences of your Bank in this regard that could be replicated where DBs could lead this effort?
(e) Is the Bank working in any project together with the Government aimed at shaping policies, revising legislation, or improving operations towards sustainable development? If so, can you share why do you consider this will contribute to the achievement of the SDGs?

(3) *Drivers and Barriers*
(a) Does the country/countries in which the Bank operates has in place an SDGs Framework Policy? How having clear comprehensive strategies within countries, regions and across sectors of SDG implementation (i.e., SDG integrated national financing frameworks) facilitate DBs role as financers of the 2030 Agenda?
(b) Which are the key enabling conditions for DBs to be agents of change in the 2030 Agenda implementation?
(c) In your regional/national experience, which market failures have you encounter that make it challenging for the bank to drive change towards an effective implementation of the 2030 Agenda? How would it look like to have 'adequate market' conditions?
(d) What are the most important factors that have prevented a substantial financial expansion? For example, low equity capital, conservative behaviour, lack of access to the international financial market?
(e) Do credit rating agencies have an impact on how DBs take decisions in terms of where to invest and what to finance? What would be the suggestions to improve the evaluation standards of these agencies?
(f) Have you identified that fiscal space in governments within your country or region is a barrier to scale up SDG financing by DBs?
(g) How can government guarantees or loans from other DFIs support this endeavour to accelerate action towards sustainable development?

(h) What are the most significant obstacles to implement SDGs in bankable projects?
(i) In your experience, what is missing for DBs to assume a more active role within countries in order to mobilise funds aligned to sustainable development priorities, either from public entities (local/regional/national), private investors or other international finance institutions?

(4) *SDG Compatible Development Pathways*
(a) How do you think the Bank can foster the emergence of projects linked to sustainable development pathways? Do you consider DBs could engage more actively in channelling funds towards these trajectories?
(b) Rather than financing projects linked to one or a set of SDGs, would you consider as a feasible path to refocus the Banks' portfolios to transformational entry points such as:
  (i) Human well-being and capabilities
  (ii) Sustainable and just economies
  (iii) Food systems and nutrition patterns
  (iv) Energy decarbonisation with universal access
  (v) Urban and peri-urban development
  (vi) Global environmental commons.
(c) How to better align lending policies with scientific and robust approaches, which may be developed via multi-stakeholder processes?

Appendix 3. Revised and interviewed banks

Bank	Description
Europe	
FMO	Bilateral Dutch entrepreneurial Development Bank.
AFD	National French development bank focused in reducing inequalities and promoting sustainable development.
KfW	National German development bank that supports economic and social progress in developing countries and finance German and European companies, municipal enterprises, public institutions and private individuals.
America	
COFIDE	National Peruvian development bank focused in generate development in 3 areas: economic, social and environmental. COFIDE is a second tier bank (they disburse and invest in to other commercial and financial corporations).
BNA	National Argentinian development bank.
Bancoldex	Bilateral Bank for the foreign commerce of Colombia. It is a second tier bank (they disburse and invest in to other commercial and financial corporations). Bancoldex promotes competitiveness and productivity of the entrepreneur sector of Colombia.
ABDE	Brazilian association for law and economy created to develop research between law and economy. It supports the Brazilian development banks.
BID	Multilateral bank in the Latin America and the Caribbean. It provides loans, grants and technical assistance to achieve development in the region in a sustainable, climate-friendly way.
BDMG	Regional Brazilian development Bank in Minas Gerais, Brazil. It aims to participate in the economic development of the Minas Gerais Federal State of Brazil.
BRDE	Regional Brazilian development Bank in the South Region of Brazil. It aims to participate in the economic development of the Rio Grande do Sul, Santa Catarina and Parana.
NAFIN	National Mexican development Bank that contributes to the economic development facilitating the access to finance SME, entrepreneurs and other development services.
BNCR	Biggest National Development bank in Costa Rica and Central America.
Bancomext	Mexican National Bank for the foreign trade that aims to contribute to the Mexican development through the Mexican foreign trade finance.
CFN	National Ecuadorian development bank that aims to promote development in the productive and strategic sectors of Ecuador.

(Continued)

Continued.

Bank	Description
BDE	National development bank in Ecuador.
BancoEstado	National development bank of Chili.
BNDES	National development bank of Brazil. It is the principal instrument of the government for the long-term investments in every sector of the economy.
BCIE	Multilateral bank of the Central America region for the economic development and integration of that region, including the country founders but also the rest of the Central American countries.
Africa	
TDB	Multilateral South and Eastern African trade and development financial institution. It finances economic integration and sustainable development through trade finance, project and infrastructure finance and business advisory services.
CDG Capital	Moroccan investment bank and subsidiary of the Caisse de Dépôt et de Gestion.
DBSA	National South African development bank that seeks to play a role in development infrastructure in South Africa and the rest of the continent.
	Asia
ADFIAP	NGO that regroups all development banks and other financial institutions engaged in the financing of development in the Asia-Pacific region (131 member-institutions), based in Makati city, Philippines.
PT SMI	Indonesian national entity under the Ministry of finance serving as a catalyst for accelerating national infrastructure development in Indonesia.
Exim	National Export-Import Bank of India. Exim provides financial assistance to support Indian exports and imports.
DFCC	National development bank of Sri Lanka, very focus in provide innovative and responsible solutions for Sri Lanka development.
FDB	National development bank of Fiji that provides financial and advisory services to assist in the economic development of Fiji and in particular in the agriculture, trade and industry sectors.
LBP	National bank of Philippines. It priories sectors as small farmers and fishers, micro and SMEs, agri-and-aqua projects, governments units and corporation, communications, transportations, housing, education, health care, environment and tourism.
DBP	First development bank of Philippines with a focus in developing the country's infrastructure.

Appendix 4. Focused literature review

In recent years, literature on PDBs — both coming from academic sources and from relevant stakeholders in the field — has been slowly growing. Academic research on PDBs has mostly focused on understanding their roles, business and lending models, financial products and the challenges the might face to fulfil their tasks (i.e., Griffith-Jones and Ocampo 2018; Mazzucato 2015; Xu, Ren, and Wu 2019). Since the 2007/09 financial crisis, interest in and support for these institutions has broadly increased and some studies (Luna-Martinez and Vicente 2012; World Bank 2018 and in Xu, Ren, and Wu 2019) have also tried to map and understand how they operate, what are their mandates, financial services, clients, governance, investment sectors, among other aspects. Little has been said by scholars on PDBs role and contribution to implement and finance the 2030 Agenda.

As presented by some studies, PDBs can play an important part in supporting one country's economy. On one hand, they can invest in sectors and give their support to long-term development projects, whereby private sector and commercial banks fear to go — because of the high uncertainty of their future success (Mazzucato 2015). On the other hand, they have the ability to carry out countercyclical lending during a crisis and are above all, suited to reignite growth after a crisis (Brei and Schclarek 2018). Nevertheless, it is essential to be careful not to generate distortions in the market that could displace or discourage private actors from investing (Mazzucato and Penna 2016; OECD, UN-Environment, and WBG 2018; Smallridge et al. 2019).

Others studies have signalled that building projects and investing in critical sectors for development might imply higher costs, as it requires designing and evaluating projects with positive impact that sometimes will entail more social returns than private returns (Spratt and Griffith-Jones 2013).

Building on this research about the roles that PDBs have in society Mazzucato and Penna (2016) developed a typology of the different functions of PDBs. They demonstrate theoretically and empirically that PDBs act contra-cyclically during economic crises, have a development role promoting projects with public good characteristics and positive externalities, addressing the funding gap for innovations and SMEs and financing the societal challenges that have costs that are not reflected in prices, such as climate change. They also conclude that 'in a time in which many countries are trying to not only stimulate growth but to address key societal challenges, State Investment Banks (SIBs) seem well positioned to effectively promote the much-needed capital development of the economy in a smart, inclusive and sustainable direction' (Mazzucato and Penna 2016).

On the other hand, studies coming from international organisations (IDFC 2019; OECD 2018, 2019; OECD, UN-Environment, and WBG 2018, 2019; Sedemund et al. 2018; Thwing Eastman et al. 2018; UNCTAD 2018), think tanks (Clark et al. 2019; Cochran and Pauthier 2019; Engen and Prizzon 2018; Griffith-Jones, Attridge, and Gouet 2020; Morris 2018a) and PDBs (BNDES 2017; Carlino et al. 2017; Fernández-Arias, Ricardo, and Panizza 2019; Olloqui et al. 2013; World Bank 2018) have recently started to assess how PDBs can contribute to climate change and SDGs implementation and have started to place more attention to National Development Banks (NDBs) and Sub National Development Banks (SDBs).

For instance, a 2019 report by the Climate Policy Initiative (CPI) shares data that illustrates that the largest amount of public climate investments comes from NDBs (Clark et al. 2019). The academic book The Future of Development Banks also confirmed that the sample of NDBs assessed, were increasing long-term finance in fostering innovation and entrepreneurship in national economies, financing infrastructure and contributing to green growth (Griffith-Jones and Ocampo 2018). Furthermore, according to a study published by the UNCTAD (2018) due to the expertise in designing and implementing long-term development projects and the experience in leveraging private resources for development purposes, PDBs are showing progress in the implementation of sustainable development in economies.

However, it is necessary to review much more in detail the internal and external changes that PDBs need to embark on at a strategic and operational level, so that their financial efforts will be aligned with the 2030 Agenda. Different papers and reports have provided some insight on the integration of sustainable development in the vision and the overall strategy of PDBs, like the one published by the Center for Global Development-CGD (Morris 2018a) which provides an interesting overview of IDFC member practices. Nonetheless, we see that they have so far remained at the scale of strategies.

In 2019, I4CE published a framework for financial institutions to align with the Paris Agreement (Cochran and Pauthier 2019). It offers a guide for selecting activities, scaling up the impact and adopting a comprehensive scope of climate action. While the framework is intended for the climate agenda, the authors suggest this proposal could also serve for SDGs, on the basis that they seek similar goals, with the difference that SDGs possess an integrated and holistic nature.

Other researchers have proposed practices and sectors that could help PDBs to accelerate the achievement of SDGs. The Interamerican Development Bank published an article (Carlino et al. 2017) of how PDBs in Latin America can contribute to the SDGs. The authors recommend PDBs should invest in critical sectors, rather than in sectors that will harm other dimensions of sustainable development. Once critical sectors are covered, it is important to maximise the positive synergies. They also recommend prioritising investments on SMEs, building programmes with specific targets, ensuring resources for the most vulnerable populations and providing preferential rates to projects with innovative ideas aligned with SDGs. In addition to the development of sustainable projects directed to critical sectors, PDBs need to accompany the projects with indicators that measure the impacts and progress of PDBs' actions (Carlino et al. 2017). Most recently, Griffith-Jones, Attridge, and Gouet (2020) suggest that PDBs, as experts in pipeline development, are capable to identify and develop bankable projects that will foster sustainable trajectories.

As generally described, current research recognises the critical role PDBs can play in solving market failures and supporting countrýs economies and development. The existing body of literature also has started to reflect upon the role and potential contribution that PDBs — from all sizes, business models and geographies — could have in terms of SDG implementation and finance. However, to date, only a limited number of studies have explored how PDBs are trying to align in practice with the 2030 Agenda. Adding on existing efforts, the present study seeks to go a step further by analysing in much more detail how PDBs — from different sizes and geographies — have interpreted and are including sustainable development priorities in their day-to-day discussions, processes and operations. For this purpose, we conducted qualitative research — through interviews with PDBs — in order to understand their business models, governance structures and the specific practices they have developed to align their whole organisation with the 2030 Agenda and its SDG. From another angle, we also assess quantitatively the lending practices and leverage capacities of a sample of PDBs, in order to observe their financial potential to contribute to sustainable development and SDGs' implementation.

Research question: what are the best practices and innovative solutions developed by PDBs, and in particular NDBs, to align all their functioning, processes and practices with the 2030 Agenda in order: (i) to have a transformative effect; (ii) at a desired scale.

From Global to Local: Subnational Development Banks in the Era of Sustainable Development Goals

Sergio Gusmão Suchodolski, Adauto Modesto Junior, Cinthia Helena de Oliveira Bechelaine and Leila Maria Bedeschi Costa

ABSTRACT

Financing the implementation of the seventeen Sustainable Development Goals (SDGs) has been a development challenge since the establishment of the 2030 Agenda — especially under the unequal circumstances imposed by COVID-19. This paper aims to better inform this debate by highlighting the nature of Subnational Development Banks (SDBs) in the context of sustainable finance and how they operate within development networks. To this end, the research method addresses a comparative study among countries that stand out for the number of subnational institutions in their development systems, Brazil and Vietnam. After comparing the Brazilian and Vietnamese particularities, we present concrete examples of SDBs working to connect local needs to the 2030 Agenda investments. As final conclusions, the study allows to demonstrate that, by being the last mile specialist on the ground, in different localities with particular backgrounds and contexts, SDBs could be available channels to international resources to address the financial needs of local firms and governments, improving both efficiency and effectiveness of development programs and funds. Highlighting the potential of SDBs, this analysis leaves possibilities for a future research agenda on more integrated national development finance systems focused on local impact.

1. Introduction

Multilateral and national development banks have been widely discussed in the literature since the iconic Bretton Woods meeting in 1944. The role of such institutions in financing long-term investments (Diamond 1957; Bruck 2001), correcting market failures (Stiglitz 1994; Levy-Yeyati, Micco, and Panizza 2004), acting in a countercyclical manner in global financial crisis (Brei and Schclarek 2013, 2018) and performing as a strategic player for governments (La Porta, Lopez-De-Silanes, and Shleifer 2002; Mazzucato and Penna 2016), has been the subject of several discussions for over 75 years. However, little academic research has been carried out around the last mile institutions on the development scale: the Subnational Development Banks (SDBs) — which undermines the capacity of scholars and public officials to fully understand and explore their potential to contribute to Sustainable Development Goals (SDG) implementation, specially under the challenging conditions imposed by COVID-19.

Alongside the discussion of development banks on the subnational level, the debate on sustainable development, increasingly pressing after the 2015 international agreements, requires an unprecedented change in the volume of investments, in the type of offer and in business models for both public and private sectors. In that regard, Griffith-Jones et al. (2018) point out the importance of development banks as institutional vehicles to support the urgency of major investment in sustainable development and consequently the need for a structural transformation in the development model. Yet, besides the international finance flows that are being focused on the sustainable frontier, the challenge remains greater for the less developed regions of the planet. The needs are still more demanding when it comes to underdeveloped regions facing a combination of high levels of income inequality, high poverty ratios and climate-related vulnerabilities. To this end, the claiming lies in how to ensure that sustainable finance available in the international market will be applied according to the needs of the local population in less developed regions.

This paper aims to better inform this debate by highlighting the nature of SDBs in the context of sustainable finance and how they operate within development networks. Questions such as: what are they, how many and where they are, how do they build their role, and how do they relate to governments and other banking institutions at regional, national, and global levels, will be explored. In order to fulfill this objective, the research method applied a comparative study among countries that stand out for the number of subnational institutions in their development systems, Brazil and Vietnam. After comparing the Brazilian and Vietnamese cases, we present concrete examples of SDBs working to connect local needs to the 2030 Agenda. These real cases studies strengthen the argument of how SDBs can act as key actors in directing international capital to finance local development impact and may present useful insights for other contexts.

The research is divided into seven parts. The Second Section explores the subnational development banks worldwide, differentiating them from national and multilateral institutions and also placing how many there are, when they were founded and where. The third and fourth sections present the Brazilian and the Vietnamese SDBs, discussing the main characteristics and peculiarities of each development system. The differences and similarities of these two systems are presented in a comparative chart in the fifth section. Section Six focuses on how SDBs have been working at the local level to address the financing demands connected with the SDGs with real examples of institutions from Brazil and Vietnam. Finally, the final conclusions of this work are presented in Section Seven.

2. Subnational Development Banks Worldwide: Who and Where Are They

According to their ownership, Xu, Ren, and Wu (2019) divide development banks into two groups, as shown in Figure 1. The first, belonging to more than one country, constitutes the group of Multilateral Development Banks (MDBs) at the regional or global levels. The second group are those created by a country or a region of a country, establishing the National Development Banks (NDBs) and the Subnational Development Banks (SDBs), respectively.

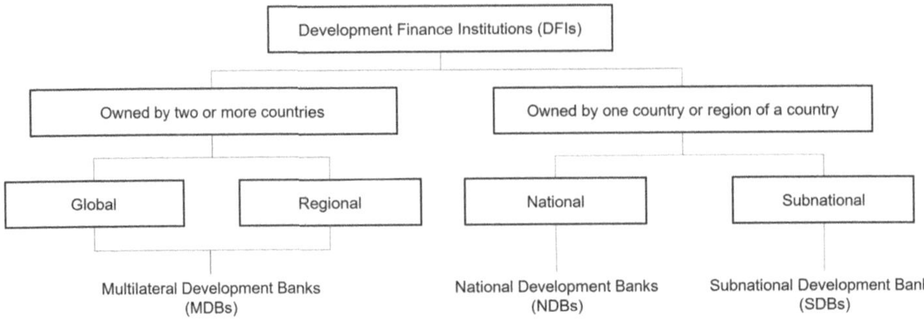

Figure 1. Category of development finance institutions by ownership. Source: Authors elaboration adapted from Xu, Ren, and Wu (2019).

The MDBs make up the core of the system designed to finance investments that promote economic growth and social development worldwide (Shelepov 2017). According to Xu, Ren, and Wu (2019), multilateral organizations are established by two or more countries and can be divided into global institutions, with global members (without distinguishing between regional and non-regional members), regional institutions, consisting of groups of countries from one or more regions.

Unlike multilateral ones, in which equity participation may vary between a set of countries with different levels of participation, a constitutive feature of NDBs is the participation of one national state, as the name suggests. As detailed by De Luna-Martínez and Vicente (2012), NDBs are essentially institutions owned, administered and controlled by the government of a nation, which must provide strategic direction and assign members of the board. According to a survey conducted by the World Bank on NDBs, about 75 per cent of the institutions surveyed have 100 per cent state ownership (De Luna-Martínez and Vicente 2012).

The predominant characteristic of SDBs, on the other hand, is the performance within a country, whether at the regional, state/provincial, or even local level. Although many academic articles have discussed how development institutions can be effective at the multilateral and national levels, SDBs are still little explored in academic research in the field of development finance.

The reason for going subnational in the establishment of public financial institutions is related to the belief that the combination of national and subnational development policies would lead to improved results in comparison to those achievable only with national ones (Ferroni 2004). In other words, by better knowing and monitoring the needs and peculiarities of their regions, SDBs would tend to act with greater selectivity e effectiveness, favoring local financing and, therefore, driving development in their territories. Another argument that advocates the institution of SDBs is that provincial or local public banks may increase regional welfare as they prevent a capital drain from poorer to richer regions by financing local projects and creditors in a more integrated economy (Hakenes and Schnabel 2010).

As difficult as can be to determine the exact number of development banks around the world, the French Development Agency (AFD), in a notorious effort to fulfill the data gap, mapped 447 institutions at the multilateral, national or subnational levels in 2020. About 76 per cent of institutions are national or subnational development banks

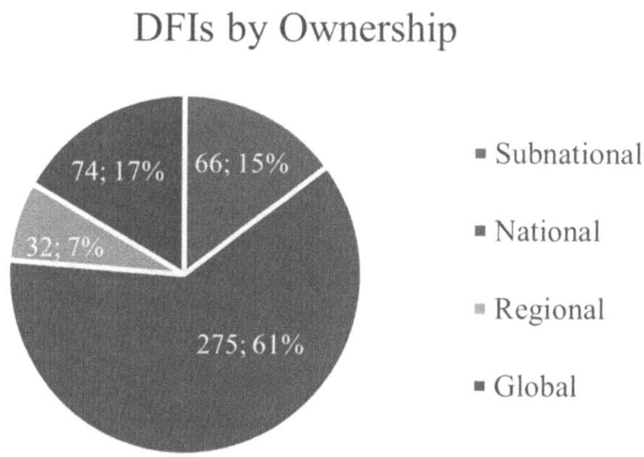

Figure 2. DFIs by ownership. Source: Authors elaboration from AFD database.

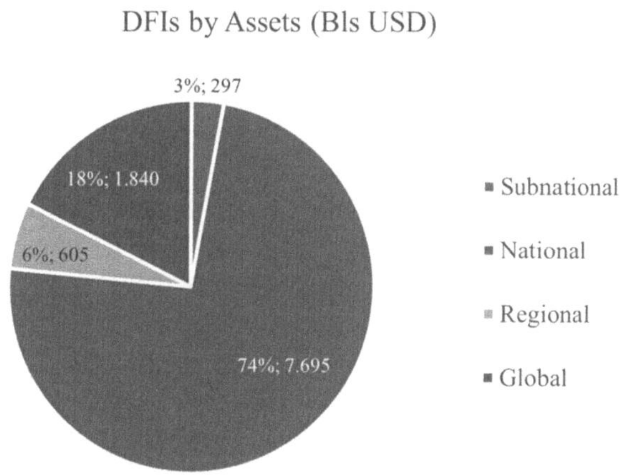

Figure 3. DFIs by assets (Bis USD). Source: Authors elaboration from AFD database.

around the world. More exactly, 15 per cent, or 66 institutions, represents SDBs in the last mile development scale (Figure 2).

Comparing these institutions in terms of total assets, NDBs appear as outliers. In fact, Griffith-Jones et al. (2018) point out as a characteristic of NDBs the considerable number of institutions around the world and the large-scale performance. In terms of total assets, Studart and Gallagher (2016), when distinguishing more than 250 NDBs with at least US $ 5 trillion in assets in 2015, point out that many NDBs surpass multilateral banks in size, scale and scope. According to AFD data, as shown in Figure 3, approximately 74 per cent of assets are concentrated at the national level, with nearly USD 7.7 trillion in assets. MDBs concentrate 23 per cent of total assets, with 17 per cent at the global level. Subnational banks account for 3 per cent of total assets, with around USD 300 billion.[1]

[1]It is important to highlight that the SDB's total assets number does not fully capture its relative importance since most of them operates as second-tier banks implementing on-lending programs from larger NDB and/or Multilateral ones.

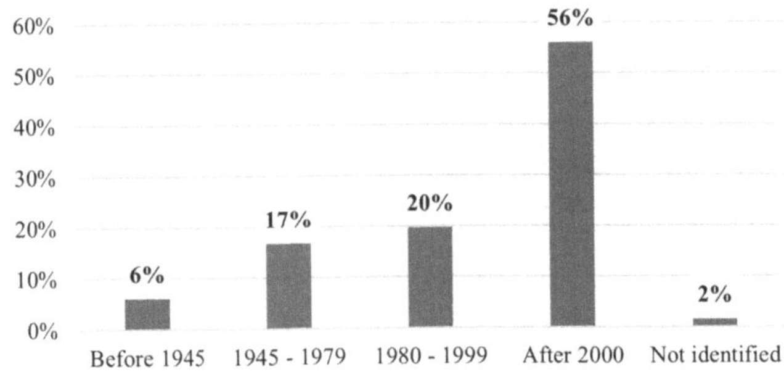

Figure 4. Period of establishment of SDBs (% of total). Source: Authors elaboration from AFD database.

The golden age of NDBs began in the 1950s, when countries from different regions sought a rapid industrialization, as mentioned by Griffith-Jones and authors (2018) and Torres and Zeidan (2016). Compared to NDBs, the establishment of the majority of SDBs has occured more rencently. Only 6 per cent were founded before the Second World War, such as Banco Ciudad de Buenos Aires in Argentina (1878), Investitions-bank and Landersbank Saar in Germany (1924 and 1941), and Bank of North Dakota in the USA (1919). Another 17 per cent were created between 1945 and 1979, including the Brazilian development banks Bank of Northeast (Banco do Nordeste do Brasil — BNB), South Regional Development Bank (Banco Regional de Desenvolvimento do Extremo Sul — BRDE), both at regional level, and the Development Bank of Minas Gerais (Banco de Desenvolvimento de Minas Gerais — BDMG) at state level, and the Colombian Instituto para el Desarrollo de Antioquia (IDEA). 20 per cent of SDBs were established between 1980 and 1999, a period marked by a massive process of public banks privatization in many parts of the world. Examples of SDBs established during this period include the Catalan Institute of Finance (ICF) in Spain (1985), the California Infrastructure and Economic Development Bank (IBank) in the USA, and the Brazilian development agencies, as discussed in the next section.

The bulk of SDB's (56 per cent of them) were established after 2000, both in developing countries and countries with sophisticated financial systems. Examples of SDBs in developing countries include Vietnamize local funds and Brazilian development agencies. New institutions in developed countries such as USA, Germany, United Kingdom and France were funded with a specific focus to provide infrastructure finance or help mitigate climate change challenges. Examples of specific SDBs in the USA include the Connecticut Green Bank (2011), the NY Green Bank and the Hawaii Green Infrastructure Authority, both funded in 2014 (Figure 4).

Among SDBs mapped, 32 per cent are located at South America — where Brazil stands out; 29 per cent in Asia — particularly in Vietnam with 18 institutions; 23 per cent in Europe, especially in Italy and Germany; and the last 17 per cent in North America and Pacific (Figure 5). According to Xu, Ren, and Wu (2019), the number of institutions in countries with different income levels corresponds to an inverted U shape: on average, middle-income economies have more development financial institutions than high and low-income economies.

Because of the complexity of their systems of SDBs and the active role that these institutions play in the implementation of development agendas within their countries, the

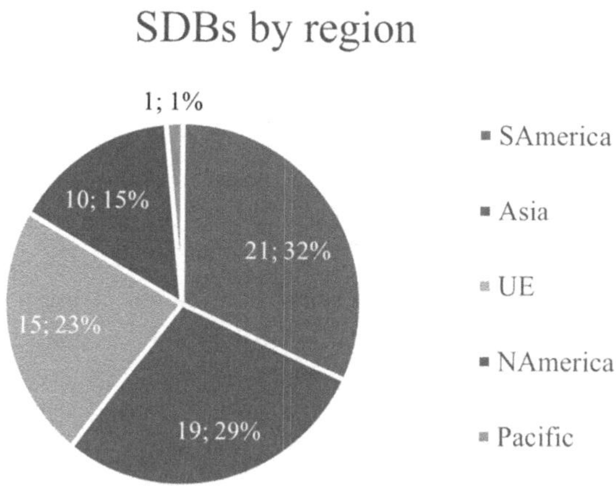

Figure 5. SDBs by region. Source: Authors elaboration from AFD database.

examples of Brazil and Vietnam will be further explored in the next two sections, in which we try to describe both systems, compare similarities and differences and draw lessons that might be applicable to other contexts.

3. Brazilian Subnational Development Banks: Boom, Shrinking and Current Outlook

Brazil is a federative republic, composed of states with a certain degree of autonomy (self-government, self-regulation and self-collection) and capable of their own government and constitution. There are 26 states, that are divided into municipalities, and one federal district. The regional or subnational economies differ from one another in several ways, with particularities in history background and development indexes, including access to credit.

The foundation of National Bank for Economic and Social Development (BNDES), in 1952, was the main milestone for the creation of the regional or state financial development institutions (Horn and Feil 2019). Brazilian SDBs originated by the developmentalist approach in the 1950s integrate, together with the BNDES, the so-called National Development System (SNF) (Araújo et al. 2013; Cunha, Prates, and Carvalho 2016). The SNF constitutes a system of financial institutions controlled by the federal government, states, or groups of states.

According to Araújo et al. (2013), the regional or state public development banks, the SDBs, were created to act in a complementary way to the BNDES, establishing themselves, at the time, as important sources of credit for the regional economy and financial inclusion of sectors without access to credit in the traditional banking market (Ferraz and Ramos 2018). According to Horn and Feil (2019), the SDBs can help break the vicious circle in which the credit supply tends to go to regions that have a higher degree of economic development, encouraging the access to local credit and increasing the capillarity of the Brazilian financial system.

The 1950s and the 1960s saw the creation of several SDBs, as stated by Araújo et al. (2013). Along with the creation of the BNDES, in 1952, the Banco do Nordeste (BNB), the bank of the northeast region of Brazil, was created, and later in 1966, the Bank of the Amazon region (Banco da Amazônia — BASA) was founded. As stated by Horn and Feil (2019), the creation of FINAME (Special Industrial Financing Agency) in 1966, following the expansion of BNDES activities, boosted the creation of development banks in the states, which started to act as resource transfer agents, expanding the capillarity of the national bank (Cavalcante 2007). By 1970, four states already had their own development bank: Minas Gerais (1962), Bahia (1966), Paraná (1968) and Espírito Santo (1969), in addition to another regional bank combining three states of the southern region (Rio Grande do Sul, Santa Catarina and Paraná) — the BRDE founded in 1962. From 1970, eight other states would also follow the same trend, with the creation of development banks of Maranhão, Ceará, São Paulo, Rio Grande do Norte, Rio Grande do Sul, Rio de Janeiro, Goiás and Santa Catarina.

According to Salviano Junior (2004), the growth of the state financial system would reach its peak in 1988, when state banks, development banks and state savings banks accounted for 10 per cent of banking system assets and deposits, for 17 per cent of operations and 6 per cent of the banks 'total shareholders' equity.

However, the trajectory of state banks has undergone several transformations until the current configuration. Changes caused by financial crises, problems of governance and internal management in banks would imply a shrinking of institutions (UN-DESA 2005), especially the state financial institutions affected by the 1980 crisis (Araújo et al. 2013).

From the 1990s onwards, in the context of market-oriented reforms, the Brazilian Program for the Reduction of the Public Sector's Presence in Banking Activity (*Programa de Incentivo à Redução do Setor Público Estadual na Atividade Bancária* — PROES) was launched in 1996, with the objective of prepare state and development banks for privatization purposes (Salviano Junior 2004). The structure of the system has changed dramatically. According to Gama Neto (2011), PROES was seen as one of the solutions to the constant financial crises of state banks and an important contribution to the efforts to reduce inflation at the time. The controlling states of the banks could opt for their subsequent privatization, extinction or transformation into Development Agencies (DAs) (Cunha, Prates, and Carvalho 2016). This reconfiguration of the Brazilian development system through the privatization of commercial banks under public control and the transformation of development banks into DAs was based on the premise of greater control over the level of states indebtedness and less exposure to popular savings, without detracting the importance of its socioeconomic role.

After the PROES, sixteen development agencies were created. According to Araújo et al. (2013), as non-financial institutions regulated by the Brazilian Central Bank (BACEN), they represented an alternative offered to states that had lost their development banks. Although they still have the same objectives and are regulated as development banks, DAs differ from banking institutions as they cannot: (i) raise funds from the public; (ii) have a reserve account at the Brazilian Central Bank and (iii) contract interbank deposits as depositors or depositaries. They operate through equity capital and on-lending funds (as BNDES) from national and international development organizations (Araújo et al. 2013). They are also obliged to establish and maintain, permanently, a liquidity fund equivalent to at least 10 per cent of the value of its obligations, which must be fully invested in federal public securities (Horn and Feil 2019). The three

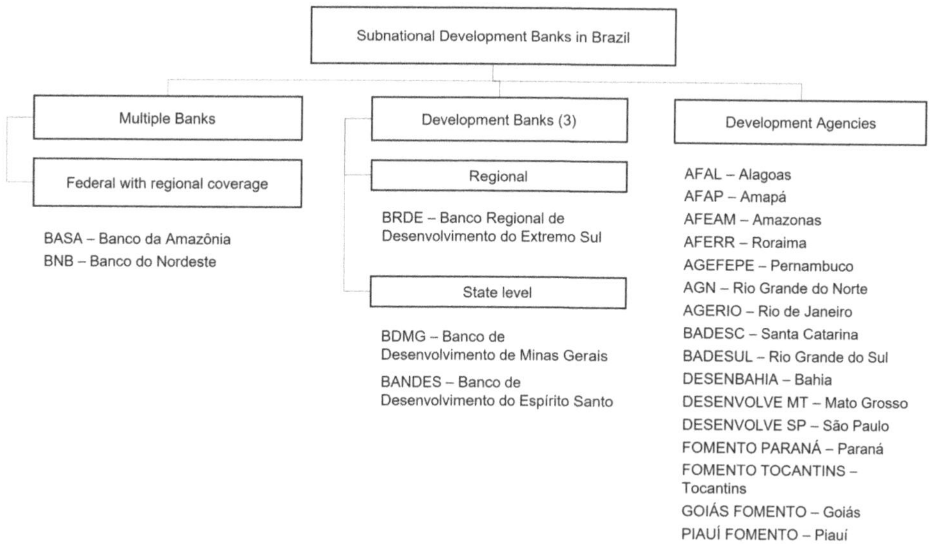

Figure 6. SDBs in Brazil. Source: Authors elaboration from Central Bank of Brazil, 2019.

development banks that remained after the execution of PROES, correspond to two state banks — Minas Gerais (BDMG) and Espírito Santo (BANDES), and the regional bank in the southern region (BRDE). Such institutions are essentially controlled by government states and have as their main characteristic the responsibility to grant credits, especially in the medium and long term, aiming at the economic and social development of the region where they operate. Its liabilities consist of long-term deposits, foreign loans, bonds and government transfers.

And there are also the two multiple banks created by the federal government with regional coverage: the Northeast Regional Bank (BNB) and the Amazon Bank (BASA). Multiple banks in Brazil have as their main characteristic the existence of diversified portfolios, such as commercial, investment and/or development, leasing and credit, financing and investment. Unlike development banks, their liabilities include direct deposits (Figure 6).

In a longitudinal analysis using data from Brazil's Central Bank, after the implementation of PROES, when there were 13 SDBs, the total assets corresponded to BRL 15.7 billion in the year 2000. By 2011, another 8 development agencies were created in the state level, and in 2019, the total assets of the 21 SDBs correspond to BRL 113.4 billion. The growth of assets is more than 600 per cent in the 20 years analyzed, an average growth of about 11 per cent per year, as shown in Figure 7.

Comparing the total assets growth of SDBs with BNDES's assets, it is possible to verify some variations. In the 2000s, the total assets of the SDBs corresponded to 16 per cent of BNDES total assets. From 2007 to 2015, there was a noticeable growth in the BNDES total assets, distancing the NDB from the group of SDBs currently existing. Part of this growth is due to the Investment Support Program (*Programa de Sustentação do Investimento* — PSI), responsible for making financing conditions more attractive for the acquisition of machinery and equipment produced in Brazil in an economic retraction context. In this period, the ratio of total SDB assets to BNDES assets corresponded to around 9 per cent,

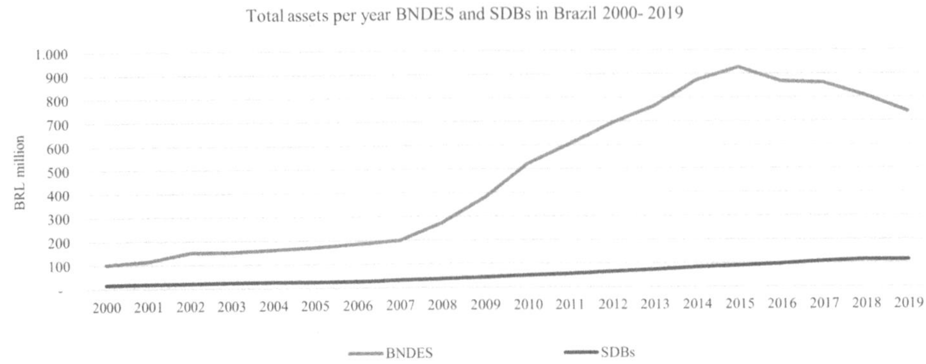

Figure 7. Total assets per year BNDES and SDBs in Brazil 2000–2019. Source: Authors elaboration from Central Bank of Brazil database.

even with the increase in the number of development agencies. From 2015, with the decrease in BNDES assets and parallel growth in SDB assets, the SDBs assets return to the level of approximately 15 per cent of the NDB assets.

In terms of mandates and development instruments of the 21 SDBs in Brazil, it is possible to verify that the operational modalities vary a lot according to their size and region. According to Horn and Feil (2019), the main mandate modalities include: long-term credit for investment projects; financing small and medium-sized companies (SMEs), rural producers and production cooperatives; pure working capital; management of fiscal funds, normally used in operations with the municipal public sector to finance urban infrastructure projects. In addition to the financing modalities, Horn and Feil (2019) also mention activities of mobilizing economic agents in support of sectoral and regional development programs, such as the dissemination of information on credit lines and incentives. Blended finance instruments, such as mobilizing the private sector through public–private partnerships, are also part of the scope of BNDES and SDBs.

Regarding their governance, there is a growing concern to improve internal management practices highly recommended by the Brazilian Central Bank in order to prevent problems occurred in the 1990s. Among other structures, SDBs organizational structure includes the operation of technical committees, whose main objective is to ensure financial suitability and decision-making efficiency in internal activities (Horn and Feil 2019). These committees are responsible for defining criteria for credit loans, risk management, accounting, among other practices. Most of the SDBs have boards of directors and directors appointed by the government of their controlling states and its composition must be approved by Brazilian Central Bank.

Considering the data from 2019, there are also significant differences when it comes to equity and asset base among Brazilian SDB's. Banks with regional coverage, as BNB, BASA and BRDE, have a higher asset and equity base than state banks. As shown in Figure 8, BNB (Norwest Bank) appears as an outlier in terms of assets and equity (BRL 58.6 billion in assets and BRL 5.4 billion in equity), while BASA (Amazon) and BRDE (South Region) have similar sizes considering the asset-equity criteria– assets between BRL 15 and 20 billion and equity between BRL 2 and 3 billion. The 18 state

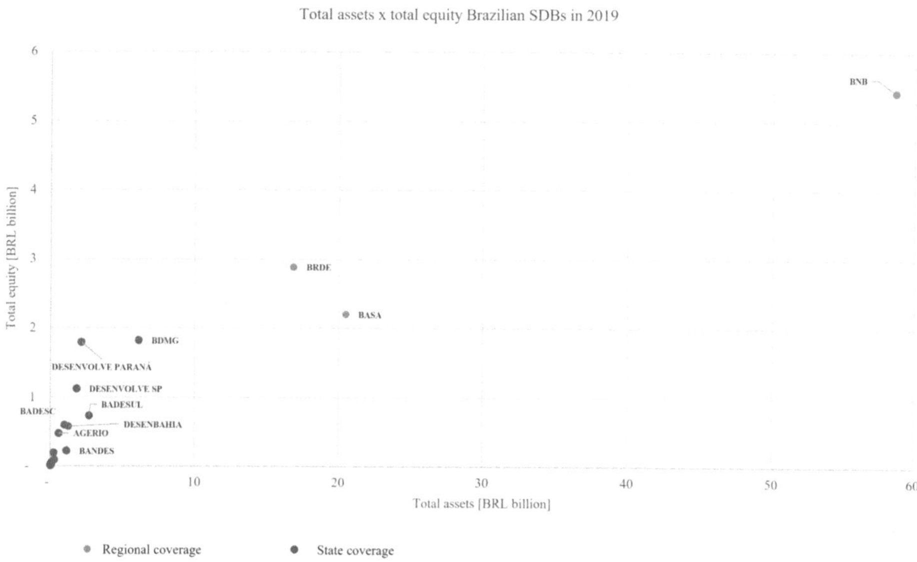

Figure 8. Comparison between total assets and equity of SDBs (regional and state) in Brazil in 2019. Source: Authors elaboration from Central Bank of Brazil database, 2019.

banks and development agencies have a maximum equity of BRL 1.8 billion and total assets between BRL 6 billion and BRL 8 million. BDMG (Minas Gerais state) stands out as the largest state development bank in Brazil. The state banks are quite diverse in terms of size: 11 development agencies have assets of up to BRL 600 million, 5 institutions have assets between BRL 1 and 3 billion and only 1 institution (BDMG) has assets greater than BRL 5 billion — Figure 9.

Another important feature of the Brazilian SDB seems to be the concentration of the system. Considering the total assets of the SDBs in 2019, 90 per cent of this amount is concentrated by four banks: BNB, BASA, BRDE and BDMG, three of them in the regional coverage and one with state coverage.

According to Horn and Feil (2019), the significant size difference between SDBs in Brazil could be explained by the disparity participation of the controlling states in the national economy. In other words, the authors point out the tendency for the states with lowest participation in the Brazilian GDP to have the smallest SDBs, in terms of assets. For example, BDMG — the largest state development bank (as shown in Figure 9), operates in Minas Gerais, the third Brazilian state economy in terms of GDP (9.2 per cent of the total country GDP). At the other extreme, the smallest state financial institution, Roraima Development Agency (AFERR), operates in a state with GDPs is equivalent to 0.2 per cent of the national GDP. Some exceptions to this rule are the states of São Paulo and Rio de Janeiro, whose agencies do not correspond to the size of the economies.

As a last essential feature, the origin of funds is a fundamental issue to increase SDBs business and financial sustainability. According to Salviano Junior (2004) and Araújo et al. (2013), the majority of SDBs in Brazil is dependent on official resources, such as government funds, transfers from official institutions and own resources. Examples of government resources are constitutional funds with a focus on regional development, as the Northeast Constitutional Financing Fund (FNE) operated by BNB. Another

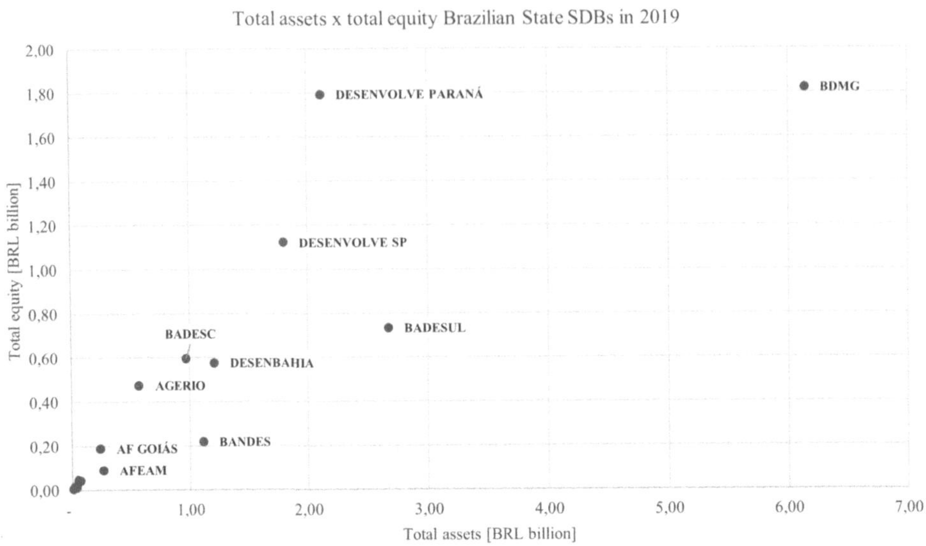

Figure 9. Comparison between total assets and equity of states SDBs in Brazil in 2019. Source: Own elaboration from Central Bank of Brazil database.

source concerns the on-lending transfers from BNDES to SDBs. In fact, as discussed previously, the origin of the Brazilian SNF had in BNDES one of the main sources of funds, since SDBs were created to act in a complementary way to the national bank (Ferraz and Ramos 2018). In addition to transfers from the BNDES, other official sources may come from institutions such as the Financier of Studies and Projects (FINEP), which is the administrator of the National Fund for Scientific and Technological Development (FNDCT), or specific funds such as the Coffee Economy Defense Fund (FUNCAFÉ) and the General Tourism Fund (FUNGETUR).

In the context of the fiscal restrictions faced by Brazilian states, governments funds have been a decreasing source of funding for state banks and development agencies, which have imposed strong incentives for them to make their operations more profitable, seeking a greater leverage in such a way that the results can be reverted to strengthen their financial position enabling a better access to funding in market conditions.

Partnerships with multilateral institutions (MDBs) also play an important role in providing funding for development. It is possible to verify a path initiated by development banks at state and regional level, as BDMG and BRDE. These resources are often directed towards specific investments such as sustainability and financial inclusion, which reinforces the argument of the need to expand and integrate risk management with substantiality standards and methods for measuring and reporting impact in line with the requirements of funding institutions, as will be discussed further in this paper.

4. The Development System in Vietnam: Local Funds on the Spot

Located in East Asia, with China, Laos, Cambodia and Thailand as neighbors, Vietnam has been configuring itself as an emerging economy since its unification in 1974. It is the 14th country in the world in terms of population, with over 90 million inhabitants

(Bulard 2017; IHOLD 2016; IMF 2019) distributed into 58 provinces and five municipalities with provincial status (Can Tho, Ho Chi Minh City, Da Nang, Haiphong and Hanoi).

According to the International Monetary Fund (IMF) Country Report (2019), Vietnam has been experiencing a robust period of sustained development, with an average growth of 7 per cent in the last 10 years. A set of factors is associated with this economic performance: market-overflowing effects of Asian nations' growth, geopolitical circumstances, which led the country to effective trade agreements, and state inductive actions. Although the attraction of foreign industrial plants represented an increase in productivity and technological progress, it has itself posed new development challenges such as income inequality, environmental issues, education gaps and local development (World Bank 2015).

The role of the banking system and development institutions has been increasing together with the country's recent evolution and is also influenced by a historical pivotal economic role played by the Vietnamese Government in the country's economy. Since 1988, the State Bank of Vietnam (SBV) accumulates functions of the country's central bank, financial regulatory agent and guardian of the monetary reserves. Simultaneously, state-owned commercial banks were restructured and had their role enhanced.

The state ownership of some commercial banks came from 1990s banking reform. Following the 1990 Ordinance on Banks, the SBV delegated its banking activities to four newly created state-owned commercial banks (SOCBs), each targeting a different segment of the economy: Vietnam Industrial and Commercial Bank — Vietinbank (industry and commerce); Bank for Agriculture and Rural Development — Agrinbank (agricultural and rural development); Bank for Foreign Trade of Vietnam — Vietcombank (international trade) and Bank for Investment and Development of Vietnam — BIDV(infrastructure).

According to the World Bank (2015), the 2008s crisis led to a major banking reform in the country with a step-by-step approach. One of these phases was the separation of development institutions and commercial banks (Tran, Ong and Weldon 2015; Bulard 2017; IMF 2019). The development banks came from inside the commercial banks, as they used to perform development roles until the reforms. For example, social policies were implemented by the Bank for Agriculture and Rural Development until the creation of the Bank for Social Policies (Agribank 2017).

A third set of development institutions operates at the subnational level — the Local Development Investment Funds — LDIF's. Founded after 2008, in the context of the financial crisis response in the major municipalities, the 18 LDIF's are regulated as non-financial institutions. Its background comes from the need to expand infrastructure and public goods' investments — as sanitation and education, by local credit institutions. According to AFD (2017), the local development fund model was chosen because of the numerous specific development challenges in municipalities, faced with the impacts of international financial crises. The government encouraged the decentralization of infrastructure investments at the provincial level: '[...] as commercial bank financing and bond issuance did not prove to be the appropriate solution for the Provincial People's Committees (PPC) during this period, the Local Development Investment Fund model was considered more appropriate in this context' (AFD 2017).

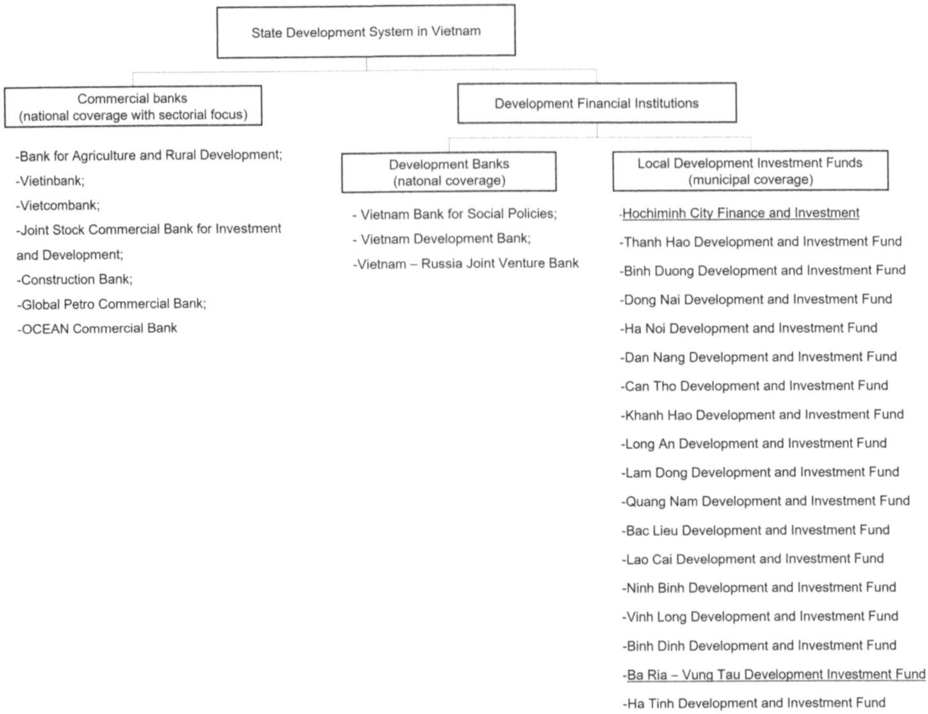

Figure 10. Vietnam development system. Source: Authors elaboration.

In AFD database it is possible to identify different levels of finance development institutions in Vietnam, including at the national and subnational coverage: three national banks — Vietnam Bank for Social Policies (VBSP), Vietnam Development Bank (VDB), Vietnam Russia Joint Venture Bank (VRB); and 18 local financing funds. Therefore, the resulting Vietnam development system combines a set of commercial banks with portfolios dedicated to specific economic sectors, with institutions focused on development, whether national or municipal coverage (Figure 10).

The Vietnamese national development system is relatively recent and is formed by this complex network of development institutions operating in a complementary way. Commercial banks with sectorial focus perform development functions by financing long-term investment while national development banks are physically present throughout the country's territory, with local branches through which they grant credit directly to local firms, fulfilling SDB's typical roles, with a certain degree of specialization in some development functions. Finally, the Local Development Investment Funds are focused on the support of improving local public services associated with a better infrastructure background.

At Vietnam provinces and its largest cities, national development banks and local funds act under complementary way. Because of the bank's dependency on limited treasury budget allocations and Official Development Assistance (ODA), Vietnam government decided to create local funds that were supported by MDB's in the beginning — World Bank and AFD (ESCAP, 2017). Because they were established to improve local investment demands with national and international funding sources, LDIFs are expected to operate as commercial-oriented entities, selecting infrastructure projects that will generate sufficient financial returns (ESCAP, 2017). The model has been expanded to a total of 36 out of 63 provinces and it supportive legal framework has been updated consistently (ESCAP, 2017). According to ESCAP (2017) funding commitments were approximately $144 million in February 2015 and each dollar invested from LDIFs has leveraged $1.73 in investment.

Based on the most populous cities, Hochiminh City Finance and Investment (HFIC) is focused on infrastructure constraints and challenges in social services, environment and other economic sectors. Founded in 2010, it is a key investment instrument, which operates according to City People Committee's planning priorities (CII 2020). With the initial capital of 55 billion dongs and 100 billion dongs expected to be internalized by 2020, HFIC funding comes from municipal bonds issuance, loans, and sponsorship (AFD 2017; CBI 2018; CEO Club of Vietnam 2020; CII 2020).

Like HFIC, Hanoi Investment Fund (HNIF) in 2017 by the Hanoi People's Committee for the purposes of receiving budget capital, mobilizing medium-term and long-term capital from organizations and individuals in the country and abroad. HNIF aims to enhance investments in projects and enterprises to develop Hanoi's infrastructure and improve its socioeconomic indicators. The fund aims to become a relevant capital mobilization channel in the city. With a charter capital by 220 million dollars (nearly, 5 billion dongs) the HADIF has expanded cooperation with local and foreign financial organizations and investors (Kiet 2018).

As the other local investment funds, they work with both credit granting and equity. According to World Bank (2012), the Ho Chi Minh City Investment Fund have been a playing a role model as local fund in terms of internal policy and procedures for investment, infrastructure, social and environmental safeguards, and establishing partnerships with the private sector to increase its participation in financing municipal infrastructure in Ho Chi Minh City (World Bank 2012; CII 2020).

It is also important to consider that, although Local Development Funds are excepted from the regulatory control by Central Bank, they can be completely appropriate to international financing market procedures. The funds have legal status, charter capital and balance sheet. It is a relevant condition to obtain international resources, especially funds for green investments, which have been a relevant funding strategy.

According to SBV Key Statistical Ratios (SBV 2020), in March 2020, the state banks represented more than 42 per cent of the banking assets — 12.4 trillion dong (VND). In equity, the state banks represent 25 per cent (617 trillion VND). Although banks and local funds are constantly working to improve development, they act under different standards about the equity and assets relationship. For the banks, the financial leverage is the rule, since they get direct deposits. For the funds, created as channels to mobilize resources and applying them in other infrastructure funds, the leverage seems less important. Instead, the Vietnamese's local funds operate by channeling MDB's resources, establishing partnerships with private local funds and becoming shareholders of private enterprises (AFD 2017; Kiet 2018; Hà 2019).[2]

[2]It is important to note that this research could not identify a common database for all local Vietnamese funds in terms of their equity and assets, which have prevented us from conducting a longitudinal analysis similar to the one that was done for the Brazilian case.

5. Comparing Subnational Development Models: SDBS as a Result of Country's Economic and Political Context

The number, model and functions of development institutions in each country, whether at national or subnational levels, vary substantially, which makes it difficult to reproduce generalizations and patterns (Além, Madeira, and Martini 2017). As emergent countries, both Brazil and Vietnam share significative development challenges. Bringing it in a nutshell, their architecture responds to the specific national development processes and the development of both financial systems. Several elements may be highlighted to allow a meaningful comparison between the two systems. Firstly, the state configuration. Brazilian SDBs have regional or state coverage, while Vietnamize funds work on municipal level.

A second comparison can be made by the year of establishment of the institutions at the subnational level. While Brazilian institutions followed the movement to create national development banks around the world, Vietnam's institutions were created more recently, mainly after the 2008 crisis. It is also important to note that while in Brazil there was a shrinking movement of these institutions regarding the 1990s liberal reforms, the significant presence of the state in its banking system suggests that the Vietnam's government didn't follow the liberal reforms from the 1990s onwards. In Vietnam case, nevertheless, the banking reform implied establishing Basel regulation rules to commercial banks and the emergency of the new development institutions.

The national development institutions also play different roles in both countries. In Vietnam, the national development banks have branches in several cities acting as first-tier institutions. In contrast, BNDES, in Brazil, acts both as a second-tier institution, offering resources to the SDB's, and as a first-tier institution.

Regarding the relationship with national development system, Wruuck (2015), using the European model, explains that subnational public finance systems can be presented as vertical or horizontal ones. Além, Madeira, and Martini (2017) explain that while some countries have more concentrated national development systems, with the existence of a strong and central role for an institution (normally the NDB) with all other funding institutions playing a secondary role within a vertical relation; in other models, horizontal ones, even if they have a prominent national institution, there are more specialized institutions to serve various segments and sectors. The German system, for example, can be conceptualized as a vertical system of development institutions, where the different levels (national and subnational) are linked. For example, the NDB KfW provides financing to subnational institutions in Germany, and at the same time, German SDBs often play an active role in implementing policies. In the horizontal dimension, on the other hand, there is greater heterogeneity, since, although there is a main development bank at the national (or even multilateral) level, regional institutions (when they exist) would work independently, not necessarily adopting policies for similar economic sectors.

Brazil and Vietnam have different approaches in this sense. Brazil has a hybrid model, which mixes vertical and horizontal aspects, due to the strong presence of BNDES as a funding provider, together with the SDBs autonomy in the state or regional levels. On the other hand, Vietnam has an essentially horizontal model, due to local funds independency.

In Table 1, we try to summarize the comparison between the two systems:

Table 1. Comparison between Brazilian and Vietnamese national development systems.

National development system	Brazil	Vietnam
Type of subnational institutions	Multiple regional banks, Development banks (regional and state banks) and Development state agencies	Local Development Investment Funds (municipal coverage)
Period of establishment	1960 and reviewed after 1996 banking restructuring program	After 2000, especially after 2008 crises
Relationship with national development system	Hybrid (predominantly vertical)	Horizontal
Funding sources	Onlending from BNDES, national funds, subnational governments funds and multilateral banks (all SDBs); national or international bonds market (only subnational public banks)	Multilateral banks; equity stakes of states banks; national and international bonds markets
Under Central Bank regulation/ Basel I or II	All SDBs (including Development Agencies)	Local funds not subjected to Central Bank regulations

Source: Authors elaboration.

This comparison, far from being exhaustive, demonstrates how a country's development system may present different aspects depending on its historical and economic context. However, these different formats do not prevent them from operating towards similar development goals in a pragmatic approach. In the next section, in terms of the recent sustainable finance frontier, the SDBs examples of Brazil and Vietnam demonstrate how such institutions can function as boosters of local impact. In addition to the Brazilian and Vietnamese examples, new subnational development banks in the United States with a clear mandate for green financing also reveals a new path for subnational institutions.

6. The New Sustainable Finance Paradigm and SDBs as the Last Mile Institutions

According to De Luna-Martinez et al. (2018), it will be necessary to mobilize trillions of dollars to achieve the Sustainable Development Goals (SDGs), fulfill the commitments of the Paris Agreement and meet the investment priorities listed in the Addis Ababa Action Agenda (AAAA). At the global level, the financing gap to achieve the SDGs was estimated to be US$ 5–7 trillion, and roughly US$ 2.5–3 trillion per year corresponds to the developing countries gap (UNCTAD 2014). As the existing sources of financing are still insufficient to meet the development aspirations of the world, sustainable finance is part of a new paradigm, whose innovative and more effective instruments are urgent to mobilize capital, mainly for less developed regions and local contexts. The SDGs brings substantial changes in sustainable financing, including a much wider range of public and multilateral actors, with the presence of local institutions, and a greater volume of private financing (Shine and Campillo 2016). It is not only a question of rethinking the volume of financing, but above all, ensuring that the financed projects have the right requirements to minimize negative impacts and enhance additionalities (Riaño and Barchiche 2020).

The AAAA, in its turn, provides the blueprint to finance the goals addressed in the SDGs and considerably expands the diversity of actors involved in the mobilization of domestic and external financial resources. Combining the call made to development banks with the emphasis on local governments (Orliange 2020), SDBs are positioned at the heart of AAAA. Following this direction, development finance could be maximized by strengthening a network of development banks at different levels — multilateral, regional, national and subnational (UNCTAD 2016). According to the United Nations, banks at different levels could perform different functions and, at the same time, explore complementarities in order to benefit from combined regional efforts to act on projects in large countries (such as China and India) and also in small countries (like the Republic of Korea in the 1950s).

The SDBs may bring efficiency and effectiveness to the implementation of development programs as their local expertise directly contribute to a less costly and more agile credit analysis process and to a better identification and selection of projects, broadening the base of bankable ones. Acting in partnerships with larger national and multilateral institutions, SDB's helps them to better channel available financial and technical resources to promote local impact by adapting sophisticated governance and operational requirements to practical and pragmatic approaches that are suited to their local environment, acting as last mile institutions. That combination of strong partnerships, availability of resources and local expertise can create a much more prosperous space for closing the financial gap in terms of SDG implementation, as advocated by the AAAA.

Following the Brazilian and Vietnamese SDBs system discussed in this paper, it is possible to show with concrete examples of how the connection between SDBs and the sustainable financing agenda happens in practice. Some banks as the Development Bank of Minas Gerais (BDMG) in Brazil and Hochiminh City Finance and Investment (HFIC) in Vietnam, are incorporating 2030 Agenda premises into financial products, lending process and funding.

Regarding the sustainability path in Brazil, BDMG was the first subnational institution to raise funds in the international market with a focus on sustainable operations in 2013. BDMG is an institution with more than 58 years old (founded in 1962) operating in the 2nd largest Brazilian state in population and the country's third largest economy. As a financial and knowledge platform, the Bank provides not only credit lines, but it is engaged into project preparation and technical assistance. It is also the main credit supplier of Minas Gerais' pool of 853 municipalities.

The encouragement of sustainable development and the concern for future generations have increasingly been incorporated into BDMG's way of acting and internal policies over the years (BDMG 2020a). In relation to the recent strategy of linking its portfolio to the goals of 2030 Agenda, a Framework was developed aiming to finance investments that have clear and significant socioenvironmental impacts and that contribute to the SDGs. The Sustainability Bonds Framework, also called SDG Framework, certifies that part of the BDMG portfolio is in accordance with the Sustainability Bond Guidelines of 2018, which combines principles for green and social financing (BDMG 2020b). In order to grant independence from the project eligibility process and ensure that the labeling process has positive additionalities, the SDG Framework was also subject to a Second Party Opinion (SPO), an external evaluation process by a specialized international company with a set of independent auditors.

Analyzing the connection of the SDGs with BDMG financed portfolio, it is possible to verify the relationship with 13 of the 17 SDG goals and 28 of the 169 targets and some concrete finance experiences related to the SDGs, both in social and green investments.

Related to green investments, to substantially increase the share of renewable energies in the global energy matrix, BDMG is acting to foster SDG 7 (clean and affordable energy) and SDG 13 (action against global climate change). In 2019, in order to obtain resources to finance clean energy generation and energy efficiency projects, BDMG signed a contract with the European Investment Bank (EIB) that resulted in the raising of EUR 100 million. The credit line was intended to finance renewable energy generation projects — solar photovoltaic energy, small-scale hydroelectric energy and bioenergy plants — and energy efficiency, such as public lighting and efficiency in buildings and industries. Since the end of 2019, almost EUR 20 million has been invested in photovoltaic plant projects in low development regions in Minas Gerais.

According to the Social Bons Principles, social categories aim directly to address or mitigate specific social issues and/or achieve positive social results, often for a well defined vulnerable population (ICMA 2020). BDMG examples of social investments consist in projects for municipalities accessible basic infrastructure (SDG 11), access to basic essential services — such as health (SDG 3) and education (SDG 4), job creation and programs designed to prevent and alleviate unemployment due to socioeconomic crises — including COVID-19 pandemic (SDG 8), gender financial inclusion (SDG 5), among others.

Vietnam banking deployment system can be seen as a carbon dependent in progress to a more sustainable path (CBI 2018). According to the ASEAN Green Finance State of the Market (CBI 2018), out of 47 public sector entitles green bonds potential issuers, six are Vietnamese. For the 2011–2020 period, the government approved the Vietnam Green Growth Strategy. On that regard, several institutions of the Vietnamese development system were considerate potential issuers: Vietnam Development Bank (VDB), Vietnam Bank for Social Policies (VBSP) and VietinBank. At the local level, some institutions have already issued bonds: Ho Chi Minh City (US$ 23 MM, 2016) and Ba Ria Vung Tau Province (US$ 4 MM, 2016). These green bonds financed projects of water management and climate adaptation (CBI 2018).

In order to promote the 2030 Agenda, Hochiminh City Finance and Investment (HFIC), in a similar path to the Brazilian SDB BDMG, have certified its credit portfolio to be a climate bond issuer. In 2016, when the Vietnam Ministry of Finance approved a pilot project for sub-sovereign green bonds issue, the municipal People's Committee decided going to the market. Ho Chi Minh City Finance and Investment State Owned Company issued a VND 523.5 bn (USD23 m) 15-year green bond with proceeds allocated to 11 projects related to the water, adaptation and infrastructure sectors (CBI 2018).

In this sense, the partnership between multilateral banks and subnational institutions to create resource lines for sustainable purposes, such as Brazilian and Vietnamize examples mentioned above, is one of the possibilities for new international cooperation agreements cited in AAAA. While multilateral organizations have global reach, access to financial resources and technical expertise for projects of this nature, subnational banks have the capacity to direct resources to the regional or local context in developing countries, implementing the global agenda on the ground.

In addition to the banks mentioned here, other countries are creating SDBs at regional or state level with a specific focus on sustainability. According to Coalition for Green Capital (CGC 2017), several local specialized institutions were created in United States aiming work with green finance. The examples include the newly created development banks at the municipal or state level as the Connecticut Green Bank (founded in 2011), Hawaii Green Infrastructure Authority and NY Green Bank (both created in 2014) and Montgomery County Green Bank (2015). Other cases, such as the California Infrastructure and Economic Development Bank (IBank), created in the 1990s, include programs for energy and environmental needs, as programs for loans to municipalities, universities, schools and hospitals.

7. Conclusions

The paper highlighted the potential of Subnational Development Banks (SDBs) as financial and knowledge platforms connecting global institutions and funds to local firms' and governments' needs. By doing so, we expect to demonstrate that these institutions may have a meaningful contribution in the global effort to make finance work for the necessary transition to a more sustainable development pattern and therefore should be empowered and better integrated to the global development community.

The examples of the Vietnamese and the Brazilian development systems illustrate several possibilities to ensure more resource mobilization to implement the 2030 Agenda. Although they are very different experiences, both provide an effective set of financial solutions to generate local impact. The two countries have also recently enforced their development systems by fostering sustainable frameworks and expanding the number of subnational entities. And they have been successful in terms of obtaining international resources to support the transition to a greener and more inclusive economy.

As mentioned before, this paper is part of a research agenda on how development institutions may better align themselves in the global effort to unleash the potential of more sustainable investments and economic practices.

We hope that it raises the interest of other scholars to keep investigating how subnational development banks may contribute to this major challenge. As future research questions, we believe that there is still a considerable amount of work to be performed in terms of better estimating the social, economic and environmental impacts of SDB's operations and, in this sense, have a clearer perspective regarding their level of additionality. We also consider very important the building of reliable, comparable and public available databases on SDB's around the world, which would allow more comprehensive and robust analysis of this group of institutions.

Disclosure Statement

No potential conflict of interest was reported by the author(s).

Funding

The author(s) reported there is no funding associated with the work featured in this article.

ORCID

Sergio Gusmão Suchodolski http://orcid.org/0000-0001-8515-8680
Adauto Modesto Junior http://orcid.org/0000-0002-0565-7648
Cinthia Helena de Oliveira Bechelaine http://orcid.org/0000-0002-5036-9012
Leila Maria Bedeschi Costa http://orcid.org/0000-0002-0709-9846

References

AFD (Agence Française de Developpement). 2017. 'Evaluation Summary of Ho Chi Minh City Finance and Investment State-Owned Company Credit Line (HFIC).' Accessed August 2020. https://www.afd.fr/en/ressources/evaluation-summary-ho-chi-minh-city-finance-and-investment-state-owned-company-credit-line-hfic.

Agribank (Vietnam Bank for Agriculture and Rural Development). 2017. 'Annual Report.' Accessed August 2020. https://www.agribank.com.vn/en/ve-agribank.

Além, A. C., R. F. Madeira, and R. A. Martini. 2017. 'Sistemas nacionais de fomento: experiências comparadas.' *Revista do BNDES* 47: 251–256.

Araújo, V. L. D., M. J. D. S. Pires, M. F. D. Silva, and D. A. D. Castro. 2013. 'O sistema brasileiro de instituições financeiras subnacionais para o desenvolvimento: um panorama.' *Nova Economia* 23 (3): 579–618.

BDMG (Banco de Desenvolvimento de Minas Gerais). 2020a. '2019 Sustainability Report.' Accessed August 2020. https://www.bdmg.mg.gov.br/report/.

BDMG (Banco de Desenvolvimento de Minas Gerais). 2020b. 'Framework de títulos sustentáveis 2020.' Accessed August 2020. https://www.bdmg.mg.gov.br/sustainable-bonds/.

Brei, M., and A. Schclarek. 2013. 'Public Bank Lending in Times of Crisis.' *Journal of Financial Stability* 9 (4): 820–830.

Brei, M., and A. Schclarek. 2018. 'The Countercyclical Behavior of National Development Banks in Latin America and the Caribbean.' In *The Future of National Development Banks*, edited by S. Griffith-Jones and J. A. Ocampo. Oxford: Oxford University Press.

Bruck, N. 2001. 'Development Banking Concepts and Theory.' In *ADFIAP-IDF. Principles and Practices of Development Banking Manila*, Vol. 1. Philippines: ADFIAP-IDF.

Bulard, M. 2017. 'Vietnã, o polo industrial da vez.' *Le Monde Diplomatique Brasil*, ed. 115. Accessed August 2020. https://diplomatique.org.br/vietna-o-polo-industrial-da-vez.

Cavalcante, L. R. 2007. 'Seis personagens à procura de um autor: a inserção das agências de fomento e dos bancos de desenvolvimento no Sistema Financeiro no Brasil.' *Revista Desenbahia.* Accessed June 2020. http://www.desenbahia.ba.gov.br/publitao/arquivos/arquivos/1314c568f7cb488e8427af9b64a7dedb.pdf.

CBI (Climate Bonds Initiative). 2018. 'ASEAN Green Finance — State of the Market.' Accessed August 2020. https://www.climatebonds.net/files/files/ASEAN_GreenFin_SotM_CBI_012019.pdf.

CEO Club of Vietnam. 2020. 'Member Directory — HFIC.' Accessed August 2020. http://ceoclubvietnam.com/members/ho-chi-minh-city-finance-and-investment-state-owned/.

CGC (Coalition for Green Capital). 2017. 'Green Banks 101 & Nevada Green Bank Study Results.' One-Day Work-Shop — July 27. Accessed August 2020. https://www.nrel.gov/state-local-tribal/basics-green-banks.html.

CII (Ho Chi Minh City Infrastructure Investment Joint Stock Company). 2020. 'Founding Shareholders: HFIC.' Accessed August 2020. http:/cii.com.vn/en/introduction/founding-shareholders.

Cunha, A. M., D. M. Prates, and C. E. Carvalho. 2016. 'O Sistema Nacional de Fomento: Formato Atual e Propostas de Reforma.' *Análise Econômica* 34 (65): 269–300.

De Luna-Martínez, J., and C. L. Vicente. 2012. 'Global Survey of Development Banks.' The World Bank. Accessed June 2020. https://papers.ssrn.com/sol3/papers.cfm?abstract_id=2006223.

De Luna-Martinez, J., C. L. Vicente, A. B. Arshad, R. Tatucu, and J. Song. 2018. *2017 Survey of National Development Banks* (English). Washington, DC: World Bank Group. Accessed June

2020. http://documents.worldbank.org/curated/en/977821525438071799/2017-Survey-of-National-development-banks.

Diamond, W. 1957. *Development Banks*. Washington: Johns Hopkins Press.

ESCAP (Economic and Social Commission for Asia and the Pasific). 2017. 'Infrastructure Financing Strategies for Sustainable Development in Viet Nam'. National Study/Paper version 15 September 2017. Accessed August 2020. https://www.unescap.org/sites/default/files/20170915%20National%20Study%20-%20Infrastructure%20Financing%20-%20Viet%20%20Nam.pdf.

Ferraz, J. C., and L. Ramos. 2018. 'Inclusão financeira para a inserção produtiva de empresas de menor porte na América Latina: Inovações, determinantes e práticas de instituições financeiras do desenvolvimento.' Informe regional, CEPAL. Accessed August 2020. https://www.cepal.org/sites/default/files/document/files/documen-to_regional_version_en_edicion.pdf.

Ferroni, M. 2004. 'Regional Public Goods: The Comparative Edge of Regional Development Banks.' Paper Prepared for a Conference on Financing for Development: Regional Challenges and the Regional Development Banks at the Institute for International Economics. Accessed June 2020. https://www.piie.com/publications/papers/ferroni0202.pdf.

Gama Neto, R. B. 2011. 'Plano Real, Privatização dos Bancos Estaduais e Reeleição.' *Revista Brasileira de Ciências Sociais* 26 (77): 129–150.

Griffith-Jones, S., J. A. Ocampo, F. Rezende, A. Schclarek, and M. Brei. 2018. 'The Future of National Development Banks: Introduction.' In *The Future of National Development Banks*, edited by S. Griffith-Jones and J. A. Ocampo. Oxford: Oxford University Press.

Hakenes, H., and I. Schnabel. 2010. 'The Threat of Capital Drain: A Rationale for Regional Public Banks?' *Journal of Institutional and Theoretical Economics* 166 (4): 662–689.

Hà, H. T. 2019. 'Hanoi Development Fund Looks to More Efficient Operation.' *Vietnam Plus*. Accessed August 2020. https://en.vietnamplus.vn/hanoi-development-fund-looks-to-more-efficient-operation/152587.vnp.

Horn, C. H., and F. Feil. 2019. 'Instituições financeiras de desenvolvimento regional e os desafios do Sistema Nacional de Fomento.' *Economia e Sociedade* 28 (1): 227–254.

ICMA. 2020. 'Social Bond Principles.' Accessed August 2020. https://www.icmagroup.org/green-social-and-sustainability-bonds/social-bond-principles-sbp/.

IHOLD Brasil. 2016. 'Vietnã: o novo milagre econômico?' Accessed August 2020. https://pt-br.ihodl.com/economics/2016-09-03/vietna-o-novo-milagre-economico/.

IMF (International Monetary Fund). 2019. 'Annex IV.' IFM Country Report No. 19/235. Vietnam. Accessed August 2020. www.imf.org/en/countries/vnm.

Kiet, A. 2018. 'Hanoi Sets Up New US$ 220-Billion Development Investment Fund.' *Hanoi Times/Investment*. Accessed August 2020. http://hanoitimes.vn/hanoi-sets-up-new-us220-billion-development-investment-fund-5679.html.

La Porta, R., F. Lopez-De-Silanes, and A. Shleifer. 2002. 'Government Ownership of Banks.' *The Journal of Finance* 57 (1): 265–301.

Levy-Yeyati, E., A. Micco, and U. Panizza. 2004. 'Should the Government Be in the Banking Business? The Role of State-Owned and Development Banks.' IDB Working Paper. Accessed June 2020. https://publications.iadb.org/en/publication/should-government-be-banking-business-role-state-owned-and-development-banks.

Mazzucato, M., and C. Penna. 2016. 'Beyond Market Failures: The Market Creating and Shaping Roles of State Investment Banks.' *Journal of Economic Policy Reform* 19 (4): 305–326.

Orliange, P. A. 2020. 'From Poverty Reduction to Global Challenges, a New Horizon for International Development Cooperation?' *Revista Brasileira de Política Internacional* 63 (2): 1–26.

Riaño, M. A., and D. Barchiche. 2020. 'Financing the 2030 Agenda for Sustainable Development: Prerequisites, and Opportunities for the Post-Covid-19 Crisis.' IDDRI Issue Brief. Accessed August 2020. https://www.iddri.org/sites/default/files/PDF/Publications/Catalogue%20Iddri/D%C3%A9cryptage/202005-IB0320-2030%20agenda_0.pdf.

Salviano Junior, C. 2004. 'Bancos estaduais: dos problemas crônicos ao PROES.' Banco Central do Brasil. Accessed June 2020. https://www.bcb.gov.br/htms/public/BancosEstaduais/livro_bancos_estaduais.pdf.

SBV (State Bank of Vietnam). 2020. 'Data Ratios 2020.' Accessed August 2020. https://www.sbv.gov.vn/webcenter/portal/en/home/sbv/news.

Shelepov, A. 2017. 'New and Traditional Multilateral Development Banks: Current and Potential Cooperation.' *International Organisations Research Journal* 12 (1): 127–147.

Shine, T., and G. Campillo. 2016. 'The Role of Development Finance in Climate Action Post-2015.' OECD Development Co-Operation Working Papers, n. 31. Paris: OECD Publishing.

Stiglitz, J. 1994. *The Role of the State in Financial Markets*. Washington, DC: The World Bank.

Studart, R., and K. P. Gallagher. 2016. 'Infrastructure for Sustainable Development: The Role of National Development Banks.' GEGI Policy Brief 007.

Torres, E., and R. Zeidan. 2016. 'The Life-Cycle of National Development Banks: The Experience of Brazil's BNDES.' *The Quarterly Review of Economics and Finance* 62: 97–104.

Tran, B., B. Ong, and S. Weldon. 2015. 'Vietnam Banking Industry Report', *Duxton Asset Managenment*.

UN-DESA (United Nations Department of Economic and Social Affairs). 2005. *Re-Thinking the Role of National Development Banks*. New York: UN-DESA.

UNCTAD (United Nations Conference on Trade and Development). 2014. 'World Investment Report 2014: Investing in the SDGs: An Action Plan.' United Nations publication.

UNCTAD (United Nations Conference on Trade and Development). 2016. 'The Role of Development Banks.' In: Promoting Growth and Sustainable Development in the South. United Nations Publication (UNCTAD/GDS/ECIDC/2016/1).

World Bank. 2012. 'ICR Review Independent Evaluation Group for Ho Chi Minh City Investment Fund for Urban Development Project (Disclosure Authorized).' Accessed August 2020. https://projects.worldbank.org/en/projects-operations/project-detail/P104848.

World Bank. 2015. 'Taking Stock: An Update on Vietnam's Recent Economic Developments (Public Disclosure Authorized). Accessed August 2020. www.worlbank.org.vn.

Wruuck, P. 2015. 'Promoting Investment and Growth: The Role of Development Banks in Europe.' Deutsche Bank Research.

Xu, J., X. Ren, and X. Wu. 2019. 'Mapping Development Finance Institutions Worldwide: Definitions, Rationales and Varieties.' New Structural Economics Development Financing Report.

Part II

Public Banks

Understanding Full Investment and the Potential Role of Public Banks

Wesley C. Marshall and Louis-Philippe Rochon

ABSTRACT
In this paper, we argue that Keynes correctly diagnosed the principles of 'sound finance' as limiting human progress, but did not map out a viable alternate solution of 'full investment', and seems to even warn against it. E.F. Schumacher critiqued Keynes's position that until the problem of production is solved, only following 'the money motive' could lead humanity out of the tunnel of economic need. Now a half century since Schumacher's critiques, the production problem can be seen in a new light, and the debate surrounding the money motive can be reevaluated with greater context. We build upon the debate and the lessons of recent history, and within the context of other thinkers such as Veblen and Polanyi, to argue that the money motive does not need to be abandoned, but rather placed within a reformed institutional and monetary framework. We argue that full investment can only be properly addressed by shifting the overall objective of economic activity from production to human advancement. We conclude the paper by offering several considerations on why public banks are ideal institutions to shepherd a transformation of mentality into the creation of new markets and activities dedicated to human advancement.

Introduction

In a seldom-mentioned quote from the *General Theory*, Keynes asserts 'that a state of full investment in the strict sense has never yet occurred, even momentarily' (Keynes 1936, p. 324). Since it is the only time that Keynes uses the phrase in the General Theory, and indeed in his *oeuvre*, it comes as little surprise that full investment is not referred to more often in Keynesian literature. In contrast, the related concept of full employment is widely discussed by Keynes and his followers, and often promoted as the principal goal of public policy.

In this paper, we take a closer look at the concept of full investment, its meaning and its implications. This is not a straightforward task: as Keynes states, it has never happened in practice, and here we argue that it has not been mapped out in theory, either. We argue that in terms of theory, Keynes's internal debate over 'the money motive,' taken together with Schumacher's critique of Keynes's ultimate position, gets us most of the way there. Building upon the work of other authors, we construct the rest of the argument.

Both Keynes and Schumacher emphasize the importance of ideas, and how perceptions of how societies function have often limited — and greatly limited — our capacity for human advancement. We argue that in order to understand full investment, we must first abandon several quiet assumptions of conventional thinking. One is that money and credit are products of capitalism, a myth perpetrated over time and space, omitting widely varying monetary experiences of different economies — capitalist and otherwise — throughout history. Another is that work is by nature to be done for individual gain. In order to more fully arrive at a theory of full investment, both credit, money, and work must be considered not in a new way, but rather in ways that have occurred throughout history, but that have been excluded from conventional thinking.

As one of the great critics of capitalism, in 1931, Keynes described the 'money motive' as 'the love of money as a possession - as distinguished from the love of money as a means to the enjoyments and realities of life,' as 'a somewhat disgusting morbidity, one of those semi-criminal, semi-pathological propensities which one hands over with a shudder to the specialists in mental disease' (Keynes 1931, p. 369). However, Keynes arrived at the conclusion that it was nonetheless necessary for another hundred years to pretend that 'foul is fair' (Keynes 1931, p. 372), until humanity emerged from the 'tunnel of economic necessity into daylight' (Keynes 1931, p. 372), and could only then focus on underlying moral problems. More than forty years after taking this position, Schumacher offered perhaps the greatest critique of Keynes in *Small is Beautiful* (1973). However, now only one year away from the half century mark of its publication, and roughly a decade shy of Keynes's hundred years of pretending that 'fair is foul,' we have the great advantage of history and its many lessons, and in this article, we attempt to build on the debate of both thinkers and to resolve the issue of full investment in theory, in order to later offer our thoughts as to the best institutional routes to bring it to reality.

As arriving at a working definition of full investment first requires situating the term in history and theoretical debate, the structure of this paper follows an accumulative progression of ideas. In the first part of this article, we analyze why Keynes could never fully assimilate the concept of full investment. We argue that it was partly due to the fact that Keynes could not reconcile the money motive with a good and decent life. It is only after the theoretical debate with Schumacher, and with an appreciation of the economy from a greater degree of abstraction, that we can offer a useful understanding of full investment. Once this is established, we can move on to considerations of the institutional transformations that would be necessary to reach full investment. We examine how public banking can connect willing workers with abundant capital to change prices and work towards attending to the most urgent needs of humanity. We round out the discussion by arguing that the concept of full investment can only be resuscitated and applied to today's reality under a new mandate from the monetary institutions of the state, and that public banking is one of the more under-appreciated and valuable tools that we have for this transformative task.

Keynes, Schumacher, and the Problem of Production

Ernst Friedrich (E.F.) Schumacher was a *protégé* of Keynes, and the two enjoyed a close relationship, both personal and intellectual. Schumacher's profound respect for Keynes and shared humanist mission make his critiques of Keynes all the more relevant. As we argue, this debate fundamentally revolves around the concept of telos:[1] the consideration of what are the end goals of our social and economic systems. Throughout this article, we confront the telos of production with the telos of human needs and advancement.

We begin with Keynes in this long quote:

> There is one more explanation, I think, of the re-orientation of our minds. The nineteenth century carried to extravagant lengths the criterion of what one can call for short 'the financial results,' as a test of the advisability of any course of action sponsored by private or by collective action. The whole conduct of life was made into a sort of parody of an accountant's nightmare. Instead of using their vastly increased material and technical resources to build a wonder city, the men of the nineteenth century built slums; and they thought it right and advisable to build slums because slums, on the test of private enterprise, 'paid,' whereas the wonder city would, they thought, have been an act of foolish extravagance, which would, in the imbecile idiom of the financial fashion, have 'mortgaged the future' — though how the construction today of great and glorious works can impoverish the future, no man can see until his mind is beset by false analogies from an irrelevant accountancy. Even today I spend my time–half vainly, but also, I must admit, half successfully–in trying to persuade my countrymen that the nation as a whole will assuredly be richer if unemployed men and machines are used to build much needed houses than if they are supported in idleness. For the minds of this generation are still so beclouded by bogus calculations that they distrust conclusions which should be obvious, out of a reliance on a system of financial accounting which casts doubt on whether such an operation will 'pay.' We have to remain poor because it does not 'pay' to be rich. We have to live in hovels, not because we cannot build palaces but because we cannot 'afford' them. (Keynes 1933, p. 363)

Keynes speaks of a reorientation of our minds, critiquing the logic that leads to slums instead of wonder cities, and clearly stating that the slums are not a result of a lack of 'material and technical resources.' Yet while Keynes speaks of wonder cities and other manifestations of human advancement, he left no real road map of how to get there, and particularly finance's role in that effort. He mentions full investment, our topic here, and the 'socialization of finance' (Seccareccia 1995, p. 48), but rarely goes further than a mention. In other words, the diagnosis of the mental limitations placed on humanity by the precepts of sound finance is not accompanied by a solution to the problem.

Schumacher offers his solution to what Keynes diagnoses as the problem, from a seemingly unlikely perspective — that of Buddhist (then) Burma. However, it is quite apt. During the last century, debate regarding different ways to organize an economy tends to center along the socialist — capitalist spectrum, and certainly with good reason, as that has been the terrain of global competition for the last century or so. Yet both systems are built around production. Who controls the surpluses created by production, and the forms and goals of production itself, are planned, implemented, and justified in

[1]In his very insightful 2018 book, Hudson speaks often of the telos of society.

different ways. However, the overall goal of producing more remains the same. The mirror image of socialism-capitalism on the plane of production is humorously captured as only Galbraith could:[2] 'in capitalism, man exploits man. In socialism, it's just the opposite.'

As we argue, the solution to Keynes's diagnosis lies in abandoning, at least partially, the mental shackles of the telos of production, and therefore it is apt that the solution was found in an economic system outside of the telos of production. It is also apt that it was only in a very different society that Schumacher found what was able to scratch what had been itching Keynes for so long. Fittingly, it was a problem of ideas and perceptions. Schumacher observed how in Burmese society, the goal was to attend to human needs rather than those of money. It was the opposite of the western materialist mentality: the eastern spiritual mentality. Importantly for our arguments, Buddhist Burma operated under the telos of human need. Much like the systems of socialism and capitalism (as well as today's global financialization) operate under the production telos, the telos of human need can accommodate other regimes of accumulation, including those that are dominated by religion.

Under the production telos, the goal of the capitalist system is to produce more, and the goal of the individual is to earn more. This materialist mindset is internalized by its constituent actors to the point that the 'whole conduct of life' is geared towards making more money; likewise, a person's social worth is determined by money. Under the different telos and mindset of first attending to human problems and solutions, the whole conduct of life is more embedded in the society in which people live and on the planet that sustains them, and individual success is more measured by standing and respect in society.

To look for alternatives to the production telos, one must look either to the future, or to other societies, living or long defunct. In Keynes's monetary research, and in Schumacher's life, they both turned to anthropology. Following in Polanyi's footsteps in his analysis of the different types of money and debt throughout history, Graeber (2011) offers a convincing account of how the social mindsets of materialism and spiritualism have alternated social dominion in great (social) geographical waves in Eurasia, and how money and debt changed with them. Importantly, and counter to the conventional assumption that these are products of capitalism, Graeber emphasizes how debt and money never disappear, but just transform.

The complacency and defeatism of today's conventional thinking acts a great social nocebo. Graeber's wider panorama is important to our argument, not because we are advocating a religious worldview, but rather because we are arguing that our current economic system is not the only possibility, and to illustrate how this mindset only limits human potential. This limitation becomes alarming when we consider that we have maintained our mentalities aligned with the production telos long after it could offer humanity anything of real value, and continuing down the same path can only lead to destruction. In order to reach humanity's potential, we will need to employ credit and money under a different, and hopefully a historically new mentality. This is certainly a tall task, but there is room for optimism, particularly regarding the first necessary step: a fuller understanding of money.

---

[2]Perhaps. The quip is only attributed to him.

As we begin to map out how we could transition from a telos of production to one of human needs and arrive at full investment, and to imagine the changes in our monetary institutions that would be necessary along this path, it is helpful to start on more common ground. Lerner (1943) ends his essay with the consideration that functional finance is applicable to both capitalism and socialism. If we can define functional finance as what finances full employment at full capacity utilization, then functional finance is ultimately at the service of full employment. It likewise loses its functionality when it is not. Under the production telos, adding more money to a system makes complete sense until all who want to be employed are gainfully employed. At full capacity, adding money to the system loses its objective, as the goal has already been met. Likewise, if we have a market whose labor share is shrinking — like is the case today — then adding more money to the system is ever less functional for workers. Both cases illustrate how functional finance can reach its limits on the plane of production. It is therefore not a matter of adding more money and then it becomes full investment.

We argue that full investment can only be understood under the telos of human need and advancement, and would be a step beyond full employment: the full realization of human potential. Its success would not be manifested by everybody living in a mansion, but by everybody living well and wisely. This is without a doubt more abstract than functional finance and full employment, yet understanding humanity is more complex than understanding markets. We emphasize that the change of telos needed to understand full investment is much easier for us to identify than it was for Keynes, and this is purely a function of time: in the last century history has advanced and so has human knowledge.

Throughout his *oeuvre* Keynes was masterful in describing and deriding the constrictions of sound finance, both in its morality and its implications for public policy, but never described the possibilities of its opposite — full finance. In terms of logic, if sound finance leads to unemployment and slums, then full investment would lead to great wonder cities. Yet even the first steps down that logical path lead Keynes to the moral problem also alluded to in the same quote: should we all live in 'palaces'? Certainly the earth could not withstand every household living in a palace. Schumacher quotes Gandhi several times in *Small is Beautiful*, always to great effect: 'there is enough for every man's need, but not enough for every man's greed' (Schumacher 1973, p. 34). And there is also the moral problem: certainly some have more of a claim to a castle than others. How to fully unleash the capacity of money and production in a materially sustainable and socially agreeable way appears to have placed Keynes in such a great dilemma that he advised to not even try it:

> For at least another hundred years we must pretend to ourselves and to every one that fair is foul and foul is fair; for foul is useful and fair is not. Avarice and usury and precaution must be our gods for a little longer still. For only they can lead us out of the tunnel of economic necessity into daylight. (Keynes 1931, p. 37)

Keynes's ultimate decision that the money motive, as repugnant as it was, must continue to guide society, was the core of Schumacher's critique:

> that avarice, usury and precaution (i.e., economic security) should be our gods was merely a bright idea for Keynes; he surely had nobler gods. But ideas are the most powerful things on earth, and it is hardly an exaggeration to say that by now the gods he recommended have been enthroned. (Schumacher 1973, p. 123)

There are two fundamental factors in Keynes's internal debate and in Schumacher's rebuke of his conclusion that can be considered separately, but ultimately go hand in hand: morals and the historical context in which those morals apply. Schumacher states that Keynes's moral stance was 'merely a bright idea.' Yet in this particular quote, Schumacher is surely giving short shrift to Keynes's argument, which is very explicit and clear in recognizing that questionable morals were necessary only as long as they were needed to lead society out of 'the tunnel of economic necessity.' As long as it requires the work of most to feed, shelter, and clothe all, one's moral responsibility to others is to be sure that all have enough to subsist. But once this changes, so do moral responsibilities: 'the critical difference will be realized when this condition has become so general that the nature of one's duty to one's neighbor is changed. For it will remain reasonable to be economically purposive for others after it has ceased to be reasonable for oneself' (Keynes 1931, p. 372).

Keynes was peeking forward to when increased production could no longer be morally justified. As long as we are immersed in the tunnel of economic need, the telos of human needs and the telos of production intersect. But once out of the tunnel, we can no longer work for both simultaneously. And as the two planes pull apart, they reveal previous contradictions that were partially recognized by both Keynes and Schumacher, and which are ever more evident today.

Schumacher's critique is much in line with Keynes's thinking, and he speaks of 'the problem of production' in a similar form[3] to our treatment of the telos of production. But rather than treating the production telos as a phase to be overcome like Keynes did, Schumacher questioned the very nature of the production problem: are we really attending to our needs, or only to the ceaseless 'cultivation and expansion of needs' (Schumacher 1973, p. 34). With a half century advantage of history over Schumacher, we can also affirm the ascendancy 'of the gods he recommended,' with more emphasis on that which Veblenian and later Galbraithian thinking always emphasized: the intentional confusion of private interests with the public interest. The very construction of the tenets that guide the production telos are certainly not natural or divine, but rather a human construction, with private interests behind them. Indeed, it could be argued that even on a subsistence level, we never need to produce so much more. The people in Burma certainly appeared to live in a harmonious society to Schumacher. But whether that is a prosperous society depends on how we define the concept.

Schumacher was unsparing in his criticism of Keynes:

> the assertion that 'foul is useful and fair is not' is the antithesis of wisdom. The hope that the pursuit of goodness and virtue can be postponed until we have attained universal prosperity and that by the single minded pursuit of wealth, without bothering our heads about spiritual and moral questions, we could establish peace on earth, is an unrealistic, unscientific, and irrational hope. (Schumacher 1973, p. 33)

Whether the moral problem must be solved before the money problem, or whether solving the money problem can lead to solving the human problem, is now essentially a moot debate, as history has now well established which went first and what were the consequences. As Keynes's protégée, we do not doubt Schumacher's sincerity in

---

[3] Albeit with some differences that we will not include here.

stating that 'Keynes had nobler gods.' Perhaps Keynes simply got his time frame wrong. Perhaps instead of a century, he should have said half a century, shortly after Schumacher's rebuttal would have come out. Perhaps it was in the 1970s that the world needed to make this conscious leap between telos, but the gods of avarice, paraphrasing Schumacher, took humanity a different route.

The Battle of Ideas: The Keynesian Revolution and Counterrevolution

With the benefit of nine decades of hindsight, we can now point to a different phrase in *Economic Possibilities for our Grandchildren*:

> The pace at which we can reach our destination of economic bliss will be governed by four things – our power to control population, our determination to avoid wars and civil dissensions, our willingness to entrust to science the direction of those matters which are properly the concern of science, and the rate of accumulation as fixed by the margin between our production and our consumption; of which the last will easily look after itself, given the first three. (Keynes 1931, p. 372)

From today's vantage point, it would at first glance appear that Keynes's great powers of prediction were errant in this case, as our path to 'economic bliss' has been systematically and ever more derailed over the last half-century, but Keynes neither mentions finance nor the possibility that the decisions of the financial elite that he so derided in his time could collapse the system as they did then. The omission invites a closer look.

For Keynes, 'the rate of accumulation [...],' is the end result of peace, population control, and the limitation of science, and this rate determines the pace at which we can reach 'our[4] destination economic bliss.' But we must emphasize that it is a certain type of accumulation: one reached through production. As countless authors have argued in varyingly similar ways, the process of financialization implies a global regime of accumulation that is ever less 'fixed by the margin between our production and our consumption.' This radical change was not due to population explosions or wars, but rather to the failure of science to limit itself to 'those matters which are properly the concern of science.' Indeed, it was in large part due to a battle of ideas, and also a battle for the spaces where ideas are formed. In both popular opinion, academic recommendation, and public policy decision, the monetarist counter-revolution against Keynesian thought has been thorough and well documented. By never explicitly mentioning finance, but rather the overly expansive science behind it, Keynes arrives at the root of the problem. As today's science once again recommends austerity as if we were in Victorian times, it is ever more clear that without winning the battle of ideas, finance could never prove a real threat to our path toward economic bliss.

Throughout his *oeuvre*, Keynes showed a deep understanding of how banks could claim to be serving the public interest while merely serving their own — perhaps most starkly in *The Economic Consequences of Mr. Churchill* (1925b) — and therefore how bank ideology could encroach upon real science, become 'the whole conduct of life,' and subvert the process of solving the 'problem of production.' In the *Treatise on Money*, Keynes states that 'it is evident that there is no limit to the amount of bank-money which the banks can safely create provided that they move forward in step'

[4]That is, of course, if 'our' can include the common person.

(Keynes 1930, p. 26). While this argument was framed as a theoretical idea, assuming a closed economy with a fully independent banking sector, Keynes certainly had political economy on his mind as well, as on the next page he comments that 'each bank chairman sitting in his parlour may regard himself as the passive instrument of outside forces over which he has no control; yet the "outside forces" may be nothing but himself and his fellow — chairmen' (Keynes 1930, p. 27).

Keynes's ambivalent attitude towards the money motive, providing many grievances and protestations but few concrete answers, is similar to Keynes never fully revealing the contrivances and machinations of money and how banks and governments create it. These could be related to his only partial success in the 'struggle of escape from habitual modes of thought and expression' (Keynes 1936, p. viii). Or it could be related to his statement that 'the *Class* war will find me on the side of the educated *bourgeoisie*' (Keynes 1925a, p. 323; italics in original). But it is also possible that Keynes thought that without knowing who — or perhaps knowing *exactly* who — would wield these incredibly powerful tools, it would be best to leave them in the toolshed, akin to Einstein's regret over his part in inventing the nuclear bomb. But if it hadn't been Einstein, someone else would have discovered the bomb. And despite Keynes's reticence, the financial equivalent of a nuclear bomb — the shadow banking system — was in any case constructed, and detonated, and the world now lives in the financial nuclear winter of austerity.

In the realm of ideas, the Great Financial Crisis (2007–2009) was a very instructive moment, demonstrating the limits of conventional macroeconomics through its abject failure to predict the easily predictable (Stiglitz 2008), and fully exposing the myth of money as being *ex-ante* and *scarce* (Parguez 2006). The sheer volumes of credit created in the private sector followed by those of the subsequent public bail out also revealed that the State, just like the private banks, could create credit–money *ex nihilo* and *ad infinitum* without the country running out of money or having it watered down in the form of inflation.

Yet by the time this *primae facie* evidence of the possibility of limitless credit/money creation by the market and the State, the ideology of what Veblen referred to as 'the vested interest' (Veblen 1919) had far surpassed its limits, ascending to the 'imperial science' (Stigler 1984) that has come to inform the 'advisability of any course of action' of both public institutions and private companies, and to govern 'the whole conduct of life' for society at large. Schumacher is again aligned with Keynes in his appreciation of the power of ideas: 'Every science is beneficial within its proper limits, but becomes evil and destructive as soon as it transgresses them' (Schumacher 1973, p. 49). The battle of ideas continues, and as much as thought must build on the work of the great economists and combine, debate and transform arguments as reality changes, one of today's great ironies is that, when it comes to money, we do not even need any greater understanding of money in order to finance any type of project, regardless of whether it creates financial profit or not.

The Separation of Telos and the Revelation of the Great Ironies of Our Time

Our current historical junction is rife with ironies that result from the ongoing superation of the production problem. We have made it out of the tunnel of necessity, but did not find economic bliss. Now that the world is awash in capital, it seems as though we cannot find anything good to spend it on. And as the urgency of massive and new spending increases, it seems as though nobody understands money and how it can be channeled to meet such needs. The conventional mindset is no longer consistent with reality: money is still considered to be all-powerful, but we continue to observe its impotence.

The gap has arguably never been greater between the real capacity of our human and economic potential, and its realized capacity. These are the results of a system out of balance, which no longer relies on all to support all, and leaves a giant surplus population that is not incorporated into the system other than as subsistence consumers. There is nothing to fulfill the vacant role of meaningful occupation, despite the fact that we arguably have never had a work force so ready and willing to confront the collective challenges facing humanity, which themselves have arguably never been greater. What is missing is a change in mentality and the institutional support to transform the new mentality into new public policy capable of connecting abundant capital with necessary work that can be fulfilling for the individual, and recuperative for nature and society.

Looking forward to a day when the production problem would be solved, Keynes states that 'for the first time since his creation man will be faced with his real, his permanent problem – how to use his freedom from pressing economic cares [...] to live wisely and agreeably and well ... ' (Keynes 1931, p. 367) Indeed, the last half century has witnessed levels of monetary creation that are historically unparalleled, but humanity's problems have only grown. Schumacher states that 'money is considered to be all-powerful; if it could not actually buy non-material values, such as justice, harmony, beauty or even health, it could circumvent the need for them or compensate for their loss' (Schumacher 1973, p. 314).

Our current situation makes it difficult to continue to countenance in good faith any debate that confronts money and morals, as it would appear ever more clearly that the only practical way forward is to ensure that the money motive is aligned with moral principles and that we mobilize state finance to bridge the great disconnects between human potential and human action; abundant capital and the investment projects that are urgent for our survival; and between an ever growing young population, eager and willing to improve society and nature, and the paying job opportunities to do so. Concerns over the negative consequences of the states' financial largess, always exaggerated, are today ever more glaringly incorrect both on the telos of production and humanity. Whereas the precepts of 'sound finance' never let us build that 'wonder city,' the losses from inaction today will be far graver than those missed opportunities. Today's much greater challenges should be spared no 'financial extravagance' and it would be 'supreme foolishness' not to marshall all of our resources for collective survival:

> This is the philosophy of materialism, and it is this philosophy — or metaphysic — which is now being challenged by events. There has never been a time, in any society in any part of the world, without its sages and teachers to challenge materialism and plead for a different order of priorities. The languages have differed, the symbols have varied, yet the message has always been the same: 'seek ye *first* the kingdom of God, and all these things [the material things which you also need] shall be *added* unto you.' They shall be added, we are told, here on earth where we need them, not simply in an after life beyond our imagination. Today, however, this message reaches us not solely from the sages an saints but from the actual

> course of physical events. It speaks to us in the language of terrorism, genocide, breakdown, pollutions, exhaustion. We live, it seems, in a unique period of convergence. It is becoming apparent that there is not only a promise but also a threat in those astonishing words about the kingdom of God — the threat that 'unless you seek first the kingdom, these other things, which you also need, will cease to be available to you. (Schumacher 1973, p. 314)

If we can see our greatest problems today in the realm of ideas, it is only fitting that a change in overall mentality — a change of telos — would be the appropriate solution. We believe that the essence of the telos needs must include human advancement, expressed as 'the truism that man's greatest resource is man, his initiative, intelligence and creativity' (Schumacher 1975, p. 9). Following this truism is another. Schumacher quotes R.H. Tawney: 'if [...] economic ambitions are good servants, they are bad masters' (Schumacher 1973, p. 1). Connecting work and finance under this basic spirit would be the essence of this change in telos. We begin with work and then move on to money and public banking.

Transforming Work Through the Transformation of Prices

Since at least the days of Adam Smith, the motivation of productive work has been envisioned as individuals seeking personal gain, in the process contributing to the market, which offers social provisioning to all. Exactly how seeking individual gain leads to social wellbeing was attributed to God's invisible hand.[5] Graeber identifies a fundamental point of divergence in the perceived meaning of work. In the middle ages of religious domination of finance, Ghazali in 11th century Persia stated that it was the hand of God that controlled prices, and that God creates markets for the benefit of man, and they are therefore not to be interfered with. The great difference is that for Ghazali, the hand of God leads us to help each other through our individual efforts, and both markets and the specialization of work are merely aids in this cause, as we must have some division of labor lest we all have to do everything (Graeber 2011, pp. 279–281). On the other hand, for Smith and the capitalist tradition of thought, specialization is a form of individualistic competition. We therefore either have a God that provides money and markets in order for each of us to look after ourself, or a God that provides money and markets in order for us to look after each other.

Much like money always exists, although changes in form and function depending upon the society and form of accumulation in which it finds itself, so does work. While the criteria of the efficiency of capital has led capitalist systems to embrace different forms of mass production, in the non-capitalist Burma that Schumacher relates, work was led by different ideals and motivations, and offered a much greater sense of harmony with nature and society. Just as the last half century has seen an incredible increase in money, while human problems only worsen, it has also seen ever more goods produced, while ever fewer find meaningful employment. Schumacher again offers a useful quote by Gandhi: 'the poor of the world cannot be helped by mass production, only by production by the masses' (Schumacher 1973, p. 79). However, we must attend to Keynes's 'doubt on whether such an operation will "pay".'

[5] Smith's 'invisible hand' has been attributed myriad meanings over time. In Smith's two major works, it always means the hand of God.

In order to offer decent pay for production by the masses — the majority of the world's population is poor — the efficiency of capital must be abandoned as the principal criteria in determining what type of work pays. However, we emphasize that the efficiency of capital and the money motive must be considered separately. In our proposed change of telos, the first must be replaced, but not the second, as once the criteria of what pays is aligned with what helps society and nature, then paying those who work towards those goals only furthers the collective effort.

It is only at the level of state financial institutions that the power exists to change our economic systems' purpose. Given the growing population and deteriorating situation of earth, there are enormous possibilities for increased investment, work, and production, simply in taking care of each other and the earth. However, these activities are rarely seen as capital efficient. But once it is recognized that 'what pays' is a completely socially determined criteria, and that money and capital are not scarce natural resources that must be socially rationed, but rather social constructions that are by their social nature abundant, then we can arrive at the conclusion that if we want to make it pay, it can pay. This is the essence of making money our servant and not our master. As stated, today this change in mentality is almost not even required, as for practical purposes the money is already sitting there, looking around for something better to do.

To be clear, our proposed change in telos is not contemplated on the spectrum of rich and poor. Likewise, a change of telos would be less of a social revolution and more of a 'mandarin revolution' (Galbraith 1977, p. 197), such as the one that brought the world the 'golden age' of capitalism. It is therefore a call for an institutional revolution, similar to the Keynesian revolution in which the change occurs at the top of the system and fundamentally alters markets and prices. The difference would be that today the goal would not be full employment within the production telos, but rather full investment within the human telos.

In terms of mentality and operation, a transition towards such a telos would demand much more from state institutions than it would from the common person, who within a transformed institutional context, could work towards typical material goals of a house and children and vacations and a comfortable retirement without guilt. As long as the criteria of the efficiency of capital is abandoned and production systems are shifted from mass production toward production by the masses, we can keep the money motive, converting 'economic ambitions' into good servants for actively working towards improving the material existence of the masses.

A telos of human needs/advancement would mean that investment and work can be directed towards a new purpose and spirit. Unlocking human potential and creativity from alienated work aimed only at profit, and returning to a general spirit of 'being economically purposive for others,' would allow individuals, groups and society to work toward do what they see best as long as it is purposed in accordance to the needs of the only space that exists for production -planet earth; and in accordance to what is socially useful.

The contrast with current mainstream debate is instructive. When speaking of work, national debates are often still grounded in a mentality that has outlasted its possible purposes. The Keynesian and post-Keynesian traditions have almost uniformly supported the goal of full employment, and its corresponding public policy application, the Employer of Last Resort (ELR). Today, the opposing Friedmanian proposal of a

Universal Basic Income (UBI) has risen to prominence (Seccareccia 2016) as ELR proposals have faded from public view, although still existing in many countries under different forms.

Polanyi emphasizes how in capitalism's earlier days in England, starvation was both the theoretical justification and public policy motivator for people to work (Polanyi 1944). Today, for practical purposes, ERL offers jobs to the unemployable, while the UBI unemploys people that could otherwise work. All are bad motivations either to work or not to work, and all are imagined on the plane of the production telos. For example, if an ELR program is conceived to subsidize private companies to take on workers that they would not have otherwise, it does little to advance human needs: 'when a minority will be able to feed, maintain, and supply the majority, it makes no sense to keep in the production stream those who have no desire to be in it' (Schumacher 1973, p. 266). Again, this is similar to Keynes's consideration regarding our changing duties to ourselves and our neighbors. Today, we most certainly need the state as an employer of first resort, as argued by Harrington (1972) and Correa and Vidal (2020) guiding the change of telos towards more rewarding employment.

In today's context, following the production telos means following the downward trajectory of markets. For the precariously employed, under an ELR program or not, the ever less fulfilling employment opportunities mean that the possibility to be paid not to work at all is often seen as a welcome alternative. Schumacher identifies the fundamental flaw:

> to strive for leisure as an alternative to work would be considered a complete misunderstanding of one of the basic truths of human existence, namely that work and leisure are complementary parts of the same living process and cannot be separated without destroying the joy of work and the bliss of leisure. (Schumacher 1973, p. 58)

The word bliss appears again. It is not that economic bliss is not working. It is having a job that one finds rewarding, even more so if one is socially recognized for the work. Understood under this perspective, paying able bodied people not to work, or remanding people to tedious and needless work, can be seen as an invitation to not realize their human potential and full personal dignity. But to insist, Schumacher's critiques belong to another era. If paying able bodied people not to work in the past was always an affront to individual dignity and social cohesion, and always impeded individuals from reaching their full potential, today it is an act of collective suicide.

In light of humanity's many urgencies, there is much work to be done, and many idle workers, and many workers willing to dedicate their efforts to nobler goals than corporate profit. A shift to the telos of human need/ advancement would promise to open an ample gamut of opportunities that have been limited by the logic and practice of producing what the market deems necessary.

Changing the telos to one of human needs under the mission of 'unlocking human potential' implies increasing the productive diversity of humans, restoring much of that which has been lost around the world, and rethinking technology. Seen not only as what is new and beyond nature, but rather as a reserve of practical human knowledge, we can incorporate traditional technology at the service of humanity and nature into the gamut of viable solutions to today's problems. This would include many lost or moribund rural occupations that are labor intensive and capital unproductive forms of producing in greater harmony with the earth. All of this can be surveyed, studied and discussed in new universities. The amount of science to be performed, plants and animals and their uses to be discovered, and productive labor to be had is particularly difficult to imagine in many developed countries where nature is less bountiful and traditional uses and knowledge of natural products were all but lost centuries ago. Where they survive in the tropical world, such populations where traditional production in harmony with the land are still alive, are one of humanity's great treasures when seen under the maxim of the human telos that 'man's greatest resource is man, his initiative, intelligence and creativity.'

Taking advantage of this greatest resource therefore means taking advantage of what we've got. And that certainly applies to the other side of the technological spectrum as well: here we can refer to the promise of fusion energy, large scale carbon capture and desalinization projects. Converting cutting edge military technology into peaceful cooperative space exploration, and to explore space for the sake of exploration and not asteroid mining. A change in telos can only be brought about by taking advantage of human potential and repurposing our productive and financial systems. A change of telos would have to be based on 'initiative, intelligence and creativity,' not paying people to do nothing as individuals, such as the UBI, or to stop moving forward as societies, such as the degrowth option.

Much like we have seen with work and finances, when dealing with overall production, the current production telos also offers the limited possibilities of more or less growth, whereas we need different growth. We don't need to slow down the ship of financialized global capitalism, we need to turn it around, as we are headed for imminent disaster. We do not need to produce less, but rather much more, but under a repurposed system, where we will need new methods and technologies, in conjunction with traditional rural technologies, in order to clean up the mess of previous production. Just like it would be criminal not to take advantage of our collective knowledge and preparation, it would also be so not to have the call go out far and wide, inviting all social classes and abilities. This is the essence of a change of telos: it is not doing less of what is destroying humanity, but rather to change what we are doing. This is fully compatible with Keynes's 'wonder city' as a material goal, although we would also add the wonder countryside.

Having now outlined our arguments in the construction of a new telos in which work and finance are repurposed toward the maximum human need of collective survival and advancement, we can add the final piece, which as suggested, is really the easiest one, the proverbial cherry on top of the cake.

Why Public Banks and Not Other Options

> I conclude that the duty of ordering the current volume of investment cannot safely be left in private hands. (Keynes 1936, p. 320)

In agreement with Keynes, we would also doubt that private hands can be trusted with our proposed change of telos. Returning the control of money to the national state, and one which can serve the public purpose, is the fundamental political task of a change of telos, and a very difficult one, if it can be achieved all.

The merits of a public bank on the production plane, and arguments as to why we cannot solely depend on fiscal spending (Marshall and Rochon 2019), have and will continue to be discussed. However, if the task at hand is a change in telos, we believe that the public bank is an instrument better served to turn the ship around than other forms of public financing. As Lerner argues, functional finance is only a way to get the ship moving slower or faster, but if the goal is to spend in new and different ways, there are essentially only two ways: either fiscal grants through specialized agencies or pubic banks. Both options would allow us to define what we want and what we need under the new course of the 'public purpose'. In practical terms, the two should be thought of complementary tools. In theory, we argue that the public banking option has distinct and often underappreciated features that make it a more precise instrument for a repurposing of our economic system.

The first step is to underline the primacy of credit in our current system: it is called capitalism because capital — in the form of credit — defines the system. Joan Robinson states that 'control of investment requires control of credit' (Robinson 1943, p. 26). For new investment to be able to chart a new course, it must be in the form of credit, and that credit must be controlled in its connections, expansions, and directions. We quickly look at these three characteristics separately.

The traditional role of private investment banks is that of picking who deserves credit, and traditionally the blessing of bank credit has been able to transform individuals into leaders and businesses into national champions. Converting money into society's servant and not master will imply a shift of financial power from the money masters of today, to the public bankers of tomorrow. The traditional guardians of money would still be the best agents to evaluate new projects, and indeed to see them through, but the criteria of creditworthiness would shift in accordance with the new telos. Public banks would bless public champions — the projects, big and small, that do the best to work toward the telos. The only thing that would change is the concept of what a champion is.

While the spirit of repurposing our current system from the top recommends banking as the key institution to be transformed, it is far from the great advantage of public banking over fiscal spending in our current context. As we have hinted at, the greatest advantage of public banking is that it can transform already existing capital, such that no new financial resources are needed in order to have trillions of dollars in new recycled credit. Nor is any great financial ingenuity required. All that would be necessary is to add a new actor to current Quantitative Easing programs and include it in the new division of existing stock of government and corporate bonds. This could be done under many forms, but as mentioned, 'what pays' is no longer an applicable criteria for new ventures, as today tens of trillions of dollars in capital lay inert, gaining nothing, and can be channeled towards any project that profits society and the environment, where they could earn just as little financial reward as is currently the case, but pay millions of salaries for decades.

In addition, with the cost of credit at low to negative rates, new state credit is virtually free as well, and much as central banks around the world accept ever greater levels of private sector corporate bonds, they could simply keep adding to their balance sheets in the form of public bank bonds. In addition, with each bond purchased by the Central bank, the public bank could expand upon this capital nine or tenfold, much like commercial banks can today.

Whichever form of public bank credit expansion could be more targeted than traditional fiscal policy. Under the precepts of functional finance, prices can be raised and lowered, but in a general fashion. The channeling of credit by public banks would allow for a more selective targeting of price change. Under a new telos, credit policy directed by public banks would be aimed at making activities destructive to humanity and nature less profitable, while those which aids humans and nature more profitable.

By directing cheap and abundant credit to some actors and sectors, public banking can effect market prices though market mechanisms, and hopefully align prices with our new telos. People would be paid, and have incentives to pay back loans, assuring to some degree that the newly repurposed money will not spill out into old patterns of spending, guiding prices and directing prices changes towards an alignment with the new telos. When thinking of turning the ship around, and the new connections, expansions, and directions of public credit, perhaps turning the ship around is not the best metaphor, as changing the direction of society will imply pulling — never pushing — many different people from different places along in the same direction. The pull of new credit with therefore be most effective when it is diverse in its purpose and scalable in size. In this sense, public banks can serve — as they do today — on the municipal, city, and state levels, as well as the national ones. And they can be dedicated to financing housing and small enterprises as has been recently common, or the management of public goods such as water management (McDonald, Marois, and Spronk, 2021) in more novel ways.

As the traditional connecting points of economic activity, and historical leaders of the production telos, banks would have to be at the forefront of our proposed change of telos. They would have to be public banks, and their definition of creditworthy would no longer be giving money to people who have already proved that they have money, but rather channeling recycled credit into new projects that fulfill the criteria of the human telos. Only when perceptions of work and finance are repurposed to human needs can we approach full finance: the amount of money necessary to bring us out of the tunnel of socially created economic need into the daylight of social and ecological harmony.

Conclusion

The Keynes-Schumacher debate regarding the money motive was always one of order and timing. While we sympathize with Schumacher's argument at the time, it is no longer a debate, as Keynes's hundred years are up, and his argument that prosperity must precede morals will have reached its statutory limit.

From today's perspective, we can more clearly understand the separation of the productive and the human telos, and perhaps better understand why Keynes could not allow for a suitable resolution to the problem of the money motive under the framework of a change in telos. Here we have argued that in theory, full investment can only be possible in a society that has moved on to the human telos, fully aware of what it needs to do with its new financial freedom. Once money and its intuitions are fully recognized as not masters, but servants to the need of humanity, can we change prices as we see fit, and use credit at will in order to approach the fulfillment of our goals of human survival and advancement. A hundred years since Keynes opened the debate, money has never been cheaper or more abundant, nor has the need for its good use ever been more morally clear.

Disclosure Statement

No potential conflict of interest was reported by the author(s).

References

Correa, E., and L. Vidal. 2020. 'Asistencialismo o trabajo: Ingreso Básico Universal o pleno empleo. Migrantes y mujeres.' *Boletín del Grupo de Trabajo: Feminismos, resistencias y emancipación*. Buenos Aires: CLACSO.

Galbraith, J. K. 1977. *The Age of Uncertainty*. Boston, MA: Houghton Mifflin Company.

Graeber, D. 2011. *Debt: The First 5,000 Years*. Brooklyn, NY: Melville House Publishing.

Harrington, M. 1972. 'Government Should Be the Employer of First Resort.' *The New York Times*, March 26.

Hudson, M. 2018. *... and Forgive Them Their Debts: Lending, Foreclosure and Redemption from Bronze Age Finance to the Jubilee Year*. Dresden: ISLET - Verlag.

Keynes, J. M. 1925a. 'Am I a Liberal?' [Part 1]. *Nation & Athenaeum*. August, 563–564.

Keynes, J. M. 1925b. *The Economic Consequences of Mr. Churchill*. London: Hogarth Press.

Keynes, J. M. 1930. *A Treatise on Money Volume I: The Pure Theory of Money*. London: MacMillan.

Keynes, J. M. 1931. *Essays in Persuasion*. London: MacMillan.

Keynes, J. M. 1933. 'Economic Self Sufficiency.' *The Yale Review* 22 (4): 755–769.

Keynes, J. M. 1936. *The General Theory of Employment, Interest, and Money*. London: Macmillan.

Lerner, A. 1943. 'Functional Finance and the Federal Debt.' *Social Research* 10: 38–51.

Marshall, W. C., and L. P. Rochon. 2019. 'Public Banking and Post-Keynesian Economic Theory.' *International Journal of Political Economy* 48 (1): 60–75.

McDonald, D. A., T. Marois, and S. Spronk. 2021. 'Public Banks + Public Water = SDG 6?.' *Water Alternatives* 14 (1): 1–18.

Parguez, A. 2006. 'Moneda y Capitalismo: La Teoría General del Circuito.' In *Confrontaciones monetarias: marxistas y post-keynesianos en América Latina*, edited by A. Girón. Buenos Aires: CLACSO.

Polanyi, K. 1944. *The Great Transformation*. Boston, MA: Beacon Press.

Robinson, J. 1943. 'The Problem of Full Employment.' Study Outline No. 10. London: Workers' Educational Association.

Schumacher, E. F. 1973. *Small is Beautiful: Economics as if People Mattered*. New York: Harper.

Schumacher, E. F. 1975. 'Alternatives in Technology.' *Alternatives* 1 (1): 7–22.

Seccareccia, M. 1995. 'Keynesianism and Public Investment: A Left-Keynesian Perspective on the Role of Government Expenditure and Debt.' *Studies in Political Economy* 46 (1): 43–78.

Seccareccia, M. 2016. 'Ingreso básico y pleno empleo: Lecciones de Polanyi, Keynes y Minsky.' *Ola Financiera* 9 (1): 1–32.

Stigler, G. 1984. 'Economics: The Imperial Science?' *The Scandinavian Journal of Economics* 86 (3): 301–313.

Stiglitz, J. E. 2008. 'It Doesn't Take Nostradamus.' In *The Economists' Voice Top Economists Take on Today's Problems*, edited by J. E. Stiglitz, A. Edlin, and J. B. DeLong. New York: Columbia University Press.

Veblen, T. 1919. *The Vested Interests and the Common Man*. New York: B. W. Huebsch.

OPEN ACCESS

A Dynamic Theory of Public Banks (and Why it Matters)

Thomas Marois

ABSTRACT

Public banks are pervasive, with more than 900 worldwide, and powerful, having assets nearing $49 trillion. Yet they are too often perceived as static financial institutions, based on economic theories that begin from fixed notions of what it is to be a publicly owned bank. This has given rise to polarized debate wherein public banks are characterized as being either essentially good or bad. This is unrealistic and unhelpful as we seek ways to confront the crises of finance and of climate finance. We need instead to rethink public banks as dynamic and contested institutions within the public spheres of states. In this view, public ownership itself predetermines nothing but it does open up a particular *public* realm of possibilities. Change becomes possible and is a result of social forces making it so, if within the structural confines of gendered, racialized, and class-divided capitalist society. A dynamic theory of public banks provides a novel theoretical alternative and a practical pathway towards financing green and just transitions in the public interest.

1. Introduction

We need now to rethink public banks. There are over 900 of them worldwide with combined financial assets nearing $49 trillion dollars (McDonald, Marois, and Spronk 2021). These public commercial/retail, universal, and development banks operate at all levels, from the local and sub-national to the national, regional, and global scales. Over the last decade or so these public banks are resurgent, re-asserting their established capacity and expertise in order to confront recurrent financial crises and assume a catalytic role in tackling the crisis of climate finance (Marois 2021). They are, however, anything but new. Public banks have an institutional legacy going back more than six centuries to the first municipal banks founded in Barcelona and Genoa, followed by Venice, Naples, Amsterdam, and Hamburg. Since the late nineteenth century and with the consolidation of capitalism globally, public banks have acquired a diverse set of political, economic, and social functions. Yet contemporary thinking about public banks has failed to account for such heterogeneity. Instead, the idea of 'public banks' has been pushed into two opposing theoretical corners: an orthodox political view, typically negative, and a heterodox development view, often positive. Despite this apparent polarization, political and development views share common and foundational conceptual ground: in both views, the *public* ownership form of these banks logically precedes their institutional functions. Put otherwise, the functions of public banks (what they do) does not alter the meaning of being 'public' within either view. This matters because historical actions and future changes in how public banks function appear to be outside of and trivial to what public banks *are* in time- and place-bound contexts. Economic theory confines the actual practices of public banks and constrains our intellectual ability to be realistically critical or creatively optimistic. For those concerned with, for example, trying to find better means of financing a green and just transition to a sustainable and equitable future, these fixed and polarized conceptualizations present real barriers to securing sober alternatives in the public interest. We need now to be able to rethink public banks, warts and wonders alike, to innovatively direct their institutional capacity and transformative potential without the straight jackets of existing economic theory.

I argue that an alternative dynamic view of public banks enables us to rethink public banks within contemporary capitalism. A dynamic view does so without recourse to essentializing tropes of 'public' banks being meant to do this or essentially failing to achieve that. It is an anti-essentialist approach that exposes public banks to changing historical, social, political, and economic determinations. To do so, a dynamic view positions the socially contested institutional functions of public banks prior to their ownership form. Change becomes possible and is a result of social forces making it so, if within the structural confines of gendered, racialized, and class-divided capitalist society. This provides a novel and substantive theoretical alternative to orthodox political and heterodox development views.

2. Political and Development Views: Ownership Form Before Institutional Function

Despite otherwise contending worldviews on economic development, markets, and states in capitalism, the orthodox 'political' and heterodox 'development' views within economics share a common interpretive approach vis-à-vis public banks. Ownership form is foundational, logically coming before institutional functions in ways that fundamentally shape their otherwise polarized understanding of what public banks are and, importantly, what public banks are *a priori* meant to do. Orthodox and heterodox economic approaches, that is, tend to share a *pre-social* conceptualization of being publicly owned. Mine is not a necessarily disputed observation, nor is the political versus development divergence derived from ownership form unacknowledged within the economic literature on public banks. In one of the most widely cited studies on the subject, economists La Porta, Lopez-de-Silanes, and Shleifer (2002, p. 67; my emphasis) write that the '*[o]wnership* of banks thus promotes the government's goals in both the "development" and the "political" theories. … In both theories, the government finances projects that would not get privately financed. In the development theories, these projects *are socially desirable*. In the political theories, *they are not*.' The line of thinking is unequivocal: ownership form logically precedes institutional function, even if the outcomes differ radically in terms of corruption or economic additionality (Figure 1; elaborated below). It has also constituted a remarkably sticky narrative organizing the theory, evidence, and policy of public banks in economic development literature (see Barth, Caprio, and Levine 2006;

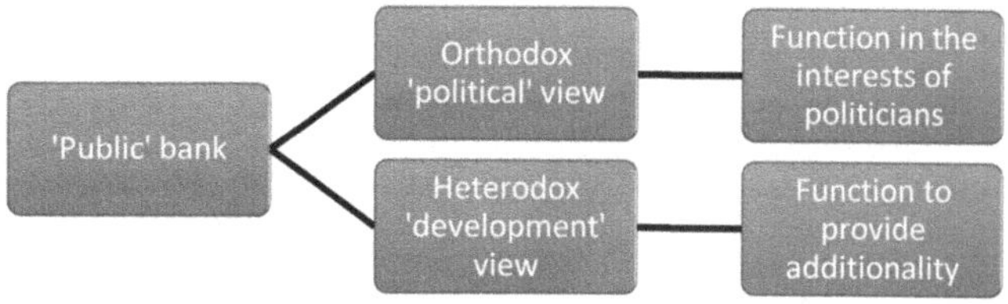

Figure 1. Political and development views: Ownership form precedes institutional function.

Levy Yeyati, Micco, and Panizza 2007; World Bank 2012; Andrianova, Demetriades, and Shortland 2012; Marcelin and Mathur 2015; Scherrer 2017; Bircan and Saka 2018).

On the one hand, there is the orthodox 'political' view. Typically advanced by neoclassical economists and liberal political economists, the political view of public banks is characteristically *negative*. Adherents argue that 'governments acquire control of enterprises and banks in order to provide employment, subsidies, and other benefits to supporters, who return the favor in the form of votes, political contributions, and bribes' (La Porta, Lopez-de-Silanes, and Shleifer 2002, p. 266). There is no ambiguity, no room for divergence, and no possibility for change. Public enterprises, like public banks, are political firms that are 'predestined for political uses' and therefore 'subject to political interference from politicians, special pressure or interest groups' (Marcelin and Mathur 2015, p. 529). Political influence entails corruption, and this in turn generates interference in financial markets (Barth, Caprio, and Levine 2006; Demirgüç-Kunt and Servén 2010). Neoclassical case study and large-scale quantitative evidence affirm that public banks correlate with (and are sometimes said to cause) economic inefficiencies, under-development, and corruption (Caprio et al. 2004; Cull, Martinez Peria, and Verrier 2017). In this worldview, the public ownership of banks is seen as a deliberate political deviation meant to displace or preempt private ownership (Megginson 2005, p. 34).

Here the root problem with 'bureaucrats as bankers' is that of individual incentives (Shirley 1999). This is a theoretical proposition derived from timeless liberal conceptions of human nature (Demirgüç-Kunt and Servén 2010, p. 99):

> As often the case in finance, incentive problems are at the root of this issue since bureaucrats do not face incentives designed to reward efficient resource allocation. Not only do government officials often lack the expertise to be effective managers, they also face conflicts of interest due to their desire to secure their political base and reward supporters, which often goes against efficient resource allocation.

Behind this orthodox political view is the hardcore ideological belief that the spread of the market and of individual exchange relations, matched by the elimination of barriers to market exchanges, increases human happiness and societal wealth via the optimal distribution of goods and services and the freedom to choose what you spend your money on or not (Friedman 1962). It is a liberal theory of social justice based on individual self-maximizing interactions and market-based coordination of social reproduction, perceived as both neutral and natural in human history (see Hayek 1984). Self-interested individuals naturally seek their advantage in markets, as do self-interested politicians in the state (Shleifer 1998; Vanberg 2005). Any failure to admit this 'truth' in relation to public banks is to court idealistic and naïve policy-making (Barth, Caprio, and

Levine 2006, pp. 34–5; *cf.* Calomiris and Haber 2014). Ownership form thus ultimately determines institutional functions.

On the other hand, there is the heterodox 'development' view. Typically advanced by Keynesian-inspired economists, the development view of public banks is characteristically *positive*. The ideas common to this view include public banks being able and willing to facilitate economic development in ways that private banks are unwilling or incapable of doing, particularly when it comes to longer-term investments and less profitable but no less socially-significant sectors and public goods (Gerschenkron 1962; Bennett and Sharpe 1980). In contrast to political views, however, very little is said on public ownership *per se* as a conceptual category. The nature of public ownership is often assumed or snuck in the back door, even though it remains the *sine qua non* of why public banks do what they do.

As with orthodox views, substantiating evidence is in no short supply within heterodoxy. Scholars argue that the 'evidence that the prevalence of state ownership in the banking sector conspires against its ultimate development thus appears to be weaker than suggested by previous studies' (Levy Yeyati, Micco, and Panizza 2007, pp. 237–8). Whereas political views attest to slow growth, development views demonstrate higher average growth rates (Andrianova, Demetriades, and Shortland 2012, p. 449). Heterodox studies even empirically challenge the bread and butter of political views, that is, endemic public bank corruption, arguing instead that the evidence of corruption is more inconclusive than political views lead us to believe (Frigerio and Vandone 2020) This is not to say public banks are incorruptible, for they are, if not any more so than a private bank. On top of this, a growing body of evidence details how public banks are effective countercyclical lenders capable of stabilizing increasingly unstable financial globalization processes and recurrent crises (Vidal, Marshall, and Correa 2011; Brei and Schclarek 2013; Griffith-Jones et al. 2018). These conclusions are now acknowledged by the World Bank (2012) and IMF (2020).

Here too public ownership remains foundational and logically prior. For example, development view advocates elaborate on what 'public banks are expected to do a priori', posed in contrast to orthodox views (Levy Yeyati, Micco, and Panizza 2007, pp. 223–24; *cf.* Griffith-Jones et al. 2018; Di John 2020). There are different expectations brought to bear, again based on a bank being owned publicly. Development views advocate that public banks should be most active where there are market failures and should do so without competing with the private sector. Public banks should operate where there is poor institutional development and do so to support private sector financial growth. Others push what public banks should do beyond market failures and financial gaps, to include regulating competitive markets, creating new markets, and functioning counter-cyclically at times of instability (often drawing more on Minsky's financial fragility thesis) (Mazzucato and Penna 2016; Ribeiro de Mendonça and Deos 2017). There is an important shared commitment within heterodox development views, however, that logically and causally link public bank ownership to institutional functions, particularly to *additionality* (Skidelsky, Martin, and Westerlind Wigstrom 2011; Mazzucato 2015 [2013]). Additionality is described as the impact beyond that which would have occurred *without* a public bank acting or intervening, and it is often seen as functioning to crowd in private investment (Spratt and Ryan-Collins 2012, p. 1; Griffith-Jones et al. 2018). The essential meaning of being public is unequivocal. As Ribeiro de Mendonça and Deos (2017, p. 24; my emphasis) specify, 'the presence of institutions [public banks] with a *logic of action that differs* from that of the market is necessary in order to counteract destabilization', in addition to assuming other roles in financial markets. It is this oft-*un*problematized logic of action for public banks that also situates ownership form prior and as foundational to institutional functions in development views.

While critically engaging with how heterodox economists otherwise deal with credit policy and public banking, post-Keynesian economists Marshall and Rochon nonetheless reinforce fixed views on what public banks are *meant* to do by virtue of their ownership form. They write, for example, that 'public banks are not subject to the discipline of the market' and that they 'do not operate for profit' (2019, pp. 65; 67). The intent is to suggest public banks are more open to functioning differently than private corporate banks, which are compelled to maximize returns, but the wording mirrors established patterns within the literature. In doing so it obscures that public banks in countries as diverse as Turkey, Canada, and Costa Rica have been made subject to market forces and that others in political jurisdictions as different as North Dakota and the Nordic region of Europe not only operate for profit but regularly reward their government shareholders with pay-outs (Marois 2021). Once you assign a variable function to public banks as an invariable feature, it is soon belied by cases that do not conform to the model but are yet 'public' banks. They are simply public banks made differently within the public sphere, a point economic theory has had trouble capturing.

That said, unlike in orthodox political views there is in heterodox development views a liveliness *to* debate and analytical room *for* conceptual innovation (see Scherrer 2017; Butzbach, Rotondo, and Desiato 2020; Mazzucato 2018). Marshall and Rochon, for example, recognize that public banks 'are subject to the discipline of the voter', signaling that the functioning of public banks 'should be left to society's discretion, voiced through a democratic process', in turn pointing towards 'constructing' public banks around 'probity, not profit' (Marshall and Rochon 2019, pp. 65; 71). This suggests that society has a say in how a public bank functions and, ultimately, in institutional change (a point I return to shortly). Yet most Keynesian scholars of public banks have yet to walk through that door conceptually. The issue is not in *what* they see public banks doing, for indeed there are cases of public banks undertaking institutional functions just as elaborated in development approaches. It is the *why* that remains problematic, insofar as *why* a public bank does (or is meant to do) this or that often, implicitly or explicitly, boils down to it being a 'public' bank. The inner, contested, and ever-evolving social forces and power relations within global capitalism that motivate the varied institutional functions of public banks rarely receive explicit conceptual treatment.

This stumbling block derives from long-standing heterodox commitments to advocating for a greater role for the 'machinery of government' in stabilizing inherently unstable and uneven capitalist development via extra-market coordination mechanisms, including public banks (Gerschenkron 1962; Shonfield 1969; Minsky 2008 [1986]). As John Maynard Keynes wrote, '[t]he important thing for government is *not* to do things which individuals are doing already, and to do them a little better or a little worse; but to do those things which at present are *not done at all*.' (1926, p. 46; emphasis added) Keynes' position on the proper role of government in capitalist economies has had a decided influence on the development view of public banks, anchoring ownership form prior to institutional function. It is this 'extra-market coordination' commitment that Joseph Stiglitz refers to when arguing that there 'exist forms of government intervention that will not only make these [financial] markets function better but will also improve the performance of the economy' (1994, p. 20). Public banks, by virtue of being public, are meant to provide market stability, filling and correcting for market failures and investor reticence, and for generating positive externalities (*cf.* Xu, Ren, and Wu 2019, pp. 6–8).

Again, the issue is *not* that public banks do not engage in these functions. They do. Indeed, the heterodox and institutional literature on public banks has certainly bested orthodoxy in capturing operational diversity and historical variegations across time and place (von Mettenheim and Del Tedesco Lins 2008; Mettenheim and Butzbach 2017; Scherrer 2017; Griffith-Jones et al. 2018; Ray, Gallagher, and Sanborn 2020). Heterodox scholars, too, are leveraging traditional ideas for novel ends, driving new debate around public banks and patient public finance as being more innovative and able to take on government missions in order to drive forward public purpose (Mazzucato 2018). Importantly, there is a strong underlying normative public interest commitment to public banks funding socially significant but low-return public good projects, especially in infrastructure (Griffith-Jones et al. 2018). Where I diverge is in connecting any such functions or any such public interest orientation to *public* ownership in and of itself. I see being public as rather more indeterminate and contested, being made and remade by class-divided social forces in capitalism. In short, more needs to be done to historicize our theories of public banks rather than continuing to let theory over-determine diverse institutional histories.

3. An Alternative Dynamic View: Institutional Function Before Ownership Form

Orthodox political and heterodox development views of public banks are stuck in fixed and opposing corners. To rethink public banks there is thus the need to shift the terrain of debate and to elaborate an alternative conceptual framework capable of making place- and time-bound context *matter* to the meanings of public banks. This can only be broached by first jettisoning the perceived need to resolve the ultimate benefits, or not, of public banks in capitalist development. An alternative approach reverses causality, so that what people make public banks do matters. This means positioning institutional functions, which are socially contested, as logically prior to ownership form. In this conceptualization, social forces shape and reshape the institutional functions of public banks, which in turn recurrently change the meaning of being a public bank in time and place (Figure 2). In turn, the evolving meaning of a public bank will again inform the struggles and strategies of social forces as they seek to shape and reshape what it is that a public bank does, how it functions, and for whom. This again leads to an evolution in the meaning of being a public bank, endlessly making and remaking a public bank in time- and place-bound contexts. This is the foundation of an alternative 'dynamic' view of public banks.

The historical, empirical, and case study evidence on public banks and financial institutions informing this alternative 'function before form' approach to public banks has been developed elsewhere (Marois and Güngen 2016; Ho and Marois 2019; McDonald,

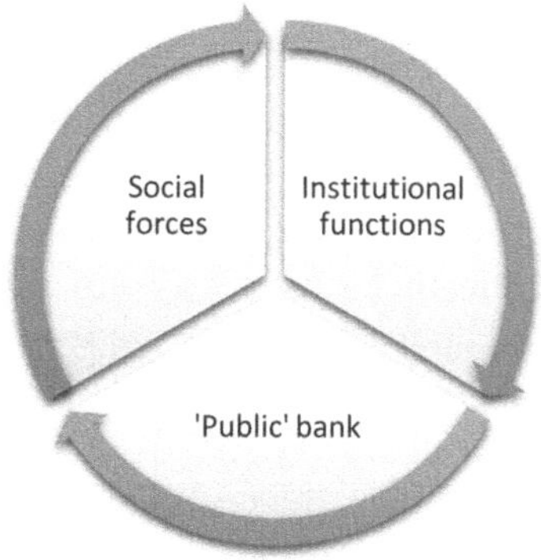

Figure 2. Dynamic view: Evolving because socially contested.

Marois, and Barrowclough 2020; Marois 2021). My purpose here is limited to setting out the conceptual framework of a dynamic view, drawing on historical institutional and materialist political economy. This involves, first and foremost, pulling the 'public' in public banks back into the historical specificity and structural influences of capitalist social reproduction that affect the actions and intentions of social forces, individual and collective. A dynamic view then interprets these institutions from the bottom up: public banks are first theorized as *institutions* in the *public spheres* of *states* within *global financialized capitalism*. This allows us to connect the shifting strategies and interests of social forces to the institutional functions and reproduction of public banks within the confines of capitalism.

At first glance, then, public banks are *institutions*. Institutions represent, crystallize, and perform patterns of behavior, customs, laws, rules, and norms in society. They are often complex in their histories, contemporary make up, and underlying power relations. Institutions, at one level of understanding, are entities onto themselves, but they are never so independently of all else. Institutions develop and evolve within a societal whole, acted upon and acting onto larger and smaller scales of existence. This leads one scholar to see institutions as 'endogenously shaped, context-determined social rules' (Ho 2017, pp. 9–10). Moreover, institutions are historical and dynamic because they are 'the *resultant* of social actors' and economic agents' interaction' (Ho 2013, pp. 1091–92; emphasis added). Put otherwise, individual and collective agents make and remake institutions, such that they are inevitably time- and place-bound entities (*cf.* Lefebvre 2016 [1972], p. 63). While we can identify and speak of specific institutional entities (like individual public banking institutions), these are inherently relational entities reproduced within the wider totality of capitalist social reproduction (Hanieh 2018, p. 15).

Public banking institutions are connected to the wider totality first through the *public sphere*. As employed here, I define the public sphere as that space *within* nation states where governing authorities can (but not necessarily do) exercise power, control, influence, and privilege over public institutions and discourses. It is similar to the 'public sector', if more expansive. It is in and through the public sphere that governing authorities can shape what public banks do, how they function, and for whom – sometimes directly and sometimes more distantly. At the same time, by seeking to influence governing authorities and/or by holding formal decision-making power within public banks' governance structures themselves, social forces can also influence and shape public banks through the public sphere. This does not occur in predetermined ways or free of contending power relationships. Social forces, be they individual or collective and acting in the public or private interest, can work to sway public banks to function and operate according to reproductive logics and rationalities different than those of private banks exposed more directly to market competition. This is *why* we see *that* public banks have acquired functions seemingly unique to public banks (but which are not themselves derived from being publicly owned). However, it is equally the case that through the public sphere social forces can also make public banks function as-if they were private profit-seeking banks (that is, 'corporatised'), strategically made to operate according to market-oriented and financialized performance indicators in the private interest (Marois 2012; *cf.* Shirley 1999; McDonald 2016). The public sphere is a field of potentiality in which social forces act and react rather than a source or site of structural determinations.

To shed the ontological surety of being this or that by virtue of being a public institution is not to suggest that the public sphere of a state may not provide potential *shielding* from competitive market and capitalist accumulation imperatives. It can and does. For public banks, such shielding can be quite direct. Public law can clearly define public banks' operations and responsibilities while legally binding mandates and missions can set their orientation and pace of operations. Public guarantees and financial resources can release public banks from unmediated dependence on fast and fickle global financial markets. Democratic governance and popular representative structures can facilitate a credible public interest operating ethos. Yet so too can public sphere shielding be rather more indirect or even effectively non-existent. When public banks are legally corporatised and operationally financialized, specific social forces have made them operate according to market imperatives regardless of the public sphere. For this reason, as and when public banks are made and remade it is because they are pulled between contending public or private interests acting in and through the public sphere.

The public sphere, in turn, is internally connected to the *state* and class-divided society (and hence, to racialized and gendered power relations). States are larger and more complex than the public sphere, but they are no less evolving institutional social formations that within capitalism condense and crystallize historically specific, contested, and class-divided power relations in society (Jessop 1990; Harvey 2010, pp. 55–6). States are therefore not independent of capitalist markets and accumulation imperatives but interconnected through wider power relations and patterns of social reproduction (Poulantzas 2000 [1978]). With the global consolidation of capitalism over the last century or so, states have evolved as integral to capital accumulation, that is, as the one institution capitalism cannot do without (Meiksins Wood 2002). Yet states, as complex institutional entities, are not smoothly determined by capitalist reproduction and accumulation as here too contentious social forces struggle over the meanings of states (Lefebvre 2016 [1972], p. 130). Capitalist states in class-divided, racialized, and gendered society are thus institutionalized social compromises that balance, to greater and lesser degrees, contradictory capital accumulation and social reproduction imperatives. States and their public spheres are therefore strategic sites of social struggles (which is one reason why privatization was perhaps the vanguard strategy of early neoliberal reformers around the world). Class-divided, gendered, and racialized forms of power, privilege, and exploitation find their way into public financial and banking institutions and how they function at different times and in different places (Dymski 2009; Roberts 2015; McNally 2020). Historically and intuitively we know this to be the case, yet to date, economic banking theory has failed to capture the reality.

In historical materialist worldviews global capitalism and capitalist social relations impart a 'particular logic upon people and make a particular form of rationality plausible to them – a pressure that takes effect behind the backs of the subjects' (Nachtwey and ten Brink 2008, p. 45). The public sphere, states, and society are all impacted and influenced, if not determined, by this shadow of capitalism (Jessop 2016). Moreover, contemporary global capitalism has taken on a particularly finance-based or financialized shadow (Lapavitsas 2009; Marois 2012; Chesnais 2016). My purpose in raising the specter of global financialized capitalism is neither to narrate its processes nor to scan the mounting definitional and conceptual debates (see Christophers 2015). Rather, it is to recognize as ontologically significant that public banks in public spheres in states are likewise located in and affected by (and in turn affect) this wider structural context (*cf.* Scherrer 2017). It is a feature of historical materialist scholarship that finance and its institutions be historicized within the totality of capitalism and its class-based exploitative structures (dos Santos 2009; Hilferding 2006 [1981]; Harvey 2010; see Marois 2012, pp. 24–35). To be sure, public banks and their functions in society have long pre-dated capitalism (Hudson 2018). Yet public banks have thrived and evolved within capitalism, even persisting through the less-than-amenable conditions of neoliberalism and financialization (Marois 2021). What a dynamic view can illuminate is how private investors and neoliberal advocates are now seeking to bend public banks to ensuring their own accumulation ends as a strategic response to the crises of finance and of climate finance (also see the 'Wall Street Consensus' in Dafermos, Gabor, and Michell 2021). As an ontological and epistemological premise of analysis, individual and collective agencies shape the world around us, but rarely, to paraphrase Engels (1959, p. 230), in the conditions of our own choosing and not always as intended. So when I speak of the shadow of capitalism over public banks what I refer to is the structural power and organizing logic of exploitative capitalist social reproduction processes, which represent the conditions of institutional existence and reproduction that can be differentially leveraged by contending public and private interests (*cf.* Lefebvre 2016 [1972]; Palermo 2019).

To rethink public banks *dynamically* is to move reflexively from and between the institution, the public sphere, the state, and global financialized capitalism as interconnected scales of reproductive existence, power, and privilege. Public banks are exposed to influence as far as the bounds of global capitalism extend while at the same moment enclosed within a hierarchy of internal relations and boundaries. Far from being this or that by virtue of being publicly owned, public banks emerge in thought and practice as complex hybridizations of social struggles and power relations that seldom correspond to any idealized notion or intended outcome. Put otherwise, public ownership itself predetermines nothing. It does, however, open a particular *public* realm of possibilities. In this, we can think of public banks as dynamic and socially constructed and reconstructed institutionalized social relations that reflect historically specific relations of power and reproduction between banks, firms, states, and contentious individual and collective social forces (*cf.* Marois 2012, p. 29).

It this way a dynamic view meaningfully and logically positions institutional function prior to ownership form. While couched in historical materialist terms, the positioning of function before form draws on a related institutional political economy literature, notably that of scholar Peter Ho. Ho argues that by focusing on historical institutional 'functions' we need not rely on timeless and essentialized notions of 'ownership' form. In this line of reasoning, public and private institutions are not essentially good or bad things, but socially constituted (Ho 2013, 2016). Where and when institutions persist, it is by virtue of context-specific factors, prevailing as 'the reflection of actors' cumulative perceptions of endogenously emerged institutions as a common arrangement' (Ho 2016, p. 1125). Institutions endure not for idealized notions of public ownership but for complex and often contradictory reasons connected to what they do, how they function, and for whom (Ho 2020; Marois 2021). In terms of public banks, this leads to a novel understanding and to unique insights. Public ownership bestows no essential or ultimate purpose on a bank. Public banks' functions are instead subject to the pull of public and private interests in class-divided society, each struggling to shape *for whom* the bank predominantly functions.

A dynamic view allows us to rethink public banks as irreducible to the 'public' ownership form yet subject to struggle. Ownership by a government, public authority, or other public enterprise becomes but one way of *positioning* a bank within the public sphere. Ownership, however, is also not the only way.[2] Having a binding public mandate and mission, being operated under public law, being subject to consequential democratic public representation and control mechanisms, and variations therein can likewise position a bank within the public sphere as a *public* bank. This then becomes the first dimension of a public bank, namely, being located within the public sphere (if not necessarily being 'publicly' owned). A dynamic view sets out three additional dimensions of what constitutes a public bank (see Marois 2021). A second dimension of a public bank is that it also performs financial intermediation and banking functions but without an innate purpose or policy orientation (reflected in the fact of their multiple mandates and missions). A third dimension is that a public bank can function in both public and private interests. A final dimension of a public bank is that it persists as a credible, contested, and evolving institution.

These four dimensions of a public bank open up research to a far wider swath of historical and empirical determinations than allowed for in existing orthodox political and heterodox development views, which assign *a priori* meanings and orientations to public banks by virtue of ownership. By contrast, these four dimensions are mean to capture their diverse histories and indeterminant futures by setting public banks in capitalist society and the class-divided struggles endemic to it without pre-determining an essential or ultimate end. The consequence of a dynamic view is neither politically vacuous nor

[2]Again, to challenge the ontological primacy of legal ownership is not to dismiss its importance. Without determining its meaning, ownership can position a bank within the public sphere. Moreover, formal ownership is often by default one of the only ways to empirically measure levels of public bank numbers and assets in existing databases, notably in Orbis BankFocus. A dynamic view offers a less quantitatively rigid but more qualitatively accurate determination that builds on scholarship already concerned with alternative banks and interested in the complex and multiple forms by which other institutions are in fact 'public' institutions, be it by full or partial state or municipal ownership, worker-owned, or producer and consumer cooperatives (see Cumbers 2012; Butzbach and von Mettenheim 2014; Hanna 2018). It too recognizes the acknowledged limits to analysis reliant on pure 'ownership' categorizations taken in the absence of understanding effective 'control' over a bank (Butzbach, Rotondo, and Desiato 2020).

normatively agnostic. Precisely the opposite. By eschewing a pre-social and ultimate end, public banks become (as in fact they are) dynamic resultants of contentious struggles within capitalism. As historical and contemporary case study research attests, public banks are made and re-made in many ways, acquiring and casting off multiple institutional functions depending on how contentious social forces struggle to make the bank within states with the shadow of capitalism.

4. Conclusion, or Why It Matters

Public banks are enjoying nothing less than a modern-day resurgence within neoliberalism and financialisation. Decades of bank privatization advocacy have quieted as public banks have proven integral to smoothing out the 2008–09 global financial crisis and in catalyzing now desperately needed low-carbon and green transition financial investments (not to mention helping to overcome the crisis of Covid-19) (Griffith-Jones et al. 2018; Mazzucato and Semieniuk 2018; UNCTAD 2019; Xu, Ren, and Wu 2019; McDonald, Marois, and Barrowclough 2020; McDonald, Marois, and Spronk 2021; Marois 2021). Yet without public banks that can be democratically commanded to function in the public interest, there is no hope of sustainable and equitable development, let alone green and just transitions for people and planet, as financial investors maneuver to control the functions of public banks for private ends. For this reason, it matters how we think about public banks. A dynamic view opens the realm of the possible public interest while being realistic about the social forces at play and struggles to come.

By contrast, orthodox political views are still desperate to constrain the potential of public banks and to gear what public banks currently do to supporting private interests and endless capital accumulation. This is the core message of the World Bank's Maximizing Finance for Development agenda and the United Nations' Finance for Sustainable Development strategy (IMF/World Bank 2015; Badré 2018; UN IATF 2019; *cf.* Dafermos, Gabor, and Michell 2021). In this new neoliberal narrative, public banks must only wrap projects in public guarantees, bending themselves to underwriting acceptable levels of private returns by socializing their risks.

Heterodox development views hold more diverse aspirations for public banks. There are calls for patient public finance and public development banks to green investments and to launch a global green new deal (Mazzucato and McPherson 2018). Others emphasize the necessity of building up public banking capacity and influence to confront the overwhelming power of private finance and global financialization (Beitel 2016; Marshall and Rochon 2019; Brown 2019). Too often, however, heterodox approaches graft specific roles and sets of expectations onto public banks, asserting a very particular vision of public banks' 'reasons to be' (notably, variations of 'additionality'). The problem is not one of imagining or advocating progressive roles and responsibilities for public banks. No. Rather, the problem resides in granting otherwise normative and contestable aspirations (which are indeed an indispensable part of being a social and political being!) a timeless status that in turn seemingly bestows fundamental meaning on a bank by virtue of it being 'public'. Far from catalyzing positive change this can overly constrain possibilities, obscure pitfalls, and undermine meaningful democratization. What good is it to command a representative and democratic say over public banks if what they are meant to do is already predetermined? Little, I suggest. Similarly, it is a grave strategic mistake to assume that, by virtue of being publicly owned, any institution, let alone public banks, will advance a green and just transition for people and planet without supportive and motivated social forces actively shaping the institution and holding it accountable to the democratic public interest. At a time when public banks are resurgent, it is a blunder of colossal proportions to either dismiss the creative energies of pro-public social forces or to underestimate the structural power of private interests to bend public banks to their own accumulation ends. Hence the practical need to rethink public banks.

An alternative dynamic view thus matters because in rethinking public banks it internalizes struggle and acknowledges the normative orientations of contending social forces. It looks to the historical and material conditions of public banks' reproduction. By doing so, a dynamic view allows us to see the operational contradictions of public banks and understand the relationships of power and politics at play within class-divided, gendered, and racialized capitalist society. In this way contending public and private interests can be brought into the light as we act on the possibilities for change. It follows that a dynamic view does not rest upon any conceptual surety that a public bank, by virtue of being public, is meant to do this or that. Nor does a dynamic view blithely right off the catalytic and public interest potential of public banks merely because they are deemed ultimately corrupt and essentially inefficient. Instead, a dynamic view concedes that this cannot be known in advance. Rather, how public banks function and for whom are the results of historical social forces acting within the shadow of capitalism. The functions that public banks do inform the evolving meaning of being a public bank. For those social forces concerned with a green and just future for people and planet, this historically and evidence-based conceptualization opens the possibility, if never the necessity, of public banks being *made* to respond in the public interest. It also accepts that public banks can be made to privilege environmentally destructive and decidedly unjust ends. What a public bank is thus ultimately depends, and that, in the final analysis, is what is most liberating about a dynamic view of public banks and why it matters.

Acknowledgement

I would like to express my gratitude to the reviewers. It is a true pleasure to have readers thoughtfully engage with your work with an eye to improving its quality and clarity. The feedback received was enormously helpful, even if my revisions do not fully give justice to their inputs.

Disclosure Statement

No potential conflict of interest was reported by the author(s).

ORCID

Thomas Marois http://orcid.org/0000-0003-0057-3987

References

Andrianova, S., P. Demetriades, and A. Shortland. 2012. 'Government Ownership of Banks, Institutions and Economic Growth.' *Economica* 79: 449–469.

Badré, B. 2018. *Can Finance Save the World? Regaining Power Over Money to Serve the Common Good.* Oakland, CA: Berrett-Koehler Publishers.

Barth, J. R., Jr., G. Caprio, and R. Levine. 2006. *Rethinking Bank Regulation: Till Angels Govern.* New York: Cambridge University Press.

Beitel, K. 2016. *The Municipal Public Bank: Regulatory Compliance, Capitalization, Liquidity, and Risk.* Roosevelt Institute. www.rooseveltinstitute.org.

Bennett, D., and K. Sharpe. 1980. 'The State as Banker and Entrepreneur: The Last-Resort Character of the Mexican State's Economic Intervention, 1917–76.' *Comparative Politics* 12 (2): 165–189.

Bircan, Ç, and O. Saka. 2018. 'Lending Cycles and Real Outcomes: Costs of Political Misalignment.' *LSE 'Europe in Question' Discussion Paper Series.* LEQS Paper No. 139/2018. London: London School of Economics.

Brei, M., and A. Schclarek. 2013. 'Public Bank Lending in Times of Crisis.' *Journal of Financial Stability* 9 (4): 820–830.

Brown, E. 2019. *Banking on the People: Democratizing Money in the Digital Age.* Washington: The Democracy Collaborative. https://democracycollaborative.org/.

Butzbach, O., G. Rotondo, and T. Desiato. 2020. 'Can Banks Be Owned?' *Accounting, Economics, and Law: A Convivium* 10 (1): 1–21.

Butzbach, O., and K. von Mettenheim, eds. 2014. *Alternative Banking and Financial Crisis.* London: Pickering & Chatto.

Calomiris, C. W., and S. Haber. 2014. *Fragile by Design: Banking Crises, Scarce Credit, and Political Bargains.* Princeton: Princeton University Press.

Caprio, G., J. L. Fiechter, R. E. Litan, and M. Pomerleano, eds. 2004. *The Future of State-Owned Financial Institutions.* Washington: Brookings Institution Press.

Chesnais, F. 2016. *Finance Capital Today: Corporations and Banks in the Lasting Global Slump.* Boston, MA: Brill.

Christophers, B. 2015. 'The Limits to Financialization.' *Dialogues in Human Geography* 5 (2): 183–200.

Cull, R., M. S. Martinez Peria, and J. Verrier. 2017. 'Bank Ownership: Trends and Implications.' *IMF Working Paper.* WP/17/60. Washington: International Monetary Fund.

Cumbers, A. 2012. *Reclaiming Public Ownership: Making Space for Economic Democracy.* London: Zed Books.

Dafermos, Y., D. Gabor, and J. Michell. 2021. 'The Wall Street Consensus in Pandemic Times: What Does it Mean for Climate-Aligned Development?' *Canadian Journal of Development Studies/Revue canadienne d'études du développement.* doi:10.1080/02255189.2020.1865137.

Demirgüç-Kunt, A., and L. Servén. 2010. 'Are All the Sacred Cows Dead? Implications of the Financial Crisis for Macro- and Financial Policies.' *The World Bank Research Observer* 25 (1): 91–124.

Di John, J. 2020. 'The Political Economy of Development Banking.' In *The Oxford Handbook of Industrial Policy*, edited by A. Oqubay, C. Cramer, H.-J. Chang, and R. Kozul-Wright. Oxford: Oxford University Press.

dos Santos, P. 2009. 'On the Content of Banking in Contemporary Capitalism.' *Historical Materialism* 17 (2): 180–213.

Dymski, G. 2009. 'Racial Exclusion and the Political Economy of the Subprime Crisis.' *Historical Materialism* 17 (2): 149–179.

Engels, F. 1959 [1888]. 'Ludwig Feuerbach and the End of Classical German Philosophy.' In *Marx and Engels: Basic Writings on Politics and Philosophy*, edited by L. S. Feuer, 195–242. New York: Anchor Books.

Friedman, M. 1962. *Capitalism and Freedom.* Chicago: University of Chicago Press.

Frigerio, M., and D. Vandone. 2020. 'European Development Banks and the Political Cycle.' *European Journal of Political Economy* 62 (March): 101852. doi:10.1016/j.ejpoleco.2019.101852.

Gerschenkron, A. 1962. *Economic Backwardness in Historical Perspective.* Boston: Harvard University Press.

Griffith-Jones, S., J. A. Ocampo, F. Rezende, A. Schclarek, and M. Brei. 2018. 'The Future of National Development Banks.' In *The Future of National Development Banks*, edited by S. Griffith-Jones, and J. A. Ocampo, 1–36. Cambridge: Cambridge University Press.

Hanieh, A. 2018. *Money, Markets, and Monarchies: The Gulf Cooperation Council and the Political Economy of the Contemporary Middle East.* Cambridge: Cambridge University Press.

Hanna, T. M. 2018. *Our Common Wealth: The Return of Public Ownership in the United States.* Manchester: Manchester University Press.

Harvey, D. 2010. *The Enigma of Capital and the Crises of Capitalism.* London: Profile Books.

Hayek, F. A. 1984 [1967]. 'The Principles of a Liberal Social Order.' In *The Essence of Hayek*, edited by C. Nishiyama, and K. R. Leube, 363–381. Stanford, CA: Hoover Institution Press.

Hilferding, R. 2006 [1981]. *Finance Capital: A Study of the Latest Phase of Capitalist Development.* London: Routledge.

Ho, P. 2013. 'In Defense of Endogenous, Spontaneously Ordered Development: Institutional Functionalism and Chinese Property Rights.' *Journal of Peasant Studies* 40 (6): 1087–1118.

Ho, P. 2016. 'An Endogenous Theory of Property Rights: Opening the Black box of Institutions.' *The Journal of Peasant Studies* 43 (6): 1121–1144.

Ho, P. 2017. *Unmaking China's Development: The Function and Credibility of Institutions.* Cambridge: Cambridge University Press.

Ho, P. 2020. 'The Credibility of (in)Formality: Or, the Irrelevance of Institutional Form in Judging Performance.' *Cities* 99 (April): 102609. doi:10.1016/j.cities.2020.102609.

Ho, S., and T. Marois. 2019. 'China's Asset Management Companies as State Spatial–Temporal Strategy.' *The China Quarterly* 239: 728–751.

Hudson, M. 2018. *... and Forgive Them Their Debts: Lending, Foreclosure, and Redemption from Bronze Age to the Jubilee Year.* Dresden, Germany: ILSET-Verlag.

IMF. 2020. *Fiscal Monitor: Policies to Support People During the COVID-19 Pandemic.* Washington: International Monetary Fund.

IMF/World Bank. 2015. *From Billions to Trillions: Transforming Development Finance Post-2015 Financing for Development: Multilateral Development Finance.* Development Committee, Joint Ministerial Committee of the Boards of Governors of the Bank and the Fund on the Transfer of Real Resources to Developing Countries. DC2015-0002. www.worldbank.org.

Jessop, B. 1990. *State Theory: Putting the Capitalist State in Its Place.* Cambridge, UK: Polity Press.

Jessop, B. 2016. 'Territory, Politics, Governance and Multispatial Metagovernance.' *Territory, Politics, Governance* 4 (1): 8–32.

Keynes, J. M. 1926. *The End of Laissez-Faire.* London: I. and V. Woolf.

Lapavitsas, C. 2009. 'Financialised Capitalism: Crisis and Financial Expropriation.' *Historical Materialism* 17 (2): 114–148.

La Porta, R., F. Lopez-de-Silanes, and A. Shleifer. 2002. 'Government Ownership of Banks.' *The Journal of Finance* 57 (1): 265–301.

Lefebvre, H. 2016 [1972]. *Marxist Thought and the City.* Trans. by R. Bononno. Foreword by S. Elden. Minneapolis: University of Minnesota Press.

Levy Yeyati, E., A. Micco, and U. Panizza. 2007. 'A Reappraisal of State-Owned Banks.' *Economia (pontificia Universidad Catolica Del Peru. Departamento De Economia)* 7 (2): 209–247.

Marcelin, I., and I. Mathur. 2015. 'Privatization, Financial Development, Property Rights and Growth.' *Journal of Banking & Finance* 50: 528–546.

Marois, T. 2012. *States, Banks, and Crisis: Emerging Finance Capitalism in Mexico and Turkey.* Cheltenham, UK: Edward Elgar Publishing.

Marois, T. 2021. *Public Banks: Decarbonisation, Definancialisation, and Democratisation.* Cambridge: Cambridge University Press.

Marois, T., and A. R. Güngen. 2016. 'Credibility and Class in the Evolution of Public Banks: The Case of Turkey.' *Journal of Peasant Studies* 43 (6): 1285–1309.

Marshall, W. C., and L.-P. Rochon. 2019. 'Public Banking and Post-Keynesian Economic Theory.' *International Journal of Political Economy* 48 (1): 60–75.

Mazzucato, M. 2015 [2013]. *The Entrepreneurial State.* Revised Edition. London: Anthem Press.

Mazzucato, M. 2018. *The Value of Everything: Making and Taking in the Global Economy*. London: Penguin-Allen Lane.
Mazzucato, M., and M. McPherson. 2018. 'The Green New Deal: A bold mission-oriented approach.' *IIPP Policy Brief* (December). London: Institute for Innovation and Public Purpose.
Mazzucato, M., and C. C. R. Penna. 2016. 'Beyond Market Failures: the Market Creating and Shaping Roles of State Investment Banks.' *Journal of Economic Policy Reform* 19 (4): 305–326.
Mazzucato, M., and G. Semieniuk. 2018. 'Financing Renewable Energy: Who Is Financing What and Why it Matters.' *Technological Forecasting & Social Change* 127: 8–22.
McDonald, D. A. 2016. 'To Corporatize or Not to Corporatize (And if so How)?' *Utilities Policy* 40: 107–114.
McDonald, D. A., T. Marois, and D. V. Barrowclough (Eds.) 2020. *Public Banks and Covid-19: Combatting the Pandemic With Public Finance*. Municipal Services Project (Kingston), UNCTAD (Geneva), and Eurodad (Brussels). https://publicbankscovid19.org/.
McDonald, D. A., T. Marois, and S. Spronk. 2021. 'Public Banks + Public Water = SDG 6?' *Water Alternatives* 14 (1): 117–134.
McNally, D. 2020. *Blood and Money: War, Slavery, Finance, and Empire*. Chicago, Il: Haymarket Books.
Megginson, W. L. 2005. *The Financial Economics of Privatization*. New York: Oxford University Press.
Meiksins Wood, E. 2002. *The Origin of Capitalism: A Longer View*. London: Verso.
Mettenheim, K., and O. Butzbach. 2017. 'Back to the Future of Alternative Banks and Patient Capital.' In *Public Banks in the Age of Financialization: A Comparative Perspective*, edited by C. Scherrer, 29–50. Cheltenham, UK: Edward Elgar Publishing.
Minsky, H. P. 2008 [1986]. *Stabilizing an Unstable Economy*. London: McGraw-Hill.
Nachtwey, O., and T. ten Brink. 2008. 'Lost in Translation: The German World-Market Debate in the 1970s.' *Historical Materialism* 16 (1): 37–70.
Palermo, G. 2019. 'Power: a Marxist View Coercion and Exploitation in the Capitalist Mode of Production.' *Cambridge Journal of Economics* 43: 1353–1375.
Poulantzas, N. 2000 [1978]. *State, Power, Socialism*. New York: Verso Classics.
Ray, R., K. P. Gallagher, and C. A. Sanborn, eds. 2020. *Development Banks and Sustainability in the Andean Amazon*. Abingdon, UK: Routledge.
Ribeiro de Mendonça, A. R., and S. Deos. 2017. 'Beyond the Market Failure Argument: Public Banks as Stability Anchors.' In *Public Banks in the Age of Financialization*, edited by C. Scherrer, 13–28. Cheltenham, UK: Edward Elgar Publishing.
Roberts, A. 2015. 'Gender, Financial Deepening and the Production of Embodied Finance: Towards a Critical Feminist Analysis.' *Global Society* 29 (1): 107–127.
Scherrer, C., ed. 2017. *Public Banks in the Age of Financialization: A Comparative Perspective*. Cheltenham, UK: Edward Elgar Publishing.
Shirley, M. M. 1999. 'Bureaucrats in Business: The Roles of Privatization Versus Corporatization in State-Owned Enterprise Reform.' *World Development* 27 (1): 115–136.
Shleifer, A. 1998. 'State Versus Private Ownership.' *Journal of Economic Perspectives* 12 (4): 133–150.
Shonfield, A. 1969 [1965]. *Modern Capitalism: The Changing Balance of Public and Private Power*. New York: Oxford University Press.
Skidelsky, R., F. Martin, and C. Westerlind Wigstrom. 2011. *Blueprint for a British Investment Bank*. London: Centre for Global Studies.
Spratt, S., and L. Ryan-Collins. 2012. *Development Finance Institutions and Infrastructure: A Systematic Review of Evidence for Development Additionality*. A Report Commissioned by the Private Infrastructure Development Group. Brighton, UK: Institute of Development Studies.
Stiglitz, J. 1994. 'The Role of the State in Financial Markets.' *Proceedings of the World Bank Annual Conference on Development Economics* 1993: 19–61.
Vanberg, V. J. 2005. 'Market and State: The Perspective of Constitutional Political Economy.' *Journal of Institutional Economics* 1 (1): 23–49.

von Mettenheim, K., and M. A. Del Tedesco Lins, eds. 2008. *Government Banking: New Perspectives on Sustainable Development and Social Inclusion from Europe and South America.* Rio de Janeiro and Berlin: Konrad Adenauer Foundation.

UNCTAD. 2019. *Trade and Development Report 2019: Financing a Global Green New Deal.* Geneva: United Nations Conference on Trade and Development.

UN IATF. 2019. *Financing for Sustainable Development Report.* New York: United Nations Inter-Agency Task Force on Financing for Development.

Vidal, G., W. C. Marshall, and E. Correa. 2011. 'Differing Effects of the Global Financial Crisis: Why Mexico has Been Harder hit Than Other Large Latin American Countries.' *Bulletin of Latin American Research* 30 (4): 419–435.

World Bank. 2012. *Global Financial Development Report 2013: Rethinking the Role of State in Finance.* Washington: World Bank.

Xu, J., X. Ren, and X. Wu. 2019. *Mapping Development Finance Institutions Worldwide: Definitions, Rationales, and Varieties.* NSE Development Financing Research Report No. 1. Beijing, China: Peking University Institute of New Structural Economics.

Public Banks, Public Purpose, and Early Actions in the Face of Covid-19

Diana V. Barrowclough and Thomas Marois

ABSTRACT
With the outbreak of the global Covid-19 pandemic and associated lockdowns, economic activity came to a grinding halt as demands for financial support in health, business, and government skyrocketed. In spring 2020 we assembled a team of experts to conduct rapid response research on how public banks worldwide responded to the Covid-19 crisis. The team employed case study methods to examine cases in the global north and south. A synthesis of our findings is presented here. We conclude that the most promising public bank responses to the crisis were those substantively guided by public purpose. Where public purpose had a more challenging relationship to public bank responses, the responses were more ambiguous and more difficult to differentiate from private banks. This rapid response study also points to promising lessons for how public banks can help to catalyse momentum to 'build forward better' and it raises a series of questions in need of further research.

Public Banks, Public Purpose, and First Actions in the Face of Covid-19

This paper presents new and original findings on the important roles played by public banks across the globe in the early months of the Covid-19 lock-down and social distancing. It synthesises a 'rapid review' global research project carried out and written up between May and October of 2020. The project has been the most ambitious effort to date to explore and document in real-time the first actions of public banks in the face of Covid-19. The research sheds light on public bank policies and actions in light of their mandates and public purpose.

We launched the research initiative because of the observation that governments and government-owned or 'public' banks were the frontline of economic defence in many countries around the world, particularly at the start of the Covid-19 outbreak. By and large, private banks were not expected to take up this role given their profit-maximising and short-term investment horizons that manifest in pro-cyclical lending. Instead, public purpose, not profitability, was needed to shape decision-making. The future of stable, sustainable and equitable societies will depend on building on the lessons now being learned.

Conducting such an immediate review was no easy task as the ground was constantly shifting: bold new policies were surpassed just weeks later by even bolder ones; programmes announced were not always put in place directly; some seemingly 'new' ones were really just being fast-forwarded. Bank officials, government policymakers and researchers alike were stumbling with 'working from home', often under difficult professional and familial circumstances. Nevertheless, this paper, and the detailed research that it synthesises, provides an important snapshot of a tumultuous time — a unique perspective on how things unfolded that contributes to a better understanding, both theoretical and empirical, of how public banks can function well, function better, and be better supported for the future. The results should help to guide policy decisions and to ensure this pandemic does not lead to another 'lost decade' and to the exacerbation of the already dire global climate crisis (UNCTAD 2020; IPCC 2021; Marois 2022b). The rapid research may also help support researchers more generally by sharing some of our experiences of working as an international team during this difficult period.

Two other contextual factors are important to gaining an understanding of the contributions of the review. The first is that Covid-19 did not strike a world economy that was otherwise stable and in good shape. The last few decades of excessive de-regulation, hyper-financialization, privatisation and globalisation had left the world economy in an unbalanced, inequitable and precarious state (Tooze 2018; UNCTAD 2019). Covid-19 served to pull back the curtains and shine a light on this fragility, but it did not create it. Second, the coronavirus is widely believed to be related to global warming and climate change. Continued clashes between humans and nature are expected, which must be addressed through socially just processes and with more equitable outcomes. This future makes it vital to learn the lessons of Covid-19 responses.

The results of our rapid response study revealed important insights into the world of public banking. The core aspect highlighted in this paper is that not all public bank responses showed the same degree of promise. Rather, where societies, governments and mandates made public purpose a guiding principle for how a public bank functions, this often translated into stronger social equity-oriented and public interest responses. In some cases, this was linked positively with the availability of adequate finance. Our research also found cases where public purpose had a more challenging relationship with public banks' Covid-19 responses. We conclude by reflecting on the lessons of Covid-19 responses for the financing of green and just transitions, and on areas for further research stemming from this project.

From Health Crisis to a Financial and Economic Crisis

When Covid-19 struck in early 2020, for most governments the only response was to impose policies of social distancing and eventual lockdown. Within weeks, or even days, this caused a previously unimaginable 'sudden stop' to the economy where consumer demand and supply dried up simultaneously, cascading across the globe even to countries that did not lockdown. The shock sparked record flows of capital in and out of financial markets and foreign exchange, interrupting productive processes and employment everywhere. At the same time as local and federal government fiscal revenues fell because of the abrupt stop to economic activity, the health, social and economic demands on their expenditures rose. No country was spared the economic effects of Covid-19 contagion, even if they yet had few confirmed cases of the virus.

Ideally, in such times, governments lead the way with responses that are rapid, bold, generous and crisis-facing, as they have done in momentous times in the past (UNCTAD 2017). Political will is essential, as is the fiscal space or economic capacity to unblock the flow of finance, to fund increased health sector bills and unemployment benefits, and to underwrite the firms, households, public services, local authorities and even banks that are reeling as the flow of money is interrupted. What individual countries in practice did varied according to their fiscal resources and the contexts of their unique political economies within global capitalism. Even just months into the crisis, when this research was being conducted, it was evident that the poorest countries and most marginalised communities were struggling with having much less capacity than their wealthy counterparts (IMF 2020). By August 2020, Japan had spent as much as 52.6 per cent of its GDP on a variety of fiscal and monetary packages; Germany 38.5 per cent, Canada 30 per cent and the United States 27.5 per cent, while even the large and higher income developing countries could manage only a fraction of this (UNCTAD 2020). In the global south the International Monetary Fund (IMF) and the World Bank scaled up their financial responses, yet many criticised them for being too little, too conditional and too unevenly distributed (Kentikelenis et al. 2020). These international financial institutions (IFIs) are not the focus of this research, however. Instead the research project aimed to investigate the responses of national and regional public banks (commercial; universal; developmental), which have too often been overlooked and under-studied despite their extremely significant roles in socio-economic development, in supporting government policies, and in providing alternative public financial capacity (see Griffith-Jones and Ocampo 2018; Marshall and Rochon 2019; Marois 2022; UNCTAD 2019).

Why Public Banks at a Time of Covid-19?

Banks were particularly important in the first months of the Covid-19 outbreak because the effect of lockdown was manifested extremely quickly in a crisis of liquidity. Firms that had been viable before Covid-19 suddenly found themselves without operational finance or reserves with which to pay loans, bills and salaries; households could not pay mortgages or rent; exporters found themselves unpaid for products that were stuck in ports and docks uncollected; importers could not access stock they had already pre-sold; municipalities, local authorities, hospitals and even national governments faced huge unanticipated and unbudgeted expenses. Hence what began as a health shock, rapidly became an economic and financial one. To unlock this, banks exercised their unique capacity to make money, and hence *time*, available, commanding where and for how long it is available.

Banks, be they public or private, are historically unique financial institutions that specialise in collecting, directing, accelerating, and magnifying money as capital and as credit. Banks do so because they have acquired over time the political right to perform these powerful economic functions in society, not least of which is the ability to create money itself by extending credits well in excess of the actual money held in bank reserves (Spratt 2009; McLeay, Radia, and Thomas 2014; Pettifor 2016; Hudson 2018). For this reason, banks have become one of the most important institutions in capitalist society, financial or otherwise. It is also a reason why governments and communities worldwide have founded *public* banks and why public banks persist as credible, if contested, financial institutions (Marois 2022).

A public bank is a bank that can be understood as located in the 'public sphere'. This can happen in different ways. A bank can be *owned* publicly — that is, by a government, public authority or public enterprise; or it can be *controlled* publicly — that is, governed according to a legally binding public purpose mandate, or according to public law, or by meaningful public purpose representation on the governing board, or by some combination of these factors. Either or both situate a bank within the public sphere and as a *public* financial institution.

Being located within the public sphere opens up the *potential* for, if not the necessity of, public banks to function differently from private banks. Private corporate banks are directly exposed to competitive market imperatives and to the short-term profit-maximising horizons of shareholders. Public banks might also be, but they need not follow these competitive imperatives. The public sphere can shield public banks from market imperatives as a matter of political will and policy frameworks. Consequently, public banks can offer and direct loans, credits, and grants in ways that are otherwise impossible for private, profit-seeking banks — and do so over longer terms, at more favourable rates, and for activities or actors that private finance would eschew because of high risk or low profitability (see Marshall 2010; Barrowclough and Gottschalk 2018; Scherrer 2017; von Mettenheim 2010; Griffith-Jones and Ocampo 2018; UNCTAD 2019; McDonald, Marois, and Barrowclough 2020; Epstein and Uğurlu 2020; Marois 2022).

This potentially special role to command money and time is of no small consequence, not least amidst crises. Public banks comprise a large and diverse part of the global financial sector. As of mid-2020, there were 910 public development, commercial/retail and universal banks worldwide with nearly US$49 trillion in combined assets, which equate to 34 per cent of 2019 global GDP (Marois 2022b, 55). If we include public central banks and multilateral banks, as well as public pension and investment funds, there are some 1,651 public financial institutions commanding just under US $82 trillion in public financial assets (equating to 58 per cent of global GDP). In general, research confirms that the scale of public banking worldwide has been systematically under-represented for decades (Xu, Ren, and Wu 2019; FiC 2020; Marois 2022b; *cf.* De Luna-Martínez and Vicente 2012; UN IATF 2019, 143). Historically many public banks and financial institutions have been created at times of or in response to crises — be they economic, developmental, financial, social, and now climate, including recent public bank examples like the new Southern owned public banks, the Scottish National Investment Bank, the Canada Infrastructure Bank, the UK Investment Bank, among many others (UNCTAD 2019, pp. 143–172; Barrowclough 2022; FiC 2020).

Research Methodology and Theory

Our research project took shape in a context too raw and fluid to have an established academic literature on public banks and Covid-19 responses. We approached the topic with a necessarily exploratory and largely bottom-up inductive and case study approach informed by existing theory about public banks in general and by previous research of team members. Our aim was to generate the first evidence on 'public banks' Covid-19 responses, with the hope of contributing useful findings to the search for useful and relevant policy responses. The research focused on accessing data and evidence from multiple sources quickly, including from the banks' data and annual reports, online media, and from semi-structured interviews. We aimed to answer the question of what public banks did in their first responses to the liquidity crisis and economic slowdown and how they did it. We sought to highlight promising responses as well as any problems and limitations.

The primary research focus was on case studies of public banks financing a variety of crisis responses to COVID-19, which was supported by several additional cross-cutting thematic topics. Potential contributors were contacted in April/May 2020, shortly after the declaration of a global pandemic. We cast a wide net from the global north and south as it was not clear who would be able to participate given the difficult circumstances and what kind of information researchers might be able to collect in light of the health and mobility issues on top of the challenges of working from home — a first for most researchers, banking officials and government policymakers alike. Our core selection criteria were pragmatic given the context: does the proposed study look at 'public bank' responses (defined below)? Is there sufficient access to information, primary and secondary? And, can a high quality 'rapid response' study be delivered in time?

Overall, the study engaged with 24 researchers and four regional public bank and development finance associations,[1] the results of which were published together in a 22-chapter online book format. Therein at least 28 cases of public banks and financial institutions were discussed, in greater and lesser detail, in addition to the wide-ranging survey reports from the regional associations. Five studies were thematic in character, looking at the initiatives and policies of development banks, central banks, microfinance alternatives, public banking movements, and south-south cooperation during those early months. It constituted the most wide-ranging study of public banks' responses to Covid-19 available.

Researchers were provided with a standardised list of questions to investigate, including background information on the bank, context of the pandemic outbreak in the study location, key actions taken in response and their intended beneficiaries, the effectiveness of these actions (as much as could be ascertained in the immediate view), and the extent of collaboration with other public service providers and public banks. The constantly shifting nature of the crisis, and the very different personal and geographical contexts of the researchers, made consistency across the contributions difficult but nonetheless rendered a valuable snapshot of a highly uncertain time.

Data was gathered from a broad range of sources. For key financial indicators, researchers used Orbis Bank Scope data and drew from bank reports and press statements. Secondary resources on individual banks provided background, although the extent of any secondary literature on the banks differed enormously (for example, there is a huge literature on some institutions, including the Latin American, the Chinese, and the German banks, but practically nothing on others, like the Council of Europe Development Bank). Researchers were encouraged to conduct online or phone interviews. Again, the ability of researchers to gain access to public bank staff amidst

[1]The Association of African Development Finance Institutions (representing 60 member institutions), the Association of Development Financing Institutions in Asia and the Pacific (87 institutions), the European Association of Public Banks (91 institutions) and Latin American Association of Development Financing Institutions (42 institutions).

the pandemic varied significantly. The strength of the research project is captured in the wide-ranging nature of the results, which illustrate both a universality of public bank experiences in advanced and developing countries, alongside very diverse realities. Subsequent studies that also find an important contribution of public banks, although without looking at them individually as in this project, include ECLAC (2021).

The rapid response research did not have the objective of making a theoretical intervention. However, our current analysis contributes to renewed theoretical debate around rethinking public banks (Marois 2022a). To date, most research on public banks has fallen into either orthodox 'political' or heterodox 'development' approaches. These views are often distinguished by polarised understandings of the 'public' ownership of banks as typically negative (orthodox) or positive (heterodox). Orthodox views are the most stark. In effect, 'bureaucrats make bad bankers' because public banks are by virtue of being publicly-owned inherently prone to political abuse, corruption, and moral hazard (see World Bank 2001; La Porta, Lopez-de-Silanes, and Shleifer 2002; Barth, Caprio, and Levine 2006; Demirgüç-Kunt and Servén 2010; Marcelin and Mathur 2015). Heterodox views are often posed in contradistinction to orthodox ones. Commonly, public banks are defined as banks that function according to a distinct extra-market logic of action and as having an *a priori* role in economic expansion and additionality, again by virtue of being publicly-owned (Levy Yeyati, Micco, and Panizza 2007; Marshall 2010; Skidelsky et al. 2011; Ribeiro de Mendonça and Deos 2017).

Heterodox approaches, however, demonstrate broader appreciation than orthodox ones for the historical influences giving shape to public banking functions, including changes in governing parties and power relations within society. Yet heterodox theory has yet to adequately capture the diverse specificities of public banking institutions across time and space. Consequently, narratives on public banking are often expressed in terms firmer than history allows for or heterodox scholars may intend (for example, stating that public banks are not subject to market competition, speculative excesses or profit imperatives, when they can be, or that public banks are meant to provide additionality, when they may not be). In short, more conceptual weight and clarity have to go into the social and political forces that give evolving and indeterminant meanings to being a public bank within heterodox views, building off of recent advances in this direction (see Butzbach, Rotondo, and Desiato 2018; Marshall and Rochon 2019). Yet in the absence of a theoretical rethinking of the meaning of the 'public' in public banks, typical orthodox and heterodox views will continue to reproduce ultimately polarised conceptualisations of public banks that over-determine otherwise historically variable institutional functions according to ownership form. In short, ownership will conceptually continue to predefine institutional function.

The results of this study support calls to rethink public banks as more complex and less historically fixed institutions, wherein mandate, sources of finance and performance appraisal matter alongside ownership form (Romero 2017; Butzbach, Rotondo, and Desiato 2018; Romero 2020; UNCTAD 2019, pp. 160–166). It is not only this research project's findings that point in this more diverse direction. Other contributions to the literature have focused on 'solidarity' as a motivating factor in one of the major new trends of the last decade, namely the growth of new and expansion of existing southern-owned and led banks (Gallagher and Chin 2019; Barrowclough 2018, 2020a). Conceptually, an alternative 'dynamic' view aims to further the rethinking of public banks, seeing public ownership not as over-determining institutional functions but as opening up 'a particular public realm of possibilities' wherein 'change becomes possible and is a result of social forces making it so' within the structures of capitalist society (Marois 2022a). In this view, historical and socially contested institutional functions give meaning to dynamic interpretations of public ownership. There remains a need for further research that engages in these deeper theoretical challenges, which have important and urgent practical implications as we confront multiple crises and societal grand challenges in need of supportive financing.

The Power of Public Banks–Promising Lessons and Findings

Based on our research at the start of the Covid-19 crisis, the most promising lessons learned from the project demonstrated that public banks could respond rapidly; act according to public purpose mandates; act boldly; mobilise their existing institutional capacity; and build on 'public-public' solidarity (Chapter 1 by Barrowclough, Marois, and McDonald 2020).[2] In these ways public banks helped to navigate the tidal wave of Covid-19, often as private lenders were turning away. Not every public bank responded in the same way or to the same extent or even showed signs of each promising lesson. Yet in general we found that funds could be found or created, often enabling generous, rapid, and bold actions, as collaborations with other public enterprises took shape with ease and in ways that reflected a clear public purpose. The project research also revealed some very weak public bank responses, underscoring the theoretical point that public ownership per se does not predefine institutional functions. At the same time, the results point to the need for greater historical understanding. Having a long organisational history helped public banks benefit from existing lines of communication, reservoirs of expertise, and established capacity to co-ordinate with others. Such historical legacies cannot be created suddenly in times of crisis. However, even when banks were relatively new, such as those from the global South, when they had a clear sense of public purpose and public-public solidarity, responses could also be bold, generous and rapid. Alongside these broad lessons, the research revealed a wide range of tools and instruments used by public banks to carry out their roles, often depending on their position within the overall global financial system.

Given the diverse range of public banks examined, with their various and varying roles in the financial system of their countries, as well as differing national developmental and political contexts, there are many different elements on which one could focus for highlighting essential lessons. Similarly with the findings of the banking associations, which synthesise almost 300 different institutions from a heterogenous mixture of countries. Here, however, we focus on and draw out the promising, and challenging, lessons relating to the banks' public purpose.

Promising Public Purpose

Whether small or large, when public banks had clear mandates and unambiguous backing from their governments and a strong public purpose, they could respond very

[2]All 'Chapter' references in this section refer to the separate researcher contributions in the edited book compilation, McDonald, Marois, and Barrowclough (2020).

quickly and generously. Italy's Cassa Depositi e Prestiti (CDP), which launched a Social Response within one week of the first Italian case registered of Covid-19 on 21 February 2020, offered up to 1 billion euros in loans for SMEs and deferred payments for local authorities (Chapter 14 by Vandone et al. 2020). Within the first few months of Covid-19, as many as 40 per cent of all firms in Italy were suffering the impact and 44 per cent of the workforce, or 4 million workers. Italy's GDP fell by 6 per cent and further declines were expected. By April, the banks 'strong prompt and relevant' response included launching a Social Response Bond raising another 1 billion euro and rolling out a series of further measures with loans and guarantees or renegotiated loans worth another 10 billion euros. These actions were firmly in line with the mission of the CDP, which was founded in 1850, and today has an explicit public purpose of fostering sustainable development and supporting employment. It is classified as a national promotional bank ('development' bank), as defined by the European Commission, and it is mandated to lend only to national and local governments and to corporate entities, not to individuals. It has a tradition of providing counter-cyclical support in times of crisis, which it had already exhibited during the global financial crisis.

The Chinese study showed a very particular example of how 'state-owned' public banks can be deployed in times of crisis, even when they have a commercial mandate (Chapter 13 by Yeung 2020). The Peoples' Bank of China (PBoC), the central bank, directed its five major state-owned commercial banks to such an extent they 'could be functioning more like ministries in the central government than private commercial banks' (p. 285). The banks' responses were focused on SMEs, who were impacted by the lockdown of Wuhan and its domino effects. More than 18 million private enterprises were under threat, affecting the jobs of 200 million people. The PBoC increased liquidity, as did central banks more or less everywhere, although they did it through reducing the reserve requirement ratio rather than the quantitative easing policies used by banks in hard currency countries. More interesting, however, in terms of public purpose, the PBoC gave the commercial banks the most explicit directions in more than a decade, to 'sacrifice profits to benefit corporate borrowers'. Banks were instructed to give up \$210 billion in profits for the year, equivalent to up to 75 per cent of profits the year before. The state banks were also required to reduce fees and defer loan repayments. Such measures reflect the hybrid nature of these banks, in which the Chinese state still holds the majority of equity and will use it to support the public policy when deemed necessary. According to Yeung, 'Ownership here translates to effective control, should state authorities choose to exercise it'. The policies were not without controversy amid claims that funds were lent to shell companies and diverted to real estate speculation. But the issue of commercial banks being required to support national goals was not in question.

The Council of Europe Development Bank (CEB) provides a different kind of example where a much smaller multilateral public bank could nonetheless play an important role, especially considering other regional institutions were more ambivalent. The CEB lent over three billion euros in emergency finance to 15 member governments in the first three months of lockdown in Europe — an amount which was a full 2/3 of total lending for the previous year. This response reflects the kind of rapid and public purpose commitment possible of a small bank with a clearly social mandate, relatively flexible governance structure and a well-established programme of lending to the public sector. Funds were raised on international capital markets in April and again in June at very favourable rates, and it quickly implemented emergency lending by amending its rules to 'fast track' public funding to health systems and small businesses under strain (Chapter 5 by Reyes 2020). Because the CEB had long-established lending schemes it could use its existing institutional history, experience and contacts to act rapidly, and its strong non-profit ethos meant that borrowers received the benefit of its ability to raise capital at favourable rates.

The benefit of the CEB's public purpose and its actions shows in the ease with which it can raise funds on capital markets, especially where investors are looking for socially responsible investments. The CEB has a history of successfully issuing 'social inclusion bonds' that are aligned with international impact investment principles. The CEB maintains a high credit rating with the major agencies despite being a non-profit institution. These both reflect the perception that the CEB's government owners will support the bank if need be. This finding chimes with pre-Covid-19 general advice from the major Credit Rating Agencies, which acknowledged that many public banks could lend more without hurting their credit ratings, especially if their lending decisions were for public purposes because this allowed the banks' owners to support it (S&P Global 2017; UNCTAD 2019, p. 164.) Moody's found that 'CEB's involvement in the coronavirus crisis response and the associated increase in lending further supports the importance of its mandate for shareholders (Member states)' (Chapter 5 by Reyes, p. 129). Reyes reports that Fitch reached a similar conclusion that the bank's strong response had increased 'its importance for its member states'.

The public purpose mandate of the Germany KfW is to provide for 'the sustainable improvement of the economic, social and ecological conditions of peoples' lives' through 'financing with a public mission'. The KfW response to Covid-19 was wholehearted as it doubled the total volume of the previous year's lending in the first half of 2020, providing more than 750 billion euros in response to the call from its government owners (Chapter 7 by Marois 2020). KfW responses involved a variety of Covid-19 support packages that included aid and loan programmes to companies, self-employed and freelance workers; instant loans to medium-sized companies that offered 100 per cent guarantees, and other packages expanding credit and guarantees to industry, credit insurers and other banks and institutions. That the KfW has acted according to a clear public purpose was expressed by the Chair of the Board of Managing Directors: *The banks and KfW have prepared intensively for today. Never before have we been able to put a full programme together this quickly* (p. 158).

The KfW is one of those public banks with a legacy of strong coherence between its public purpose mandate and the support of its government owners. This is expressed in a formal guarantee of its financial stability and is further evident in the fact that the bank has a track record of winning the lowest possible rates for its bond issuances. In the current low rate environment the KfW is borrowing at negative yields — meaning that the market essentially pays the Bank to borrow and not the other way around. As with the CEB, not only has the KfW's public purpose been good for a rapid Covid-19 response, it has also been good for financial terms.

Some national public banks were conduits for development finance and aid to other countries. The KfW committed up to 5 billion euros of new lending and grants to developing countries, reflecting that its public purpose can extend beyond national borders. Development banks owned by and lending to developing countries also played an extremely important role for their members in the first phase of the response, which was particularly important given the muted response of the World Bank and International Monetary Fund. The Inter-American Development Bank (IADB) doubled its disbursements to $26.7 billion and offered more than 600 individual loans to its members, many of whom had already severely under-financed health systems and limited social welfare capacities (Chapter 11 by Carreras and Griffith-Jones 2020). The IADB was officially founded in 1959 and is owned by 48 countries, but only 26 of them can borrow. Its mandate is 'to foster the economic and social development of the IDBs borrowing member countries, both individually and collectively'. While its institutional strategies do not include health issues, the social and economic impact of Covid-19 fitted the mandate sufficiently that within just a few months the IABD adapted flexibly. In addition to increasing sharply the number of loans offered, it increased non-conditional transfers and fast-tracked systems so as to save processing time by 2/3, which meant it took less than one month or maximum two to issue loans.

At the same time however, the IADB case study hints at tensions and constraints that can occur when banks have a multi-government structure with heterogeneous countries as shareholders and a wide spectrum of duties around shareholders' country-specific and general priorities. The new development banks that are either entirely Southern-owned or are Southern-led have shown ways, like the CEB, that multilaterally-owned public banks could respond very quickly, as their public purpose and governing structures were flexible enough to be readily aligned with new demands. These southern banks had from the outset been established to offer a southern-led alternative to the Bretton Woods institutions and this purpose guided their relief responses (Chapter 18 by Barrowclough 2020a). For example, the Asian Infrastructure Investment Bank (AIIB) adapted its priorities beyond the long-term infrastructure purpose for which it had been initially established in 2016. In the first days of March, the AIIB announced a $5 billion Covid-19 Crisis Recovery Facility and within a month requests from members were so high that it doubled the facility to $10 billion. In order to meet the 'urgent and extraordinary' needs, it not only identified new priorities for funding but adapted operations to work closely with other international financial institutions and create a network of support options, especially for the most vulnerable economies. Similarly, the New Development Bank had to be flexible as its existing policy framework did not support the special needs of members when Covid-19 struck. Established in 2014, its mandate was to mobilise 'resources for infrastructure and sustainable development projects in BRICS and other emerging economies and developing countries'. The urgent needs of Covid-19 did not fit the profile and a special waiver was needed for its first loans to China in March and a second to India in April. By June 2020, the New Development Bank announced a new fast track emergency assistance response facility with $10 billion to disburse (divided equally between health and social assistance, and economic recovery). Subsequent loans did not need a waiver. The policy changes are interesting because the New Development Bank adopted a new way of thinking about so-called 'emergencies'. Previously these were defined as being the consequence of natural disasters or conflict but after Covid-19 fallout included urgent gaps in finance for government welfare and social support — a public purpose for which the Bank had not been initially designed.

Argentina's public bank, the Banco de las Nación Argentina (BNA), is an example where a state-owned but commercially mandated public bank played a role, if perhaps not a leading role, in providing counter-cyclical lending as part of its government's Covid-19 relief programme (Chapter 10 by Schclarek Curutchet 2020). Established in 1891, at a time of crisis in Argentina, the BNA is today the country's largest commercial bank, with pre-Covid-19 loans accounting for 18 per cent of the total financial system. The BNA responded swiftly and within one month of the central bank initiating a series of new policy sticks and carrots, disbursing as much as 15 per cent of the total credit offered by the entire banking system. The central bank's carrots included offering new credit lines to the banking system that were provided at a relatively low fixed nominal rate of 24 per cent (remembering that inflation was over 40 per cent), to be on-lent for purposes such as working capital for micro-, small-, and medium-sized enterprises (MSMEs); teleworking expenses to set up home offices; salary payments of MSME employees; and credit to firms that previously had no credit profile in the banking system. There was also a policy stick, whereby banks that did not lend were charged increased costs for their liquid and short-term assets in the central bank. In this case, the BNA's response is less bold and more in line with its commercial imperatives rather than any bold public purpose.

Challenging Public Purpose

There are differences in how public banks responded to the Covid-19 pandemic, with some cases challenging the notion of public purpose having much influence. In the case of Brazil, public banks had a very different Covid-19 experience, reflecting a significant change in their mandates and the roles expected of them compared to the 2008–2009 global financial crisis years when they had played a major role providing credit to support recovery (Chapter 12 by de Oliveira 2020). Since 2015 when Brazil adopted a more neoliberal approach, the role of public banks 'could not be more different'. When the pandemic struck private financial institutions were just as able as public ones to operate the government's special Covid-19 credit lines. Of the 31.5 billion real Federal Government credit programmes implemented by Brazil's banks, 51 per cent was done through public banks, especially the Caixa Economica Federal (a 100 per cent government owned bank serving Brazil's housing credit programme). However, semi-private banks and foreign banks provided the rest and the offer was similar whether banks were privately owned or public. From the borrower's point of view, it made little difference which bank they dealt with — they were 'indifferent.' Other differences emerged when comparing the outcomes of those early months to other countries, where public banks played a more pivotal role. Firstly, implementation was slow. When government released its measures to expand liquidity in April, a few weeks after the first lockdown, it was not until June that small firms received their loans from either public or private banks. This is a long time compared to the more promising examples above. Secondly, loans through the banks, both public and private, were more expensive to borrowers than those provided directly by government — meaning that all the banks were making a cut. The costs depended on borrowers' profiles rather than bank ownership and some were charged up to 20 per cent for working capital loans. Moreover, it seems the loans were granted mostly to large companies, even when mediated through public banks, rather than favouring MSMEs who would find it difficult to access capital otherwise.

Similar delays in rolling out credit relief occurred in the case of the European Investment Bank (EIB), where it was not until April that a package could be agreed by all the member governments. Even by August, the EIB's lending in the health sector was only 18 billion euros out of an estimated lending for the year of 63 billion euros, compared to other public banks that substantively reconfigured their lending (Chapter 6 by Clifton et al. 2020). Even then some expenditures were ambiguous or seen as 'Covid-washing' with the major beneficiaries being private financial investors rather than MSMEs or social and environmental beneficiaries.

India's experience generally spells a cautionary tale about the importance of mandate and public purpose, and it points to the need for consistency between the expectations of public banks and the broader macroeconomic situation in which they are embedded (Chapter 9 by Chandrasekhar 2020). At the time of the research, India was the country, after the United States, with the second largest number of known Covid-19 infections. This was a reflection of its high population but also of India's underfunded and overwhelmed health system. Public banks were given the responsibility for providing relief to the devastated economy but they were unable to do so effectively because their mandates had changed, their public functions had been undermined, or even their institutions had been dismantled in the liberalizations and privatizations of the 1990s. India's public banks had social mandates in the past but now they have been largely commercialised. Their institutional purpose is more about making profit, incentivizing private investors and innovating service delivery. The public banks are in turn judged by their ability to maximise earnings. The government also relied heavily on monetary policy as the sole stimulus, and the public banks were unwilling or unable to lend the augmented funds made available. Some credit was targeted specifically to the National Bank for Agriculture and Rural Development (NABARD), the Small Industries Development Bank of India (SIDBI) and EXIM Bank but, apart from those parts of credit creation that were guaranteed by the government, the risk was carried by public banks and it came at a time when these banks were already burdened with large scale debt defaults caused by the contraction. Hence, credit growth did not pick up during those difficult months, rather it fell. This suggests that without a clear public purpose and the tools to implement it, public banks cannot be expected to do the heavy lifting independently of government support.

Mexico is a case where a newly-founded, high-profile public bank, the Bank of Welfare or Banco del Bienestar, was not able to play the positive role anticipated. Even though it is publicly-owned and seemingly has a public purpose, in practice its public functions are ambiguous if not downright negative (Chapter 8 by Reis 2020). The Banco del Bienestar was seen as central to Mexico's ambitious project of developing 'an alternative to neoliberalism' and creating 'a moral state'. The mandated purpose is to support 'the economy of the people' and it has been used to distribute cash benefits to the elderly, disabled and students providing cash transfers of $12 billion per annum to at least 18 million people. In practice however, the study finds that the public bank is being used to capture a lucrative market — the poor — for private sector financiers. When Covid-19 hit Mexico, more than 12 million people lost their jobs between April and May, 2/3 of whom were in the informal sector and without income support, and another 8 million became under-employed. The Banco del Bienestar expanded programmes that were already existing, in particular relating to social transfers. Pensions were paid four months in advance, existing microcredit programme users were granted deferment of payment for three months, and two million new credits were created without requiring paperwork or a credit history. Typically, this would be positive. However because the bank did not have many branches or outlets, the programmes relied on collaborations with other banks, in particular a private domestic bank tied to a larger retail conglomerate that offered spaces for branches and ATMs in its department stores. The retail conglomerate has a reputation for extremely high interest rates (around 88 per cent) and aggressive debt collection tactics. Egregiously, to receive the government's social benefits, borrowers had to open accounts at this bank if they did not have one already. It seemed that the Banco del Bienestar functioned as a kind of bond between the poor and private global financial markets, that is, in the private interest, opening the door to the 'financial inclusion' programme of the World Bank and acting to cement and increase marginalised communities' debt and dependence.

For public banks in Turkey, the research found that the early Covid-19 responses highlighted both the potential contribution and the limitations of public banks whose historic mandates have been chipped away over the last decade (Chapter 16 by Güngen 2020). When Turkey went into a severe economic slump following lockdown in April and May of 2020, the public banks emerged at the forefront of support to low-income households and MSMEs. Public banks have increasingly followed a profit-maximising stance since the early 2000s but, at the same time, the three largest Turkish public banks stepped up lending significantly and provided low-interest loans with a repayment holiday for the first six months to some seven million people who applied for basic needs credit. They lent also to shops and other businesses. These loans were backstopped by the Turkish Treasury, who assumed part of the counter-risk. While private banks also played a role in credit creation it was the public banks that provided the lion's share. On the back of this, Turkey experienced the biggest credit expansion of its history. Almost 40 per cent of the additional credit came from public banks, while only 17 per cent from private banks and 27 per cent from foreign ones, and their shares would have been even lower were it not for government regulations pushing lending. At the same time, however, the public banks are considered opaque and non-transparent, and overly connected to the big business interests of the ruling party. The Turkish public banks lack transparent and accountable public purpose. Lending to the poorest parts of society is considered miniscule, compared to trends in other countries. Their somewhat contradictory role is raising concerns about what will happen in the future and if the remnants of a social mandate to public banking is further eroded by the ruling government. At present, the Treasury automatically compensates public banks for non-performing loans, or what are called 'income losses' each month, and this amount was three times as high as usual for the early months of 2020. While the public banks showed they could respond to the crisis, they have not been able to respond to longer-term issues that are essential to turn around the deteriorating economy and to address social and environmental concerns.

The results of the rapid response research point powerfully in the direction that at times of crisis, notably the outbreak of the Covid-19 pandemic and lockdown, meaningful public purpose can have an impact on how a public bank responds. Weaker public purpose leads to more ambiguous action. The case studies, and the complementary thematic papers in the book, show that public purpose is about more than public ownership. Public purpose is inter-related with the political economy of mandates, institutional history and legacies, sources and scales of finance, and the ways that public banks fit into the broader landscape of the financial system (Chapter 2 by Romero 2020; Chapter 4 by Barrowclough 2020b). When these are well aligned, transparent and accountable, public banks have a more promising chance to play a significant role–whether in an unexpected crisis, as during the first months of the pandemic covered in this paper, or in future efforts to finance climate change adaptation and mitigation.

From Covid-19 to Building Forward Better for People and Planet

The promising lessons of how public banks responded with public purpose to the global pandemic crisis can help inform debate of how to finance responses to the climate crisis in ways aiming to build forward better for people and planet. What we know from public banks' Covid-19 responses is that public purpose can be a powerful force setting directionality for public banks — when credibly backed by society and public policy. Where public banks have eschewed public purpose for profit mandates or have been made to function predominantly in private interests, then the public banks show more muted responses to the Covid-19 crisis. To build forward better for people and planet in response to the global climate crisis, our conclusion is that transparent and accountable public purpose must play a causal role in how and what public banks do. Therein it is vital not to see public banks as essentially better or worse than private banks by virtue of being 'public', but rather as contested and dynamic institutions made and remade by social forces in capitalist society. This is significant given the already existing institutional numbers and combined assets worldwide. Be they public or private, banks uniquely command 'a power to make available time' (Konings 2018, p. 79). However, only through the public sphere can public banks command time and money according to (contested) public purpose.

It is here that public banks offer the most viable pathway for urgent financing of a green and just global transition to a low-carbon future. There is widespread agreement around the failure of private banks to respond to the financing needs for mitigating global warming, making room for the potentially catalytic role of public banks to respond in new and innovative ways (Campiglio et al. 2017; Carney 2015; Scott, van Huizen, and Jung 2017; UNCTAD 2019, pp. 143–172). Empirical evidence suggests that public investors are a main reason that renewable energy finance grew at all in the years following the global financial crisis (Mazzucato and Semieniuk 2018). Sustainability criteria for public banking has passed from niche debate to increasingly mainstream action across the globe, in low-income countries just as much as in wealthy ones (UNCTAD 2019; Barrowclough 2022). Even in the United States , where the researchers found that Covid responses were aimed more at Wall Street than the High Street and public banks did not respond to the Covid needs as one might have expected (Brown 2020), the opportunities for creating entirely new public banks are now a window "flung open". These findings support other evidence from case studies that point to public banks as existing financial institutions. Case study evidence points to public banks as existing financial institutions that can combine effective decarbonisation financing with democratic governance structures capable of integrating just transition criteria (Marois 2022b).

To suggest that public banks should lead efforts to build forward better for people and the planet is not, however, to naively assert that a bank is necessarily better by virtue of being publicly owned. There is no innate purpose or essential policy orientation that is common to all public banks. This is because public banks are contested institutions and pulled between contending public and private interests. Some of our case-study findings find that even public interests can be competing — for example, where regional banks have to reconcile differing interests and priorities of multiple stakeholders, including the IADB and CDC banks (Carreras and Griffith-Jones 2020, 246) compared to the more solidarity-driven Islamic Development Bank (IsDB) and New Development Bank (NDB) and the foreign reserve fund Fondo Latinoamericano de Reservas FLAR (Barrowclough 2020a, pp. 361–375). They too are but one element within the landscape of all financial institutions, nested within a global financial market characterised by an unequal hierarchy of national and international economic and political forces.

Yet the Covid-19 crisis has shown the financial vulnerabilities and inequalities of today's hyper-globalised, just-in-time, and hyper-financialised economy. So too it has shone a light on otherwise hidden public bank coordination networks and collaborative practices — and above all the importance of public purpose in public banking. This lesson needs to be better understood and expanded upon, with knowledge sharing, policy innovation, and capacity building being critical to a more sustainable and financially powerful global public banking network capable of catalysing a global green and just transition for people and planet.

As the first study of public bank responses to Covid-19, our research project raises as many questions as it answers, highlighting the need for further case study and empirical work. We conclude by setting out six research areas in need of further study.

- What have been the medium-term economic, social, and environmental impacts of public banks' initial Covid-19 responses? This research should look at impacts both on local authorities and communities that received support and at the impacts on public banks' own operations and sustainability.
- What 'publics' and communities have been represented in the public banks' Covid-19 responses? This cuts to questions of social equity, representative decision-making, transparency, accountability, and governance, not to mention the democratisation or not of finance in the face of crisis-related responses.
- What have been the main challenges limiting public banks' Covid-19 crisis responses? How do banks resolve the tension between remaining financially viable and supporting lending at low, no or negative return?
- How has success been measured and has Covid-19 moved forward the long-standing calls for new public purpose indicators beyond conventional financial measures and cost–benefit analysis? What metrics can effectively capture (and valorise) these public purpose collaborations?
- What lessons can be learned from further public bank case study and historical research into the impact of public purpose mandates amidst crisis responses, particularly among lesser-known and smaller public financial institutions?

- Finally, and this is perhaps the most pressing question, can the promising practices (and pitfalls) of public banks' Covid-19 responses be translated into urgent and effective responses to global climate change that better serve people and planet? Are there instances where Covid-19 responses supported green transitions? Research will also need to identify where the money came from that enabled public banks to respond rapidly and at scale and if different sources of finance differentially affected how public banks could respond.

Acknowledgements

We would like to acknowledge the work of all the authors who contributed to the original research project, producing excellent papers in a very short period of time under difficult circumstances, as well as to the bank officials who generously gave their time in interviews. Partial funding for the research project came from the Social Sciences and Humanities Research Council of Canada (SSHRC), with additional financial support from the European Network on Debt and Development (Eurodad) and the United Nations Conference on Trade and Development (UNCTAD). The project was coordinated by the Municipal Services Project (MSP), under the direction of Prof. David McDonald, Queen's University, Kingston, Canada. We must also acknowledge the generous efforts of the *ROPE* peer reviewers for reviewing this article and for providing useful feedback. It is no exaggeration that academics and researchers are under enormous and increasing personal and professional strain to teach and publish more and more. So, we gratefully acknowledge the service of reviewers in sharing (in our case especially) their time, knowledge and guidance. It is invaluable to our academic community, and indeed much appreciated. In this same vein, we are grateful to the *ROPE* Editors for putting together and shepherding this unique collection of research on public banks.

Disclosure Statement

No potential conflict of interest was reported by the author(s).

References

Barrowclough, D. 2022. 'South-South Financial Integration – New Directions in the Global Economy.' In *The New Palgrave Dictionary of Economics*, edited by M. Vernengo, E. Perez Caldentey, and B. Rosser. London: Palgrave MacMillan Ltd.

Barrowclough, D. 2020a. 'South-South Public Finance: A Rapid Review of Co-operation and Resilience to Face Covid-19.' In *Public Banks and Covid-19, Combatting the Pandemic with Public Finance*, edited by D. McDonald, T. Marois, and D. Barrowclough. Municipal Services programme. Kingston: Municipal Services Project; Geneva: UNCTAD; Brussels: Eurodad. Accessed October 6, 2021. https://publicbankscovid19.org/index.php/publications.

Barrowclough, D. 2020b. 'Coronavirus and the Evolving Roles of Central Banks: Avoiding a Climate Minsky Moment.' In *Public Banks and Covid-19, Combatting the Pandemic with Public Finance*, edited by D. McDonald, T. Marois, and D. Barrowclough. Kingston: Municipal Services Project; Geneva: UNCTAD; Brussels: Eurodad. Accessed October 6, 2021. https://publicbankscovid19.org/index.php/publications.

Barrowclough, D., and R. Gottschalk. 2018. "Solidarity and the South: Supporting the New Landscape of Long-Term Development Finance." UNCTAD Research Paper, No. 24 UNCTAD/SER.RP/2018/6.

Barrowclough, D., T. Marois, and D. McDonald. 2020. 'Public Banks Matter at a Time of Covid-19.' In *Public Banks and Covid-19, Combatting the Pandemic with Public Finance*, edited by D.

McDonald, T. Marois, and D. Barrowclough. Kingston: Municipal Services Project; Geneva: UNCTAD; Brussels: Eurodad. Accessed October 6, 2021. https://publicbankscovid19.org/index.php/publications.

Barth, J. R., G. Caprio, and R. Levine. 2006. *Rethinking Bank Regulation: Till Angels Govern*. New York: Cambridge University Press.

Brown E. 2020. 'Covid-19 and Public Banks in the United States; a Moment of Opportunity.' In *Public Banks and Covid-19, Combatting the Pandemic with Public Finance*, edited by D. McDonald, T. Marois, and D. Barrowclough. Kingston: Municipal Services Project; Geneva: UNCTAD; Brussels: Eurodad. Accessed October 6, 2021. https://publicbankscovid19.org/index.php/publications.

Butzbach, O., G. Rotondo, and T. Desiato. 2018. 'Can Banks be Owned?' *Accounting, Economics, and Law: A Convivium* 10 (1): 1–21.

Campiglio, E., A. Godwin, E. Kemp-Benedict, and S. Matikainen. 2017. 'The Tightening Links Between Financial Systems and the Low-Carbon Transition.' In *Economic Policies Since the Global Financial Crisis*, edited by P. Arestis and M. Sawyer. Basingstoke, UK: Palgrave Macmillan.

Carney, M. 2015. "Breaking the Tragedy of the Horizon – Climate Change and Financial Stability." Speech by the Governor of the Bank of England and Chairman of the Financial Stability Board, London, 29 September 2015.

Carreras, M., and S. Griffith-Jones. 2020. 'National and Multilateral Banks During the 2020 Pandemic: The Role of IADB and CDC During the First Phase of Covid-19.' In *Public Banks and Covid-19, Combatting the Pandemic with Public Finance*, edited by D. McDonald, T. Marois, and D. Barrowclough. Kingston: Municipal Services Project; Geneva: UNCTAD; Brussels: Eurodad. Accessed October 6, 2021. https://publicbankscovid19.org/index.php/publications.

Chandrasekhar, C. P. 2020. 'Public Banks and India's Ineffective Covid-19 Crisis Response.' In *Public Banks and Covid-19, Combatting the Pandemic with Public Finance*, edited by D. McDonald, T. Marois, and D. Barrowclough. Kingston: Municipal Services Project; Geneva: UNCTAD; Brussels: Eurodad. Accessed October 6, 2021. https://publicbankscovid19.org/index.php/publications.

Clifton, J., D. Diaz-Fuentes, D. Howarth, and H. Kavvadia. 2020. 'The Role of the European Investment Bank in Times of Covid-19.' In *Public Banks and Covid-19, Combatting the Pandemic with Public Finance*, edited by D. McDonald, T. Marois, and D. Barrowclough. Kingston: Municipal Services Project; Geneva: UNCTAD; Brussels: Eurodad. Accessed October 6, 2021. https://publicbankscovid19.org/index.php/publications.

De Luna-Martínez, J., and C. L. Vicente. 2012. *Global Survey of Development Banks*. Washington: World Bank Group.

Demirgüç-Kunt, A., and L. Servén. 2010. 'Are All the Sacred Cows Dead? Implications of the Financial Crisis for Macro- and Financial Policies.' *The World Bank Research Observer* 25 (1): 91–124.

de Oliveira, A. 2020. 'The Role of Public Credit Programmes in Mitigating the Economic Effects of the Covid-19 Pandemic: Brazil's Experience.' In *Public Banks and Covid-19, Combatting the Pandemic with Public Finance*, edited by D. McDonald, T. Marois, and D. Barrowclough. Kingston: Municipal Services Project; Geneva: UNCTAD; Brussels: Eurodad. Accessed October 6 2021. https://publicbankscovid19.org/index.php/publications.

ECLAC. 2021. *Financing for Development in the era of COVID-19 and Beyond*. Santiago: United Nations. Economic Commission for Latin America and the Caribbean. Accessed October 16, 2021. https://www.cepal.org/en/publications/46711-financing-development-era-covid-19-and-beyond.

Epstein, G., and E. N. Uğurlu. 2020. 'Are Bankers Essential Workers?' *Catalyst* 4 (2): 33–81.

FiC. 2020. *Finance in Common: The First Global Summit of Public Development Banks*. Paris: Conference Booklet. Accessed July 24, 2020. https://financeincommon.org/.

Gallagher, K., and G. Chin. 2019. "Coordinated Credit Spaces: The Globalization of Chinese Development Finance.".' *Development and Change* 50 (1): 245–274.

Griffith-Jones, S., and J. A. Ocampo2018. *The Future of National Development Banks*. Oxford: Oxford University Press.

Güngen, A. R. 2020. 'Turkey's Public Banks Amid the Covid-19 Pandemic.' In *Public Banks and Covid-19, Combatting the Pandemic with Public Finance*, edited by D. McDonald, T. Marois, and D. Barrowclough. Kingston: Municipal Services Project; Geneva: UNCTAD; Brussels: Eurodad. Accessed October 6, 2021. https://publicbankscovid19.org/index.php/publications.

Hudson, M. 2018. *... and Forgive Them Their Debts: Lending, Foreclosure, and Redemption from Bronze Age to the Jubilee Year*. Dresden, Germany: ILSET-Verlag.

IPCC. 2021. *Climate Change 2021: The Physical Science Basis*. Accessed October 4, 2021. https://www.ipcc.ch/report/ar6/wg1/#FullReport.

IMF. 2020. *Fiscal Monitor: Policies to Support People During the COVID-19 Pandemic*. Washington: International Monetary Fund.

Kentikelenis, A., D. Gabor, I. Ortiz, T. Stubbs, M. McKee, and D. Stuckler. 2020. 'Softening the Blow of the Pandemic: Will the International Monetary Fund and World Bank Make Things Worse?' *The Lancet Global Health* 18 (6): E758–E759. https://www.thelancet.com/journals/langlo/article/PIIS2214-109X(20)30135-2/fulltext.

Konings, M. 2018. *Capital and Time: For a New Critique of Neoliberal Reason*. Stanford: Stanford University Press.

La Porta, R., F. Lopez-de-Silanes, and A. Shleifer. 2002. 'Government Ownership of Banks.' *The Journal of Finance* 57 (1): 265–301.

Levy Yeyati, E., A. Micco, and U. Panizza. 2007. 'A Reappraisal of State-Owned Banks.' *Economia (pontificia Universidad Catolica Del Peru. Departamento De Economia)* 7 (2): 209–247.

Marcelin, I., and I. Mathur. 2015. 'Privatization, Financial Development, Property Rights and Growth.' *Journal of Banking and Finance* 50: 528–546.

Marois, T. 2022a. 'A Dynamic Theory of Public Banks (and Why It Matters).' *Review of Political Economy*.

Marois, T. 2022b. *Public Banks: Decarbonisation, Definancialisation, and Democratisation*. Cambridge: Cambridge University Press.

Marois, T. 2020. 'The KfW and Covid-19: Coordinating Public Finance Responses at Home and Abroad.' In *Public Banks and Covid-19, Combatting the Pandemic with Public Finance*, edited by D. McDonald, T. Marois, and D. Barrowclough. Kingston: Municipal Services Project; Geneva: UNCTAD; Brussels: Eurodad. Accessed October 6, 2021. https://publicbankscovid19.org/index.php/publications.

Marshall, W. C. 2010. 'Banco del Sur and the Need for Downstream Linkages: The Role of National Publicly Owned Banks.' *International Journal of Political Economy* 39 (3): 81–99.

Marshall, W. C., and L. P. Rochon. 2019. 'Public Banking and Post-Keynesian Economic Theory.' *International Journal of Political Economy* 48 (1): 60–75.

Mazzucato, M., and G. Semieniuk. 2018. 'Financing Renewable Energy: Who is Financing What and Why It Matters.' *Technological Forecasting and Social Change* 127: 8–22.

McDonald, D., T. Marois, and D. Barrowclough. 2020. *Public Banks and Covid-19, Combatting the Pandemic with Public Finance*. Kingston: Municipal Services Project; Geneva: UNCTAD; Brussels: Eurodad. Accessed October 6, 2021. https://publicbankscovid19.org/index.php/publications.

McLeay, M., A. Radia, and R. Thomas. 2014. 'Money in the Modern Economy: An Introduction.' *Bank of England Quarterly Bulletin* 54 (Q1): 4–13.

Pettifor, A. 2016. *The Production of Money: How to Break the Power of Bankers*. London: Verso.

Reis, N. 2020. 'The 'Bank of Welfare' and Mexico's Moral Economy.' In *Public Banks and Covid-19, Combatting the Pandemic with Public Finance*, edited by D. McDonald, T. Marois, and D. Barrowclough. Kingston: Municipal Services Project; Geneva: UNCTAD; Brussels: Eurodad. Accessed October 6, 2021. https://publicbankscovid19.org/index.php/publications.

Reyes, O. 2020. 'The Council of Europe Development Bank and Covid-19.' In *Public Banks and Covid-19, Combatting the Pandemic with Public Finance*, edited by D. McDonald, T. Marois, and D. Barrowclough. Kingston: Municipal Services Project; Geneva: UNCTAD; Brussels: Eurodad. Accessed October 6, 2021. https://publicbankscovid19.org/index.php/publications.

Ribeiro de Mendonça, A. R., and S. Deos. 2017. 'Beyond the Market Failure Argument: Public Banks as Stability Anchors.' In *Public Banks in the Age of Financialization*, edited by C. Scherrer. Cheltenham, UK: Edward Elgar Publishing.

Romero, M.J. 2017. *Public Development Banks: Towards a Better Model.* April 2017. Brussels: Network on Debt and Development. Accessed October 10. 2021. https://www.eurodad.org/public_development_banks_towards_a_better_model.

Romero, M. J. 2020. 'Reclaiming Public Development Banks to Finance a Sustainable and Equitable Recovery Post Covid-19.' In *Public Banks and Covid-19, Combatting the Pandemic with Public Finance*, edited by D. McDonald, T. Marois, and D. Barrowclough. Kingston: Municipal Services Project; Geneva: UNCTAD; Brussels: Eurodad. Accessed October 6, 2021. https://publicbankscovid19.org/index.php/publications.

Scherrer, C.2017. *Public Banks in the Age of Financialization: A Comparative Perspective.* Cheltenham, UK: Edward Elgar Publishing.

Schclarek Curutchet, A. 2020. 'Argentina's Countercyclical Credit Policy Response: Macroprudential Regulation and Public Bank Credit During Covid-19.' In *Public Banks and Covid-19, Combatting the Pandemic with Public Finance*, edited by D. McDonald, T. Marois, and D. Barrowclough. Kingston: Municipal Services Project; Geneva: UNCTAD; Brussels: Eurodad. Accessed October 6, 2021. https://publicbankscovid19.org/index.php/publications.

Scott, M., J. van Huizen, and C. Jung. 2017. 'The Bank of England's Response to Climate Change.' *Quarterly Bulletin* Q2: 98–109.

Skidelsky, R., F. Martin., and C. Westerlind Wigstrom. 2011. *Blueprint for a British Investment Bank.* London: Centre for Global Studies.

S&P Global. 2017. *Key Considerations for Supranationals' Lending Capacity and their Current Capital Endowment.* May 18. Accessed October 10, 2021. https://www.standardandpoors.com/en_US/web/guest/article/-/view/sourceId/10098975.

Spratt, S. 2009. *Development Finance: Debates, Dogmas, and New Directions.* London: Routledge.

Tooze, A. 2018. *Crashed: How a Decade of Financial Crises Changed the World.* New York: Viking.

UNCTAD. 2017. *Beyond Austerity, Towards a Global New Deal. Trade and Development Report 2017.* Geneva and New York: United Nations.

UNCTAD. 2019. *Financing a Global Green New Deal. Trade and Development Report 2019.* Geneva and New York: United Nations.

UNCTAD. 2020. *From Global Pandemic to Prosperity for All; Avoiding Another Lost Decade. Trade and Development Report 2020.* Geneva and New York: United Nations.

Vandone, D., M. Frigerio, C. Zatti, and D. Bakry. 2020. 'Covid-19 and Measures to Support Enterprise and Local Authorities in Italy: The Role of Cassa Depositi E Prestiti.' In *Public Banks and Covid-19, Combatting the Pandemic with Public Finance*, edited by D. McDonald, T. Marois, and D. Barrowclough. Kingston: Municipal Services Project; Geneva: UNCTAD; Brussels: Eurodad. Accessed 6 October 6, 2021. https://publicbankscovid19.org/index.php/publications.

von Mettenheim, K. 2010. *Federal Banking in Brazil.* London: Pickering and Chatto.

World Bank. 2001. *Finance for Growth: Policy Choices in a Volatile World.* Washington: The World Bank.

Xu, J., X. Ren, and X. Wu. 2019. "Mapping Development Finance Institutions Worldwide: Definitions, Rationales and Varieties." Research Report No. 1. Institute of New Structural Economics. Peking University.

Yeung, G. 2020. 'The Public Banks and Peoples Bank of China: Confronting Covid-19 (If Not Without Controversy).' In *Public Banks and Covid-19, Combatting the Pandemic with Public Finance*, edited by D. McDonald, T. Marois, and D. Barrowclough. Kingston: Municipal Services Project; Geneva: UNCTAD; Brussels: Eurodad. Accessed October 6, 2021. https://publicbankscovid19.org/index.php/publications.

Index

accountability 3, 121, 199
active banks 61, 62
Addis Ababa Action Agenda (AAAA) 143–145
African Development Bank (AfDB) 28, 35, 39, 42, 44–46, 53
agenda 43, 96–98, 101–105, 107, 109, 112–114, 116, 120–123, 127
Agenda for Sustainable Development 96
agenda, 2030 96–98, 101–107, 109, 112–114, 116, 120–123, 127
Além, A. C. 142
alignment 87, 94, 96, 100, 101, 103, 105, 106, 112–114, 116, 122
Anginer, D. 19
Araújo, V. L. D. 133, 134, 137
architecture 2, 34, 35, 48, 53, 85, 88, 92, 142
Arrow, K. J. 19
Asian Development Bank (ADB) 35, 39, 42, 44–46, 53
Asian Infrastructure Development Bank 2
Asian Infrastructure Investment Bank (AIIB) 39, 53, 194
assets 22, 48, 49, 65, 66, 69, 80, 83, 131, 135–137
Attridge, S. 47, 126

Banco Nacional de Desenvolvimento Econômico e Social (BNDES) 26–28, 70–75, 133–136, 138, 142
bank credit, pro-cyclical nature 67
bank's key characteristics 70
Barrowclough 175, 179, 188, 190, 191, 194, 198
Basel III 59–62, 64–72, 74, 75
beneficiaries 98, 107, 108, 122, 123
Benford, J. 27
Blended Finance Partnerships 113
Brazil 73, 75, 129, 132–137, 142–144, 195
Brazilian Central Bank 134, 136
Brazilian development agencies 132
Brazilian development systems 134, 146
Brazilian SDBs 133, 136, 137, 142

capital requirements 62, 65, 67, 71–74
capitalism 154, 156, 157, 163, 164, 166, 169, 170, 174–177, 179, 180
capitalist development 174
capitalization 3, 43, 44, 54
Castro, L. B. 65n12
central banks 63, 67, 73, 84, 139, 141, 166, 189, 192, 195
China Development Bank (CDB) 26, 28, 61, 69–71, 73–75
Chinese development banks 21, 31
climate finance 46, 47, 59, 64, 68, 69, 75, 86, 169, 177
climate risks 73, 75
commercial banks 7, 8, 10, 18, 24, 30, 59, 60, 73, 75, 139, 140, 142, 192
complex financial instruments 30
complex projects 59, 64, 68, 74
compliance 60, 69, 70, 75
concentration risks 67, 73
Correa, E. 164
COVID-19 pandemic 8, 9, 11, 23–28, 84, 145, 185–187, 189, 191–196, 198, 199
credit rating agencies 116
credit risk 24, 62, 66–68, 72
critical sectors 125, 126
currency risks 22, 68

DBFIs 78–80, 83–85, 90, 91, 93
de la Torre, A. 19
De Luna-Martinez, J. 143
De Luna-Martínez, J. 130
Deos, S. 173
development agencies 68, 134–138
Development Bank of Minas Gerais (BDMG) 25, 29, 106, 132, 135, 137, 138, 144, 145
development finance 59, 63, 130, 144, 193; institutions 52
development financing institutions (DFIs) 2, 3, 112, 116
development functions 140
development goals 3, 8, 143
development institutions 113, 130, 139, 140, 142, 146
development roles 126, 139
development systems 129, 146

developmental roles 67, 70, 71
direct loans 10, 30, 70, 188
du Toit, C. 114
dynamic theory 169–180

economic bliss 159, 161, 164
economic crisis 186
economic development 79, 98, 115, 133, 170, 172
economic development bank 132, 146
economic vulnerability 115
Engels, F. 177
environmental social governance (ESG) 106
equity investment 4, 13, 20, 80, 93
ESCAP 141
Eurodad 98
ex-ante verification 105
ex-post impact assessment 107
exclusion criteria 106
external engagement 107, 114, 122

fast-track procedures 24, 25, 29
Feil, F. 133, 134, 136, 137
financial actors 88, 89, 116, 117
financial crises 8, 9, 11, 19, 22, 35, 36, 39, 43, 51, 53, 54, 62, 83, 134, 186
financial institutions 23, 24, 34, 36, 48, 51, 60, 62, 63, 65, 132–134, 188, 189; regulating 61
financial instruments 2, 8–10, 20, 22, 23, 100, 110–112
financial market risks 13
financial markets 36, 37, 52, 62, 63, 78, 100, 113, 171, 173, 186
financial regulation 2, 3, 61–63, 83
financial systems 19, 63, 81, 84, 87, 132–134, 142, 191, 198
financing sustainable development strategies 116
first-tier institutions 142
functional finance 157, 166

Gallagher, K. 131
Gama Neto, R. B. 134
global financialized capitalism 175, 177
global financing architecture 92
global governance 92
Gouett, M. 47, 126
Graeber, D. 156
green bonds 39, 47, 111, 122, 145
green climate fund 4, 47, 90, 92, 113
green investments 141, 145, 179
Greenwald, B. 36
Greenwald, B. C. 19
Griffith-Jones, S. 37n2, 47, 51, 126, 129, 131, 132
guarantees 10–13, 18, 19, 24–27, 30, 39, 68, 110, 193

Harrington, M. 164
health crisis 186
health sector 28, 29, 196
heterodox approaches 190
Horn, C. H. 133–134, 136–137
human telos 163, 165, 167
humanity 154–156, 159, 161, 164, 165, 167

idiosyncratic risks 11, 12, 19, 22, 27
impact assessment 121
innovation 9, 11, 30, 31, 36, 38, 45, 46, 51, 53, 63, 64, 67, 68, 126
institutional functions 170, 172–175, 178, 190, 191
instrument choice 22
insurance type products 13, 22
Inter-American Development Bank (IADB) 28, 35, 39, 42, 44–46, 53, 194
internal models 65, 66, 68, 72, 74
interregional banks 43, 53
investment 2, 9, 13, 20, 21, 37, 80, 87, 91, 106, 111, 113, 116, 121, 139, 141, 145, 153, 154, 157
Islamic institutions 42
Ize, A. 19

Keynes, J. M. 63n10, 154, 173
Knight, F. H. 8

La Porta, R. 170
labelled bonds 111
Lacker, J. M. 19
largest state development bank 137
Last Mile Institutions 143
legal risks 68
lending practices 101, 117, 127
Lerner, A. 157
Lind, R. C. 19
liquidity 12, 23–25, 27–29, 66, 187, 195; problems 65, 75
local development investment funds 139, 140
London 2, 43
Lopez-De-Silanes, F. 170
low-income countries 2, 21, 37, 43, 44, 78, 81, 86, 93, 198

Madeira, R. F. 142
market failures 4, 35–37, 62, 63, 80, 123, 172, 174
market risks 62, 67, 68, 72–74
Marois 167, 169, 173–179, 186–188, 190, 191, 193
Marshall Plan 34, 70, 82
Martini, R. A. 142
Mazzucato, M. 38, 51, 126
McKinnon, R. I. 35
Minsky, H. P. 63n10
motivation 91, 92, 162
multilateral banks 86, 92, 131, 145, 188
multilateral development banks (MDBs) 2, 12, 35–39, 42–44, 46–48, 51–54, 105, 113, 129
municipal funding banks 28

national development banks (NDBs) 2, 3, 13, 20, 38, 48, 49, 51, 52, 54, 59–61, 64–69, 74, 75, 92, 94, 98, 111, 126, 128, 129, 131, 140, 142
national development system 133, 140, 142
national regulators 60, 61, 65, 67, 71, 75
national risks 12
new development bank 39, 194, 199
new financial instruments 109, 112
new sustainable finance paradigm 143

Ocampo, J. A. 37n2, 51
OECD 86, 89, 105, 125, 126
operational level 105, 107, 126
operational risks 62, 67, 68, 71, 73, 74
Ostry, J. D. 27
ownership form 170, 172–174, 178, 190

panorama 80
Paris Agreement 3, 92, 103, 126, 143
partnerships 29, 82, 107, 112, 113, 123, 138, 144, 145
Penna, C. C. R. 38, 51, 126
political instability 115
political risks 8, 12
prices transformation 162
private banks 60, 64, 78, 81, 83, 172, 176, 185, 188, 195, 197, 198
private capital markets 10, 30, 80
private commercial banks 108, 192
private finance 10, 30, 35, 52, 85, 87, 179, 188
private interests 158, 176–178, 180, 197–199
private investment 19, 88, 110, 113, 172
production telos 155–158, 161, 163, 164, 167
public bank functions 170, 173, 179, 186
public banking institutions 175, 190
public development banks (PDBs) 4, 78, 79, 81, 83, 87, 92, 94, 96–99, 101, 102, 105–110, 112–117, 126, 127, 133, 179; nomenclature 98
public financial institutions 63, 81, 130, 188, 199
public ownership 171, 172, 174, 177, 178, 190, 191, 198; form 170, 178
public policies 80, 109, 115, 153, 157, 192, 198
public policy instruments 82
public purpose 165, 166, 185, 186, 188, 191–199
public sphere 173, 175–178, 188, 198

rating agencies 11, 27, 31, 100, 116, 123
real economy risks 9, 11, 13
redirect private finance 87
regional banks 39, 72, 82, 112, 134, 135, 199
regional development banks 35, 36, 39, 52, 53
regional public banks 187, 189
regulatory framework 62, 68, 73–75
Ren, X. 129, 130, 132
responsible demand 91
Ribeiro de Mendonça, A. R. 173
risk categorization 11
risks 7–13, 19, 22, 23, 31, 62–65, 67, 68, 81, 83, 115

Salviano Junior, C. 134, 137
Schumpeter, J. A. 63n10
SDG-focused pipelines 104
securitization 11, 13, 22, 30, 64
Shaw, E. S. 35
Shiller, R. 27
Shleifer, A. 170
small and medium-sized companies (SMEs) 20, 25–27, 29, 51, 90, 92, 126, 136, 192
social forces 170, 174–176, 179, 180, 191, 198
social policies 139, 140, 145
social responsibility 90
solvency 62, 65
sound finance 155, 157, 161
stakeholders dialogue 108
standstill approach 27, 29
state banks 134–138, 141, 192
state-owned commercial banks 79, 83, 139
state-owned financial institutions 48
Stern, N. 37
Stiglitz, J. E. 19, 36, 62
strategic level 101–103, 106
Studart, R. 131
sub-regional banks 43, 53
subnational development banks (SDBs) 18, 91, 98, 99, 128–133, 135–138, 142, 144, 146
subnational development banks worldwide 129
subnational development models 142
subnational institutions 129, 142, 143, 145
subsidized credit 18, 52
support innovation 20, 68
sustainability policies 103, 104
sustainable development 2, 3, 86, 92, 96, 105, 107, 109–111, 114–116, 122, 123, 126, 129
sustainable development goals (SDGs) 4, 36, 59, 79, 84, 86–88, 97–102, 104, 105, 112, 117, 121–123, 126, 128, 129, 143, 145
sustainable development projects 105, 108, 194
sustainable development transformations 108, 110, 112, 117
sustainable finance 85, 112, 117, 121, 129, 143
systemic risks 22, 26, 61–63, 65, 66, 71

telos 155–160, 162–167; change of 157, 162–165, 167
Thorne, J. 114
Torres Filho, E. 70
Torres, E. 132
trade-offs 86, 103, 105, 107, 112, 121
transformative alignment 96
transition funds 89
Turkey 82, 173, 197

UNCTAD 126, 143, 144, 179, 186–188, 190, 193,198
universal basic income (UBI) 164

venture capital 13, 20, 72, 110, 111
Vicente, C. L. 130
Vidal, L. 164
Vietnam 129, 132, 133, 138–144
Vietnam banking deployment system 145
Vietnam Development Bank 140, 145
Vietnam development system 140

working capital 23, 25, 27, 136, 195
World Bank 47, 49, 51–53, 79, 81, 82, 125, 126, 139, 141, 187, 190
World Bank Group (WBG) 35, 39, 43–47, 49, 52–54, 125, 126
Wruuck, P. 142
Wu, X. 129, 130, 132

Xu, J. 70, 129–130, 132

Zeidan, R. 132